GREECE UNDER MILITARY RULE

GREECE
UNDER
MILITARY RULE

Edited by

RICHARD CLOGG
and
GEORGE YANNOPOULOS

BASIC BOOKS, INC., PUBLISHERS
NEW YORK

Printed in Great Britain

CONTENTS

v

Editors' Introduction

The publication of this book is timed to coincide with the completion of the Greek military regime's fifth year in power, a year which has seen Greece enter the longest period of dictatorship in its post-independence history. This in itself is a telling commentary on the assertions that are too frequently made that Greece's modern history is a dreary succession of *coups*, counter-*coups* and dictatorships.

One of the paradoxical consequences of the *coup* has been to stimulate a flood of books on post-war Greek history and politics. Some of these books attempt to show the dictatorship in its historical perspective and to untangle the complex web of Greek politics. Others have emphasized specific aspects of the regime, such as the machinery of repression it employs against its political opponents. Yet others recount the personal experiences of some of the chief protagonists in Greece's post-war history. The extensive bibliography included in this volume clearly indicates the growing interest in Europe and the United States in the problems of Greece and its people.

Yet another addition to this plethora of books clearly requires some justification. We feel that during these past five years enough evidence has been accumulated to study the regime on the basis of its record. This is precisely what this book is trying to do. It seeks to show the regime's impact on Greek society by analysing the Colonels' policies in the fields of education, the press, the arts, the economy, foreign policy, trade unions, public administration, local government and peasant co-operatives, as well as setting the regime in its historical context. Particular attention has been paid to structural aspects of the regime's policies. Only passing reference is made to its employment of repression and torture, since these have been given wide publicity in the press and have been thoroughly documented in the four-volume report of the European Commission of Human Rights of the Council of Europe.

It is particularly important from the European viewpoint that not only the regime's policies but the factors that have enabled it to survive relatively unchallenged for this length of time are subjected to scrutiny. It is important, moreover, to see what kind of society and political regime the Colonels are seeking to impose on a country which is both a member of the NATO alliance and an associate member of the European Economic Community, membership of both of which organizations presupposes an attachment to democratic institutions.

Each of the contributors has a close acquaintance with the country; some are actually living in Greece. Each has been given a completely free hand to write on his topic as he pleased, and there has been no attempt to present any common view, or to harmonize conflicting viewpoints. Each contributor bears responsibility only for what he himself has written. On the part of the editors there has been a deliberate attempt to invite contributions from those who view the Greek situation from differing standpoints. It is significant that, despite these differences in approach, a broad consensus emerges that the military dictatorship was neither deserved nor desired by the Greeks. And those who are concerned with an examination of the regime's actual policies come to the broad general conclusion that these policies are essentially regressive, despite the pseudo-revolutionary slogans of the Colonels and their often proclaimed identification with the toiling masses.

Given the space at the contributors' disposal and the general approach of this book, the reader will not find a detailed discussion of pre-*coup* politics or an in-depth socio-political analysis of the nature of the regime. A number of studies on these questions have recently been published, and are listed in the bibliography. What the reader will find, however, is a detailed examination of the military regime's policies. On this very little has been written in the form of systematic analysis, and it is hoped that this present volume will fill an important gap in the literature on contemporary Greece. The contributors to this volume have tried to portray the regime as it is, to show what it stands for on the basis of what it does, rather than on the basis of what its propagandists say. The impact of an authoritarian regime on the society on which it is imposed is of interest not only to those who study, or will study as future historians, the development of this particular society, but also to those who are aware of the authoritarian tendencies in the free societies of the West and wish to devise means that will render them less effective.

Moreover, the interdependence of nations in the present-day world community means that it is imperative to look at possible repercussions of events in one country on future developments in others. Greece, apart from being a member of the NATO alliance, has also been an associate member of the European Economic Community since 1962, on the basis of a treaty signed a year earlier which stipulates that this associate status will be changed to full member status by 1984. The EEC Commission has managed to avoid more decisive action by declaring the association agreement 'frozen'. This matter of mutual interdependence has assumed greater significance in post-war Europe, with the establishment of the principle of a collective enforcement of human rights. Undoubtedly the most important expression of this principle is the European Convention on Human Rights. But here again, the Greek case before the Council of Europe has given rise to displays of hesitation, reluctance and expediency based on short-term considerations by the major European governments, despite the fact that public opinion in all member countries continues to be strongly hostile to the Colonels' regime. In Britain, this climate of hostility was clearly manifested in the resolution passed at the 1967 Labour Party Conference, which called for the expulsion of Greece from NATO and supported 'all action taken by the Greek working class to bring down the regime'. The National Executive responded to the spirit of this resolution by making an offer of £100 to Andreas Papandreou's Pan-hellenic Liberation Movement (PAK). As this response might indicate, the conference decision only marginally influenced the Labour Government's policy toward Greece. In the Council of Europe the Wilson government was prepared to follow the lead given by the Scandinavians in con-demning the 'bestialities' perpetrated in the Colonels' Greece. But following Greece's withdrawal from the Council, the Labour Foreign Secretary, Michael Stewart, sided with the United States in blocking attempts to raise the Greek issue in the NATO Ministerial Council.

The Conservative Government has taken steps to develop more cordial relations with the Colonels. Senior Cabinet members now attend Greek Embassy receptions, and, in a drive further to improve relations, an official invitation was extended to the Commander-in-Chief of the Greek Armed Forces, General Odysseus Anghelis, who was warmly received in official quarters during his visit to Britain in October 1971. Somewhat ironically, the Undersecretary of State for Defence for the Royal Navy at the time of Anghelis' visit was Peter Kirk, who had been outspoken in his opposition to the Greek military regime in the Con-sultative Assembly of the Council of Europe.

Across the Atlantic, the Nixon administration, and, more particularly, Vice-President Spiro Agnew, have given open support to the regime, following in this respect the practice if not the rhetoric of the Johnson

administration. In the early months of the *coup*, however, the US administration could clearly have taken a host of actions to bring about the
immediate collapse of the *coup*, or significantly to shorten its life, when
the Colonels activated the 'Prometheus' plan, a plan elaborated by NATO
strategists to contain an internal uprising.

Once the Colonels had survived the first crucial hours after the *coup*,
their remaining in power depended upon a combination of the following
three factors: (*a*) the degree of their determination to infiltrate the whole
power structure of the state, (*b*) the degree to which others were prepared
to tolerate them, and (*c*) the level of the opposition's organization. The
opposition, despite much rhetoric in the months before the *coup*, proclaiming its intention to meet force with force, had not been effectively
organized to face the eventuality of an armed *coup*. Those, inside and
outside Greece, who were in a position to make life more difficult for
the Colonels, were not prepared to take decisive action, limiting themselves to generalized expressions of regret and pious hopes for an early
return to parliamentary democracy.

Meanwhile, the junta, a group of twelve colonels styling themselves
as the 'Revolutionary Council', having survived the first crucial post-
coup days, proceeded methodically to build its own power structure.
Until the King's abortive counter-*coup* of 13 December 1967, it was
obliged to share power with him. But it soon became apparent that the
King's key men in the first post-*coup* cabinet, former Attorney General
Kollias and General Spandidakis, were mere figureheads with no hold
on the levers of power. A major purge of officers of the three services
took place in August 1967, which enabled the 'Revolutionary Council'
to infiltrate its own trusted supporters into crucial command posts in the
Armed Forces. Such purges were intensified after the failure of the
King's *coup*, enabling the regime to increase its hold on the Armed Forces,
a remarkably large segment of whose higher echelons had proved themselves loyal to the King in the December counter-*coup*. Further inducements to officers to throw their hand in with the regime were made in
the form of substantial pay rises and perks (e.g. cheap mortgages, advantageous hire-purchase terms, etc.). Suggestions that General Odysseus
Anghelis, appointed Commander-in-Chief of the Greek Armed Forces
by the regime, did not enjoy good relations with the 'Revolutionary
Council', and in particular with Papadopoulos himself, have not been
substantiated by any visible split within the army, although in May
1971 there were reports of a revolt in a tank unit in Polykastron near
Thessaloniki. Opponents of the regime (e.g. Karamanlis in 1969, Papan-

dreou in 1971) have appealed, especially after the King's counter-*coup*, to sections of the Armed Forces to overthrow the ruling junta, pointing particularly to the regime's bungling of the Cyprus issue, but with no result.

Parallel to the building of its own power basis in the Army, the regime has managed to subjugate, almost completely, the Civil Service. Almost all Ministry officials of the grade of Director and above were either shadowed, or replaced, by military men or relatives and cronies of the Colonels. Indeed, nepotism has become one of the distinctive features of this regime, despite its declared intention to eliminate corruption from Greek life. The regime has also tried to destroy or effectively neutralize the power of organized social groups which might become foci of opposition. In this connection, they have packed local government councils, agricultural co-operatives, trade unions, and a host of professional organizations. The Church was not left untouched. Apart from replacing the aged Archbishop of Athens and All Greece within days of the *coup* by Ieronymos Kotsonis, a former royal chaplain, in whom the regime had more confidence, they imposed changes on the ruling body of the Greek Orthodox Church, the Holy Synod. They also replaced metropolitans who showed signs of non-co-operation, among them the Metropolitan of Thessaloniki, Panteleimon.

The Church's fate was also shared by the judiciary, when in 1968 a special decree abolished for three days the tenure of judges, and enabled the regime to dismiss thirty of Greece's most distinguished judges, and even deprived them of the right to practise as lawyers. When the judges challenged the constitutionality of this action before the Council of State, Greece's highest court in administrative matters, the Council sided with the dismissed judges, whereupon the military government declared the President of the Council to have resigned, despite his protestations to the contrary.

Another innovation – for Greece at any rate – was the creation of a network of commissars (most of them former officers) to act as the arbiters of the regime's policies and as sources of information to the security services. Commissars were appointed to a number of organizations, to public bodies such as the universities as well as private enterprises. Not even the Boy Scouts were spared their ministrations. On the instructions of the commissars, the regime systematically attempts to eliminate opponents, or potential opponents, from positions of responsibility. University professors have been dismissed, and employees of public utilities have lost their jobs, while private enterprises, even branches of foreign companies (such as the Athens offices of BEA) have been 'advised' to discharge persons whom the commissars chose to consider as 'dangerous to the security of the state'.

After the initial wave of purges, forced resignations and other measures of control, the most important development taken by the regime in consolidating its power has been the reorganization of the country's system of public administration in August 1971. The country was then divided into seven administrative regions, and a governor with the rank of undersecretary was appointed to each district. This is not, in fact, as the regime would have it, an experiment in regional decentralization, but an attempt to ensure on-the-spot supervision of the entire apparatus of public administration operating in a given region. This supervision was carried out by governors, who, in addition to their functions as rural satraps, also formed part of the central government in Athens. Most of these governors were selected from the group of the initial twelve members of the 'Revolutionary Council'. Through this system the regime is trying to institutionalize its control of the countryside, should discontent manifest itself in the rural and semi-rural areas. Moreover, should the regime decide to accede to international pressure to conduct elections, this system would have obvious advantages in ensuring that they went the right way for the Colonels.

This gradual consolidation of their power was accompanied by a mushrooming of the state's police and security apparatus. The budgetary allocation for the Ministry of Public Order was increased from 1,798 million drachmas in 1966 to 2,170 million drachmas in 1967, and 2,520 million drachmas in 1968, i.e. an increase (at current prices) of 40%. Security and police tasks in the country are now increasingly assumed by the Military Police (ESA) as well as by other special army units such as the Marines, a special body formed after the *coup*, under the command of Papadopoulos' brother Konstantinos. With such wide-ranging tasks now being carried out by the Armed Forces, it is not surprising to find that in 1969 the expenditure of the Ministry of Defence absorbed 49.8% of government expenditure on current account. By comparison, the share of public expenditure devoted to education declined from 15% in 1966 to 13.1% in 1969. Another indicator of the amounts spent in maintaining an extensive machinery of police surveillance abroad is to be found in the enormous increase since 1967 in expenditure allocated for the maintenance of government services abroad (embassies and other governmental agencies). Such increased sums are employed not only in carrying out propaganda on behalf of the regime (as emerged from the affair of

Maurice Fraser and Associates), but also in maintaining networks of informers engaged in spying upon, and even openly intimidating, the regime's opponents active outside Greece.

Another avenue that the regime has profitably explored in order to consolidate its position has been co-operation with, and in many instances complete servility towards, the domestic economic oligarchy, foreign business interests in the country (and especially those of Greek Americans) and the powerful group of Greek shipowners operating out of New York and London. Under the Colonels, the 'colonization' of the Greek economy has proceeded at a rapid rate. By a special article of the 1968 Constitution, all legislation granting concessions to foreign investors cannot be amended by subsequent government action or parliamentary legislation. Such concessions have in fact substantially increased as a result of the introduction of Emergency Laws 465/1968 concerning ship taxation, and 89/1967 concerning the establishment in Greece of foreign commercial and industrial undertakings, decrees which offer protection far in excess of that afforded by a legislative decree of 1953. The preferential treatment of shipowners is not limited to their shipping interests. It is further extended to their participation in the industrial sector. Thus, as time passes, the industrial, financial and commercial capital of the country will be increasingly concentrated in the hands of a small group of economic oligarchs, whose own economic interests are closely bound up with the survival of the Colonels. But despite the extremely attractive terms offered to foreign investors, the regime's experience in this field can scarcely be described as successful. An agreement with Litton Benelux S.A., concluded amidst much fanfare within a few days of the *coup*, whereby the company was to introduce investment to the value of $800 million over a period of ten years, receiving both its expenses and a commission on the investment introduced, was terminated in 1969 after proving an almost complete failure. Another $600 million investment package deal concluded with Onassis in January 1970 similarly collapsed in November 1971, while the American Macdonald Company, which had been awarded a substantial contract on unusually favourable cost-plus terms in 1968 to build a road across Northern Greece, was indicted late in 1971 in the Greek courts for alleged failure to pay its Greek subcontractors.

It should be pointed out that, although since December 1967 political power had been vested in the 'Revolutionary Council' of twelve Colonels (who between April and December of that year had been obliged to share power with the King), from early 1970 it became clear that the regime was moving ever closer to a personal type of dictatorship, with Papadopoulos increasingly wielding absolute dictatorial power. This was the clear implication of the drastic government reshuffle of late August 1971. A few troublemakers were completely removed from government posts. One of them, Col Stamatelopoulos, had been removed earlier, and assumed the role of the conscience of the 'revolution betrayed'. And Nikolaos Makarezos, a member of the original ruling troika, lost his control over the economic sector, and was relegated to the ornamental post of Second Deputy Prime Minister, with the implication that he was in future to report to the Prime Minister through the First Deputy Prime Minister, Pattakos. The latter too had earlier suffered a major setback to his own position in the hierarchy of power when he lost control of his tank unit based at the Goudi barracks near Athens.

The turning-point in Papadopoulos' ultimately successful attempt to monopolize all political power occurred in the spring of 1971. After a prolonged struggle with the 'Revolutionary Council', a struggle which severely strained his relations with Makarezos (and possibly with the Regent, Zoitakis) he managed to disperse to the provinces those officers who, by commanding crucial units in the Attica area, were instrumental in ensuring the initial success of the *coup*. These officers, who were well aware of their vital role, had often been manipulated by members of the 'Revolutionary Council' in order to influence power relations within it. With Papadopoulos' eventual success in depriving trouble-makers in the 'Revolutionary Council' of their friends in key Army units, Greece, for practical purposes, moved from a regime based on the rule of a junta to a personal, Bonapartist, dictatorship. This major shift in emphasis has also manifested itself in the propaganda line now adopted by the pro-regime newspapers, as well as in the speeches of Papadopoulos, who now consistently employs the first person singular in speaking of the 'Revolution', and maintains that he, and he alone, has been entrusted by the people to interpret their will.

The shifts in the power relationship between Papadopoulos, the junta, and the machinery of state power are also reflected in the changing nuances of the regime's propaganda. When the junta shared power with the King, the main line of propaganda was the 'communist danger' which Greece had allegedly faced. During the period of rule by junta, the emphasis switched to the 'corruption' of the politicians, to the 'decadence' of Greece under parliamentary rule, and an attempt was made to single out the former politicians as the prime architects of the country's ills. With the move to a personal dictatorship, Papadopoulos has tried to play down this emphasis by extolling the virtues of reconciliation among all Greeks, and has claimed that all Greeks were responsible for the under-development of their society and their economy. Papadopoulos, in this phase of his personal ascendancy, cannot afford to allow the old *politikos kosmos*, or political world, to remain united in its opposition to the regime. He has created personal enemies within the original junta, and it is thus important to him to try to build some kind of support among the old politicians. Hence his attempt in 1971 to start discussions with a few of the former politicians, who only a few months earlier had been described as corrupt, decadent and irresponsible.

Late in the summer of 1971 Papadopoulos, in a speech in Thessaloniki, made the extraordinary statement that the real revolution had in fact only just started. Government spokesmen now also declare that demo-cracy has already been achieved in Greece, or, in another variant, that 'Greece is the most democratic country in South-East Europe and the Middle East.'

This brief summary of the military regime's attempt to consolidate its power indicates adequately that the claims often made by the regime's spokesmen and its foreign apologists, that it intends to lead the country back to parliamentary democracy and that the military dictatorship is only a 'parenthesis' in this evolutionary process, are not convincing. These claims, frequently made in the early months and years to foreign politicians and journalists, were in fact a simple device to buy vital time to allow the regime to consolidate its power. These declarations often achieved the desired effect. On the first anniversary of the *coup*, for instance, Russell Johnston, the Liberal Party's spokesman on Foreign Affairs and four other MPs, two Labour and two Conservative, following a trip organized by the regime's PR man Maurice Fraser, declared their faith in Col Papadopoulos' word as 'a man, a soldier, and an officer' that he intended to bring about a return to democratic government. In January 1968, the Consultative Assembly of the Council of Europe was prepared to give the regime a fourteen-month period to put its promises into effect. At that time the Assembly's rapporteur stated that, in a private meeting in Athens with the then Foreign Secretary, Pipinelis, the latter had indicated that the regime was acting on the basis of a timetable which specified the various phases of progress towards elections. The moment the report was published the regime denied the existence of the timetable. We now know that such a timetable never existed. The fact that the regime is not prepared openly to admit that dictatorial government is a permanent feature in its design for Greece's political future stems from

one of the basic contradictions which beset it. The regime's dependence
on the Armed Forces for its maintenance in power means that the regime
is ultimately dependent on those who supply these forces, i.e. the US
Government. The American administration, following the so-called
'Schwartz Doctrine' of 1964, according to which the US will not interfere
with extra-constitutional, authoritarian rule by anti-communist governments, gives support to the regime, but this support has produced internal
opposition within the United States. Thus the regime is 'advised' to
maintain an image which would minimize internal opposition in the
United States. James Lowenstein and Richard Moose, the two investigators who visited Greece in February 1971 on behalf of the Senate
Foreign Relations Committee, noted that the US Embassy in Athens
'often appears to be more concerned with the regime's "Image" than
with the substance of its actions. Time and again we heard (from US
diplomats in Athens) expressions of regret at the regime's poor sense of
public relations.' This same obsession with the regime's image also
manifested itself in hearings before a Sub-Committee of the US Senate
Foreign Relations Committee the previous June. Rodger Davies, Deputy
Assistant Secretary of State for Near Eastern and South Asian Affairs, in
his evidence conceded that there had been 'some excesses' in Greece, and
added that 'the regime has not been conscious of its public-relations
responsibilities, and its responsibilities as a government to publicly
dissociate itself from these excesses.'

It is difficult to forecast if and when the Greek situation will disintegrate
into a new European Vietnam. Predictions of this sort are clearly hazar-
dous, but the Hudson Institute's Herman Kahn since 1969 has identified
Greece as a future crisis area, as 'a real possibility for future trouble'. Be
this as it may, it is perhaps encouraging that, as the governments of
Western Europe tone down their protests, Americans are becoming
increasingly aware of the dangers inherent in the US administration's
present policies. The attempt by the House of Representatives in the
summer of 1971 to block the budget appropriations for increased military
aid to Greece was clearly a reflection of this growing concern on the part
of informed public opinion in the United States. Despite support for this
move by its Foreign Relations Committee, the Senate did not endorse
this recommendation. Nonetheless, the pressure of public opinion will
certainly not lessen within the United States, particularly if the inflammatory statements made by Vice-President Spiro Agnew during his
visit to Greece are continued. While any political change in Greece will
ultimately come from inside the country, through action by the Greeks

themselves, one should not underestimate, in view of the basic contradictions within the regime, the importance of a concerned world public opinion, and especially of European and American opinion.

We hope that this book will contribute not only to the creation of a concerned, but also of an informed, public opinion. For in the propaganda battle between the regime's apologists and opponents it is easy to lose sight of the underlying trends of the regime's policies, trends which this volume seeks to analyse. Before concluding this introduction it may be useful to point to some of the salient features of the individual contributions and to provide some kind of link between them. It should be borne in mind that inevitably a book of this sort cannot hope to be wholly up to date at the time of publication. The dates of composition of the individual contributions are given at the end of each chapter.

C. M. Woodhouse in Chapter One places the 'Revolution' firmly in the context of the troubled history of Greece between 1936 and 1967, partly drawing on his own experiences as head of the Allied Military Mission to the resistance forces in occupied Greece. He finds that wherever the blame for the political crisis of 1965–67 may lie, it was not the Greek political system that was at fault. The crisis could have been resolved within the established political framework. Yet Professor George Zaharopoulos in Chapter Two, takes the view that a major contributing factor leading to the Army's intervention was Greece's 'level of political culture'.

Why then did the political system not prove capable of forestalling military intervention? Professor Zaharopoulos provides one answer in analysing the whole course of civil–military relations in Greece during the post-war period. Maurice Goldbloom, who served as labour attaché to the US aid mission in Greece in 1950–51, points to another factor, the 'external factor', namely Greece's relationship with the United States, which since 1947 has taken over Britain's role as the protecting power. This factor is also emphasized in the contributions of Alexander Xydis (Chapter Ten) and Arne Treholt (Chapter Eleven).

While Chapters One and Two fill in the background to the *coup*, the remaining chapters seek essentially to analyse the regime's ideological orientation, the effects of its policies on Greece's economic, social and cultural development and its relations with both East and West. Richard Clogg in Chapter Three similarly looks at the regime's attempts to erect an ideological superstructure which would justify its continuance in power. Although the regime came to power without any serious ideological orientation, save a strong anti-communism and a propensity for populist rhetoric, a number of attempts have since been made to provide it with an ideological *raison d'être*. He concludes that the terms populist and fascist, which are often used to describe the regime, do not adequately describe its 'ideology', which is essentially that of a peasant-dominated paternalist society, and which closely resembles that of the pre-war dictator General Metaxas.

An important element in the regime's efforts to indoctrinate the mass of the Greek people with their pseudo-ideology, was, of course, the press and the communications media. Helen Vlachos, herself a publisher of wide experience in Greece, recounts in Chapter Four the trials and tribulations of the Greek press and of Greek journalists since 1967. A further important vehicle of indoctrination has been the regimentation of the educational system to serve the Colonels' own interests. The anonymous author of Chapter Seven, who has close personal experience of the Greek educational system since 1967, analyses the way in which the educational clock has been turned back in Greece. His article demonstrates how the Colonels have manipulated the country's educational system to produce long-term effects which may well influence the development of Greek society for many decades to come.

Rodis Roufos in Chapter Eight completes this picture of the regime's attempts to influence cultural developments, drawing, in the process, an important distinction between the cultural policies of totalitarian and authoritarian regimes. He documents on the one hand the regime's efforts to influence cultural life, and on the other the attempts of writers and artists to challenge the regime by exploiting the loopholes that an authoritarian regime such as that of the Colonels provides.

Other forms of resistance to the regime as well as efforts to consolidate the opposition to it are discussed by George Yannopoulos in Chapter Nine. As is shown in this chapter, passive and active resistance have assumed various forms and have frequently made themselves felt, despite a sophisticated degree of police repression and the widespread use of torture. An additional factor, according to Yannopoulos, has been the fact that in the course of these years the structure of Greek politics has been in a state of flux, under the impact of what he terms a national ideological crisis. He analyses these new political alignments that have emerged under the 'shadow of martial law'.

The articles by Arne Treholt (Chapter Eleven) and Maurice Goldbloom (Chapter Twelve) seek to analyse the efforts that have taken place both in Europe and the United States to isolate the regime and force a change in the policy of the US administration towards the Colonels. Treholt's emphasis is, of course, on the Scandinavian efforts to expel Greece from the Council of Europe and to move NATO to take action against the military regime. This is entirely appropriate, as the Scandinavians have taken the lead in Europe in seeking to isolate the Greek dictatorship.

The regime's efforts to prevent its international isolation are described in Alexander Xydis' article (Chapter Ten). Xydis also describes the regime's attempts to counterbalance its relative isolation in Western Europe by improving relations with the Eastern bloc and with the Arab world by promoting both diplomatic and trade links. He also emphasizes the extent to which Greece's bargaining position *vis-à-vis* Turkey over Cyprus has been weakened as a consequence of the military takeover.

Professor John Pesmazoglu in Chapter Five also points to the effects of Greece's international isolation in preventing the further integration of her economy with the EEC, with which she has been associated since 1962. The regime's attempts to develop trade links with the countries of East Europe and the Arab world have failed to bring any significant improvement in the balance of payments, which has been deteriorating since the *coup*. These and other structural weaknesses of the Greek economy are analysed in the same article. All in all, the regime has managed, by increased borrowing abroad, to maintain a certain momentum of growth in the economy (despite the fact that it has yet to reach the rate of the years immediately preceding the *coup*).

The fruits of this growth, however, have not been distributed in such a way as to improve the relative income positions of either the Greek workers or peasants. This aspect of the regime's policies, as well as other policies which affect the economic welfare of these social strata, are examined in Chapter Six by George Yannopoulos. His analysis indicates that the populist rhetoric of the regime has, in fact, been belied by its economic policies which are aimed at promoting the interests of the economic oligarchy.

Clearly a book of this kind cannot hope to deal exhaustively with all facets of the Greek military regime's policies during the past five years. A major gap of this kind in the present study is the absence of any systematic analysis of the way in which the regime has tried to institutionalize its power and to construct permanent foundations for authoritarian rule in Greece through the 1968 Constitution and associated legislation. Similarly, there is little discussion of the regime's efforts to bring the judiciary under political control, or examination of the workings of martial law which has remained in force since the day of the *coup*. We had hoped to include a contribution on these highly important topics from one of Greece's most distinguished constitutional lawyers, but for technical reasons were unable to do this.

It is, however, vital for an understanding of present-day Greece to investigate the way in which the regime has sought to entrench the armed forces' position as the permanent arbiter of future developments in Greece. This has been done through the 1968 Constitution, which the International Commission of Jurists has described as 'no more than a legal instrument devised to keep the Government in power', and Law 58/1968, which outlines the very substantial powers now accruing to the Commander in Chief and the Supreme Council of National Defence. According to Article 130 (para. i), the armed forces owe 'faith and allegiance to the Country, the national ideals and traditions, and serve the Nation'. (This and the following extracts from the Constitution are taken from the official translation.) Significantly, however, according to Articles 30 (para. ii) and 66 (para. i), the King and MPs owe allegiance more specifically to the Constitution and the laws of the country. Needless to say, what precisely constitutes 'national ideals and traditions' is solely a matter for the armed forces to determine. According to Article 130 (para. ii), 'the mission and the capacity of a military man is absolutely opposed to ideologies aiming at the overthrow or the undermining of the existing *political* or social order or the corruption of the national convictions of the Greeks' (our italics).

Under the 1968 Constitution, the armed forces themselves, as a self-governing entity, acquire absolute control over promotions, retirements, assignments and transfers. Decisions in these matters are taken by 'service councils constituted of high-ranking officers, as provided by Law'. If the Minister of National Defence, who is now reduced to a mere figurehead, disapproves of these decisions, he has fifteen days in which to appeal to 'an appellate council of broader composition, by high-ranking officers' (Article 131, para. i–iii). Parliament is specifically precluded from establishing select committees to investigate 'matters pertaining to foreign policy or the defence of the country' (Article 77, para. iii).

Under the new Constitution, ultimate power in the State clearly resides with the armed forces, and the whole concept of political control of the military is negated. The Constitution contains a number of other provisions designed to ensure that the particular political order sought by the 'National Revolutionary Government', which is specifically charged with carrying out the first elections (Article 135), need never fear serious challenge from whatever quarter. Those 'irrevocably convicted to any penalty whatsoever for acts or activities directed against the existing political or social system shall be denied the right to vote'

(Article 56, para. ii). In that the regime treats virtually any opposition, whatever form it may take, as directed against the existing political or social system, and tries it in the courts as such, virtually all those convicted of opposition to the present regime will be excluded from the right to vote. Somewhat paradoxically, to be deprived of the right to stand as a parliamentary candidate necessitates a life sentence 'for active participation in a party, organization, association or union aiming at the propagation and application of ideas tending to overthrow the existing political or social system or the detachment of part of the State territory' (Article 61, para. f). Candidates must also be Greek citizens (Article 61, para. i), which also rules out a future political role for Greeks active in opposing the regime abroad who have arbitrarily been deprived of their citizenship.

Having arbitrarily and unilaterally ruled its most determined opponents *hors de combat*, the regime has taken further steps to ensure that if it does eventually condescend to restore a semblance of parliamentary life, this will be conducted in accordance with its own idiosyncratic rules. The primary instrument of this control is to be the Constitutional Court. The function of the Court, initial appointment to which, of course, lies wholly in the hands of the regime, is to 'approve' those parties seeking to contest the elections. The organization, programme, and activity of a party 'must be governed by national and democratic principles' (Article 58, para. ii). The precise definition of 'national' principles presumably lies within the competence of the Constitutional Court. Wholly excluded from the political arena are 'parties whose aims or activities are manifestly or *tacitly* opposed to the form of government or tend to overthrow the existing social system or endanger the territorial integrity of the state or public security' (Article 58, para. v) (our italics). Once candidates have overcome these various hurdles and have been elected to parliament, their function is to represent not the people but the 'Nation' (Article 59). Moreover, the deputy's parliamentary immunity is seriously curtailed, and he will in future be liable for prosecution according to the law for insulting and defaming, slanderously or not, a person or an authority' in Parliament (Article 67, para. ii).

The rights of the ordinary citizen are scarcely less hedged about with ambiguities. Article 14, for instance, purports to guarantee freedom of speech and prohibits censorship and the seizure of printed matter. But these rights are immediately qualified by the provision that the public prosecutor may authorize seizure of printed matter, among other things, 'because of insult to the person of the King, the Crown Prince, their wives and children; because of a publication which (i) discloses information on the organization, composition, armament and employment of the armed forces, or on the fortifications of the country, (ii) is patently rebellious, or aims at overthrowing the regime, or the existing social system or is directed against the territorial integrity of the State or creates *defeatism*, or provokes or instigates the commission of a crime of high treason, (iii) intends to project or diffuse for political exploitation, views of outlawed parties or organizations' (our italics). These restrictions are further reinforced by the draconian Press Law 346/1969.

Moreover, the individual citizens can be deprived of 'all rights safe-guarded under the Constitution' if the Constitutional Court decides that an individual has been using his civil rights and liberties 'for the purpose of struggling against the prevailing political system, the civil liberties, or of endangering the national independence, and territorial integrity of the State' (Article 24, para. ii). Strikes 'for the purpose of achieving political or other ends irrelevant to material or moral interests of the workers' are prohibited (Article 19, para. v). A number of the most important provisions of the 1968 Constitution have yet to be implemented. But the regime's systematic violation of articles that have been activated, such as Article 10 on *habeas corpus*, does not engender confidence that it will respect its own 'revolutionary' law.

Such then, in very brief outline, are some of the salient features of the military regime's concerted plan to ensure that it, or something very similar to it, retains permanent control of the key areas of state power for the indefinite future. While it is clearly no substitute for the detailed analysis we had hoped to include, this brief sketch will, it is hoped, throw some light on the regime's manipulation of the country's constitutional and legal framework so as to entrench itself in power. In this context it is worth recalling the words of Robert McCloskey, the State Department spokesman, in justifying the resumption by the us Administration of heavy arms shipments to Greece in September 1970: 'the trend towards a constitutional order is established'. The credibility of the regime's assurances on this point was not strengthened by reports late in 1971 that not only did the coup-makers play little or no part in the wartime resistance, but that some may also have been collaborators.

In conclusion we would like to thank our contributors for the way in which they have met very tight deadlines, John Blackwell of Secker & Warburg for the skill with which he had handled a complex manuscript, S.P.G. for the index, and Mary Jo Clogg for much help in the preparation of this book.

London, November 1971   *Richard Clogg*   *George Yannopoulos*

CHAPTER ONE

The 'Revolution' in its Historical Context

The purpose and justification of the 'Revolution' of 21 April 1967 can best be read in the slogans which cover the countryside on blue-and-white notice boards. They are simpler and clearer than the statements of policy made from time to time by the Prime Minister. They vary from fairly precise factual statements, such as the 'Communists are traitors to the nation', 'Greece has risen', or 'The revolution was an historical necessity', to exclamations of pure faith, such as 'Tranquillity – progress – regeneration', 'Greece of the Christian Greeks', or even '1972 – year of management – G. Papadopoulos'. Although many of the notice boards are now battered and tarnished, they should not be ignored. They all carry a sophisticated message, which reveals the handiwork of able propagandists.

It is worth examining the subtlety of the message before considering to what extent it is valid. It weaves together a number of themes which have a natural appeal to most Greeks. One of these is religious and moral. Take first the word for revolution itself. The word *epanastasis* means literally 'uprising', and it is etymologically related to the word for the resurrection of Christ. The same root re-appears in the slogan already quoted, 'Greece has risen', which is a simple modification of the phrase every Greek utters on Easter Day, 'Christ has risen'. This adaptation of religious phraseology to the cause of the Revolution is certainly not accidental. It is part and parcel of the basic theme of 'Greece of the Christian Greeks'.

In parenthesis, it may be remarked that such verbal skill in the use of slogans was once characteristic of the Greek Communist Party (KKE). For example, when they founded their Resistance Army in 1942, they gave it a name which produced the initials ELAS; and this acronym differs by only one letter in spelling, and not at all in pronunciation, from the Greek word for Greece. The point is worth making because of the startling fact, to which attention is drawn in later essays in this book, that a number of ex-communists are among the most dedicated supporters of the Revolution of 1967. Among them are several skilled propagandists. Another echo of the tactics of the KKE will be found in the following example.

A frequent epithet for the Revolution on the display boards is 'nation-saving'. If it be granted that on 21 April 1967 the revolutionaries saved the nation, then they are entitled to identify patriotism with support for themselves; opposition or criticism is therefore anti-patriotic: so runs the official argument. People are divided into two categories, patriots (*ethnikophrones*) and anti-Greeks (*anthellines*); and these two categories are identical and co-extensive with supporters and opponents of the regime. The government is thus identified with the nation. It is interesting to recall that precisely the same identification was made by the KKE during the German occupation. Many Greeks (and some foreigners, including myself) have found themselves described as *misellines* or 'Greek-haters' thirty years ago and as *anthellines* or 'anti-Greeks' today. The same psychology, and perhaps even the same minds, lie behind both descriptions. The criterion for such a designation was in each case the failure to appreciate that criticism of the ruling group, whether communist in the 1940s or militarist in the 1970s, amounted to an attack on the Greek nation.

A kind of Manichaean dichotomy between the forces of good and the forces of evil was thus common to both forms of authoritarianism. In both cases it was necessary to identify with the enemy a significant element in Greek life, namely the class of patriotic nationalists who believed in constitutional liberties. These were the Greeks who fought in the nationalist resistance or in the armed forces of the Middle East from 1941 to 1945; who kept the flame of democracy alive throughout the civil war from 1946 to 1949; and who made the constitutional monarchy an increasingly viable reality from 1950 to 1967. They were once identified *by* the communists as 'traitors to the struggle'; now they are identified *with* the communists as 'traitors to the nation'. Clearly, to traduce their motives or suppress their existence involves a serious distortion of history. At least three critical periods in the last generation have to be misrepresented in order to justify the claim that the Revolution of 21 April 1967 'saved the nation'. These are the periods of the resistance (1941–45), of the civil war (1946–49), and of the breakdown of parliamentary government (1965–67).

There is a myth common to the extreme left and the extreme right in Greece that the resistance to the Nazi occupation was a monopoly of the communists. Both extremes find the myth convenient: the left because it enables them to claim that they alone were patriots in those years, and the right because it enables them to justify their own attitudes of passivity or even collaboration with the occupier. The military revolutionaries of 1967 (whose role under the occupation was at best undistinguished) share this view. In their propaganda in praise of the armed forces many campaigns are given due prominence, but the resistance is left a blank.

The same myth enables both left and right to lay the blame for everything that they disapprove about the years of occupation on the British participation in the resistance. The communists blamed the British for failing to acknowledge that they alone *were* the resistance. The opposite extreme blamed the British for the very existence of the armed communist forces. The revolutionary government shares the latter view. Like the communists again, the Colonels show a marked streak of xenophobia, which takes the positive form of constant declarations of independence from any foreign power. All the misfortunes of Greece are to be blamed on the succession of foreign interventions. 'We intend to be masters in our own house' is an expression I have heard from Aris Veloukhiotis, the wartime leader of ELAS, and from Brigadier Pattakos, the First Deputy Prime Minister and formerly Minister of the Interior.

This is not the place to argue the merits of British policy towards Greece during the occupation, which certainly was not free from tactical errors. Two things, however, are certain. One is that the British presence in Greece did not create the communist resistance, which would have come into being in any case; the other is that the nationalist resistance would never have existed at all without the British intervention in 1942. To be specific, communist-controlled bands called ELAS were in the field months before the first British mission landed in the mountains at the end of September 1942; whereas the only nationalist band of any significance, led by General Zervas, was in action only because its leader had been induced to take the field by British agents. It may reasonably be argued that without the British intervention, the whole of Greece would have passed under communist control by default when the German occupation ended. The nationalist resistance would barely have existed without British support.

The point has been well put by one of the outstanding figures in the nationalist resistance: 'The great mission of organizing, consolidating and guiding the Greek people in the direction of resistance was naturally the privilege and duty, first and foremost of the nation's political and military leaders. Unfortunately, however, neither the political nor the military leaders proved equal to their mission.'[1] Those words were true of the senior generation. The politicians were either compromised by association with the dictatorship of Metaxas, or preoccupied by prior considerations of hostility to the monarchy, or simply lacking in courage and determination. The generals looked to their commander-in-chief, General Papagos, for guidance, and received none except to wait and see; and in any case Papagos was arrested and deported to Germany in the summer of 1943, after which there was no effective leadership of the military hierarchy.

Junior officers and civilians might be excused for doing nothing in the gloomy circumstances of defeat. To their credit, many refused to take advantage of that excuse. Names are invidious, but they are also important to establish the nationalist character of important elements in the resistance. Among the younger political figures were George Kartalis (formerly a monarchist and later a senior minister in several post-war governments) and Panayiotis Kanellopoulos (the last legitimate Prime Minister of Greece). It is also right to emphasize the impeccable role played by George Papandreou, who was more than once arrested by the occupation authorities. The contribution of such men was not merely to fortify the resistance with respectable political backing, but to understand and foresee the course that Greek history was taking under the impact of enemy occupation in succession to the Metaxas dictatorship. For an acute contemporary analysis of the country's current and future problems, from the point of view of patriotic minds of different political persuasions, it would be impossible to improve on the documents drafted by Kanellopoulos in February 1942 and by Papandreou at the end of 1943, both published after the war.[2]

Among the soldiers, it is only necessary to mention the names of Zervas and Psaros; but it should also not be forgotten that many patriotic soldiers, like General Kalambalikis, joined ELAS in a valiant effort to mitigate the communists' control of that force and to turn it into what it claimed to be, an army of national liberation instead of a tool of alien domination. Nor should it pass unremembered that many future generals of the highest rank and ability served in the nationalist resistance – Agoros, Nikolopoulos, Katsadimas, Papadatos and others. The army also provided important links in those years between the resistance and the Greek forces in the Middle East: for example, General Tsakalotos, an early member of the resistance in Athens who later commanded the victorious Greek Brigade in Italy; and the brothers Tsigantes, of whom one commanded the Sacred Squadron and the other was killed by enemy secret police on a clandestine mission to Athens.

Among the many junior officers who followed these examples, I will mention for reasons of personal admiration and affection only Leonidas Petropoulakis, a second lieutenant killed in action in 1943, whose name is now commemorated in a military camp in Epirus. He exactly fitted the description given in Chapter Two of the contemporaries of the present-day colonels in the Army Cadet School. If he were alive today, Petro-poulakis would no doubt be a colonel, but it is unlikely that he would be a military governor. It is indeed upon such as him, especially those who served under General Zervas in the occupation, that the conservative, nationalist opposition to the present government is chiefly based.

The distortion of history by which the resistance is generally identified with communism is naturally resented by the tens of thousands of men and women who took part in it. At the time of the celebrations of the armed forces in 1971, when all the wars fought by the Greek army were commemorated except for the period 1941–45, it was the subject of a bitter leading article by the president of the National Union of Resistance Organizations, Alexander Papadopoulos, an officer under Zervas and later a Member of Parliament.[3] Mr Papadopoulos (no relation of the Prime Minister) addressed his namesake thus: 'If it had not been for Zervas and the national resistance, everything else would have been superfluous – you would now be living (for we should be dead) full of prosperity in the communist paradise.' Searching for reasons why government propaganda has systematically ignored the nationalist resistance, the writer came as near as prudence permitted to an outright accusation: 'Do they regard it as devoid of historic value, or are they embarrassed because . . .?' That eloquent aposiopesis points directly at the record of Greece's present rulers during the enemy occupation.

It is not hard to understand why the myth which identifies the resistance with communism is readily accepted. In certain areas of Greece, particularly Macedonia and the Peloponnese, the extremists of ELAS eliminated their nationalist rivals so quickly and thoroughly that few were aware of any resistance other than the communists. In Macedonia ELAS was closely associated with Bulgarian communists, who were in turn scarcely distinguishable from the Bulgarian occupation authorities. In the Peloponnese, the indescribable atrocities committed by Aris Veloukhiotis' men in Kalamata, Meligala and other towns are remembered as vividly as the Germans' massacre at Kalavryta. As Mr Papadopoulos' article points out, Greek nationalists had two enemies in the mountains. There were in fact two distinct occupations, and two distinct resistances.

One occupation was by the Germans and their allies, and one by the communists and their allies. (The Bulgarians were the allies of both.) The two occupations overlapped both in area and in time. One of the two occupations (the communist) was also one of the two resistances. That is the reason why the other resistance (the nationalist) found itself confronted by two enemies at once. It is also the reason why it has been possible ever since to confuse public opinion by identifying resistance with the communist enemy. The climax to the succession of events which caused this confusion was of course the armed rising in Athens in December 1944, following the liberation of Greece from the Nazi occupation.

No one yet knows for certain the real motives behind that appalling tragedy. It had long been obvious that the primary objective of the KKE was to obtain power after the war, and that fighting the Germans was, as I wrote in the summer of 1944, 'a secondary but not for that reason a negligible purpose'. As the day of liberation approached, however, it began to look as if the communists did not after all have in mind a seizure of power by force. A series of agreements between the communists, their Greek rivals and their British allies – at the Plaka bridge in February 1944, in the Lebanon in May, at Caserta in September – all pointed to a bloodless liberation and the establishment of an all-party coalition government under Papandreou. That was indeed the initial outcome. But a few weeks later came the disastrous 'December events', which burned themselves into the memory of the Greek people.

When all allowance is made for the mistakes of others, it is beyond doubt that the major blame for the 'December events' must lie with the fatal errors of judgement committed by the KKE. 'The British fooled us,' said Siantos, the secretary-general of the party, to a former communist in 1946, meaning presumably that he had misjudged the weakness of the liberating force to signify that the British government was indifferent to the consequences of the German withdrawal.[4] He equally misjudged the reaction of the Soviet government, which loyally carried out Stalin's undertaking to Churchill not to interfere in Greece. Only the communist government of Yugoslavia gave the KKE some encouragement but negligible help at this date. The Greek communists had no one to blame but themselves; but tens of thousands of patriotic Greeks have had to share the discredit with them. How lively the memory is to this day can be seen in one of those simple, persuasive slogans which now cover the Greek countryside: 'Better a bloodless April than a bloody December.'

If any Greek was not misled by the 'December events' into believing that resistance and communism were one and the same thing, the process of conviction was likely to be completed by the civil war of 1946–49, which is usually called 'the anti-bandit struggle'. The 'bandits' were popularly identified with ELAS under another name. This is ironic, because the communists themselves were anxious to make their so-called 'Democratic Army' as unlike ELAS as possible. Zakhariadhis, who resumed the leadership of the KKE on his return from a German concentration camp in 1945, held the fantastic notion that Siantos was a British agent and that ELAS had 'facilitated British plans' under his guidance.[5] The new Democratic Army, commanded by Markos Vaphiadis (who had himself been a political commissar in ELAS) was to be made 'free from the bad, negative, unacceptable tradition and heritage of ELAS', and almost no effort was made to recruit trained officers who had sympathized with ELAS, presumably because they had shown themselves unable to stomach communist policy once they realized what it was.[6] The struggle of 1946–49 should not therefore be seen simply as a continuation of the resistance.

Although it is too early to attempt a definitive history of those years, certain common distortions of the record can already be identified and corrected. The motive forces behind the civil war are clear, but their relative strength and priority may well be misconstrued. There was the Soviet government's desire for an outlet to the Mediterranean, but it was offset by Stalin's cautious anxiety to avoid a direct clash with the Western powers. There was the perennial aim of Yugoslavia and Bulgaria to annex Greek Macedonia, offset by the mutual rivalry of Tito and Dimitrov over the spoils. There was the ambition of the Slavophone minority in Greece for autonomy and the ambition of the Greek communists for absolute power. There were also genuine grievances among the provincial population of Greece in the aftermath of the Varkiza agreement, which a succession of weak governments was never able to enforce effectively. So arranged, these factors form a logical chain of causation, but the historical order was perhaps more nearly the reverse. The great conflict began with local quarrels and disorders, which were exploited but not generated from above and from abroad.

Part of the mythology of the 1967 Revolution is that the Slav powers (the Soviet Union, Yugoslavia and Bulgaria) deliberately launched the 'bandit war' of 1946–49, and would readily do the same again if the Revolution were not there to prevent them. There is, in fact, no positive evidence to suggest that the civil war was launched on the initiative of any of the Slav powers, though certainly they encouraged it with moral and material support. The writings of Yugoslav leaders since the breach between Tito and Stalin show clearly that Stalin was very ignorant of the Balkans and had no enthusiasm for the Greek communists' rebellion. He told the Yugoslav leaders early in 1948 that it should be terminated as quickly as possible.[7] There is no reference to the Greek civil war in the Soviet–Yugoslav correspondence preceding the rupture in 1948; and it is clear that the Yugoslav and Bulgarian communists were far more preoccupied with their own internecine struggle over Macedonia than with helping the Greeks.

It often happens that revolutions are provoked by militant opportunists at lower levels than by the central authority which is supposed to have them under control. Thus, the Cuban fiasco of the Bay of Pigs in 1961 was forced on the American government from below rather than initiated from above. Something similar may have happened in Greece in 1946: certainly Stalin seems to have thought so later on. It may equally be doubted whether the Central Committee of the KKE was as much in control of events as it would have liked to think. Reconsideration of the evidence openly available at the time suggests that the Party was subject to divided counsels (as indeed it had been before the 'December events' in 1944), and that its official policy was lagging behind the initiative of its militants in the provinces. This was a repetition of the history of 1942, when Aris Veloukhiotis took the initiative out of the hands of the Central Committee in forming an armed force in the mountains.

Popular history has it on the record that the decision to launch the 'third round', as the communists called the civil war, was taken by the Second Plenum of the Central Committee of the KKE on 11 February 1946; and that the first deliberate blow was struck at Litokhoro, on the eastern slopes of Mount Olympus, during the night before the General Election of 31 March 1946. Careful examination of the sequence of events in that year does not bear out such categorical interpretations or such an absolute chronology. Just as the Byzantine Empire did not end punctually on 29 May 1453, so the civil war did not begin precisely on the conventionally accepted date. It had begun to get under way months earlier, and continued to get under way for months afterwards. The Central Committee of the KKE lacked direction from abroad and had no clear idea what it intended to do.

Zakhariadis wrote in 1950 that the Second Plenum 'in effect decided that the new armed struggle should begin', but he preceded those words with a more precise account of what happened.[8] Some members of the Plenum wanted to continue what he called the 'submissive line' which had prevailed since the Varkiza agreement; others wanted an 'immediate transition to armed struggle'. But the majority rejected both proposals, and decided to combine a policy of seeking 'reconciliation' with the government and a policy of 'hastening and completing the technical and organizational military preparation for the progressive reinforcement of the armed struggle of the people'. The die was not cast, in other words, on 11 February; and the incident at Litokhoro on the night of 30/31 March was just another in the long series of violent clashes which had been provoked by lawless elements on one side or the other for many months. The communist press was evidently taken by surprise by the incident: early reports in *Rizospastis* were confused, and even mis-spelt the name of Litokhoro.[9] No escalation of violence ensued until the autumn, after the plebiscite on the monarchy. Markos Vaphiadis left Athens for the mountains in August, but the headquarters of the Democratic Army was formed only in October.

Other evidence tends to confirm that the communists slid down the agonizingly slippery slope into civil war faster than their Central Committee could take its decisions. Certainly they were preparing for that eventuality, but they still hoped it could be averted, for instance by a weakening of the government or by a British withdrawal. Their more prudent and worldly-wise leaders, such as Tzimas and Karayiorgis, had reason to know that their preparations were inadequate and to suspect that the international balance of power would turn against them. But the trend to war became irreversible. The notion that it was launched by an international communist conspiracy is as fanciful as the communist myth which attributes it to a 'monarcho–fascist tyranny' promoted by the British, and later by the Americans. Both myths were passionately believed, and that was all that mattered at the time; but it will not do for history.

Two things deserve emphasis about the winning of the civil war: first, it was essentially a victory for the Greeks alone; and secondly, it was achieved without any significant departure from democratic rule. Both facts exemplify the underlying strength and stability of the Greek political system, which it is nowadays fashionable to decry. No two stories could be more different than those of Greece and Vietnam, and no miscalculation could be greater than that of the Americans in believing that what had been achieved in Greece could be achieved in Vietnam. Apart from the boost in morale produced by the Truman Doctrine in March 1947, the American contribution to the Greek government's military victory was relatively slight. American equipment began to arrive on a massive scale only when victory was already in sight. It did not make a decisive contribution even to the final operations in August and September 1949, which would have been successful without it. Indeed, it is reasonably clear that if the Greeks had had the efficient generalship in 1947–48 which they enjoyed in 1949, they could have won the war earlier with their own unaided resources. This can be asserted notwithstanding the importance of the Yugoslav decision to close the frontier to the rebels in July 1949; Tito's support for their cause had already been waning since the previous summer, when his breach with Stalin became absolute.

If the victory over the rebels was primarily a Greek achievement, not less important is the fact that it was won with virtually no diminution of political liberties. The defect of the governments of 1946–49 was not that they were tyrannical but that they were weak. They could not control their own fanatical supporters, but equally they made no deliberate effort to harass their fanatical opponents. The communist press in Athens was not suppressed until October 1947; the KKE was not outlawed until the end of that year, when Markos Vaphiadis set up his rebel government; and martial law, though intermittently proclaimed earlier at various places and times, was not extended to the whole country until October 1948. These actions may be criticized as belated, but they can hardly be criticized as undemocratic.

The same determination to respect democratic procedures continued after the war. Although the KKE as such remained outlawed, communists were allowed to re-enter politics under the banner of a left-wing front as early as 1950, when eighteen of them were elected to Parliament. At no time (until April 1967) was it suggested that the threat of communism could only be contained by suspending the constitution and abolishing Parliament. Even the strongest and most autocratic of post-war prime ministers, Field-Marshal Papagos, never contemplated taking power except as the result of a constitutional election. He knew very well that there was no necessity to do so.

That sardonic philhellene, George Finlay, used to say that the Greeks were 'unfitted both by nature and circumstances for any but constitutional government'; and furthermore he rebutted the charge that they were a difficult people to govern.[10] There could be no better confirmation of his judgment than the years from 1952 to 1964. For eleven years Greece was governed by what was virtually a single party under Papagos and Karamanlis, which won four consecutive elections. Karamanlis, leader of the National Radical Union (ERE), had a longer tenure of office than any British prime minister since Asquith. Accusations can be, and were, brought against Karamanlis' system of government, but hardly on grounds of instability. Nor can any accusation at all be brought against the two elections which terminated his administration in 1963–64 and

brought to power the opposition Centre Union (EK) under Papandreou.
Such a sequence of events is taken for granted in Britain. Elsewhere in
Europe it is rare.

It may well be asked, then, why the military revolutionaries of April
1967 were able to claim that Greek democracy had broken down into
irremediable bankruptcy, and that a communist conspiracy to seize power
was about to be put into effect. The communist conspiracy has long been
exploded as a myth. If it is necessary to disprove it again, the evidence is
very simple. A great many reputed communists were arrested on 21 April
1967, and many documents were seized which were alleged to prove the
existence of the conspiracy. Since that date many 'treason trials' have
been held and many men and women have been convicted of conspiracy
against the revolutionary regime; but not a single indictment, trial or
conviction has ever been recorded for subversive action before 21 April
1967. It is inconceivable that if such a trial were legally possible on the
basis of genuine evidence, it would not have taken place.

The KKE has in fact been in a state of progressive disintegration for a
number of years, certainly since long before April 1967. At least five
distinct factions, each with its own leader and committee, can be distinguished; but it is not any direct action of the present government (as
it was when Maniadakis was Minister of the Interior under Metaxas in
the 1930s) that has produced the disintegration of the Party. One schism
was caused in the 1950s by recriminations over defeat in the civil war,
another by the Sino-Soviet dispute in the 1960s. The most recent division
has been caused by recriminations over the failure of the Party to be
ready to react against the *coup* of April 1967, which it entirely failed to
foresee. Such a state of unreadiness, which was certainly a fact, is in
significant contrast with the claim that the Revolution forestalled a
communist plot.

The reality seems to be very different. On the one hand, there has been
an increase of subversive activity labelled as communist since the Revolution; and it seems that a greater number of Greeks than before think they
are communists or would like to be communists. On the other hand, the
Revolution has perhaps added a sixth faction to the five already identified.
It consists of those ex-communists who find their authoritarian instincts
better satisfied today by a successful dictatorship than by an ineffective
KKE. But although the 'communist plot' of 1967 was a myth, it should
not be overlooked that very many of the government's innocent supporters (though not the Colonels themselves) still sincerely believe in it.

The contention that parliamentary democracy was itself on the point of breakdown, irrespective of communist activity, deserves more serious consideration. No one would dispute that Greek democracy was at a point of crisis by early 1967. What is at issue is whether the crisis was correctly diagnosed and treated. The detailed history of the period can hardly yet be written, but one or two salient facts are unlikely to be disputed. One is that the point of crisis was reached not in April 1967 but in July 1965. In that month a quarrel between the young King Constantine and his prime minister, George Papandreou, culminated in the fall of the Centre Union government. So uncertain are the precise details of what passed between the King and his prime minister that it cannot be confidently stated whether the latter resigned or was dismissed. But it is clear that their dispute had both a general and a specific character. The general aspect was, as became apparent when their correspondence was later published, that the King thought he was being kept inadequately informed about the government's policy, and was therefore being prevented from fulfilling his constitutional role. The specific aspect concerned the control of the armed forces, particularly the appointment of Minister of Defence.

Superficially, again, the facts are fairly clear: what lay behind them is not. Two things were troubling the government about the officer corps of the army. Having been out of office for over eleven years, Papandreou considered that senior appointments were unduly biased in favour of supporters of his predecessor. More seriously, it was well known that there were two active conspiracies at work among army officers: a right-wing group (IDEA or The Sacred Bond of Greek Officers), whose antecedents went back to World War II, and a left-wing group (*Aspida*, or The Shield). It was widely believed, moreover, that the Prime Minister's son, Andreas, was associated with the latter. Papandreou found his own Minister of Defence insufficiently assiduous in dealing with the former problem, and therefore dismissed him. The King accepted the dismissal, but resisted Papandreou's intention to assume the Ministry of Defence himself, on the grounds that it was inappropriate at a time when his own son was under suspicion of complicity in a conspiracy within the army. Papandreou's insistence resulted in his own fall, whether by resignation or dismissal, and in the formation of a succession of weak and unstable governments until April 1967.

The crisis of July 1965 proved fatal both to the monarchy and to parliamentary democracy in Greece. It need not have proved fatal to either. Although the country was troubled by many problems (including a recrudescence of the Cyprus dispute), the year 1964 had been one of hopeful augury. On the death of his father, King Paul, the young King Constantine II had come to the throne in the most favourable circumstances. As a result of the General Election in February 1964, he had both a loyal government of the centre and a loyal opposition of the right. (Had the election gone the other way, as in the previous eleven years, he would have had a loyal government but a disloyal opposition.) For the first time since World War II, the two-party system was actually beginning to work. Whether or not the King was right in his dispute with his Prime Minister eighteen months later, his subsequent conduct was imprudent. Although he certainly did not act unconstitutionally, he disregarded a long-established constitutional convention that the King should offer the mandate to form a government to the party leader who commanded the largest number of supporters in Parliament. Since Papandreou still had a majority at the time of his resignation (or dismissal), convention required that the King should either dissolve Parliament or call on Papandreou to form a new government. In fact, he did neither: instead, he helped to procure the defection of a sufficient number of Papandreou's supporters in Parliament to enable another Prime Minister to form a government. After several false starts, Stephanopoulos succeeded in this task, with the support of Kanellopoulos, the leader of the opposition.

It has been much debated whether the King or Papandreou was to blame for the crisis of July 1965. Both men certainly acted intemperately, and neither can be wholly acquitted. But a considered judgment must be that a greater share of blame falls on the King and his advisers. This may seem paradoxical, given that the King was a much younger and less experienced man than Papandreou, but the judgment follows from the nature of the Greek constitution. Constitutionally there was no means by which, and no human authority by whom, sanctions could be imposed on the King if he acted wrongly: he could only be deposed, which is not a constitutional but a revolutionary sanction. The position of the Prime Minister was different. His errors, if he committed them, could be duly punished – not, of course, by the King but by the people at the next election. Unlike the King, he committed errors at his own risk. That is what the constitution meant when it declared that the King was without responsibility. He was obliged to be more careful, not less careful, about exceeding his rights. That is also what Papandreou meant when he said that 'the King reigns, but the People rule'. In the manoeuvres which he adopted against Papandreou, the King undoubtedly flouted that maxim. With his mother and his advisers at his elbow, it is doubtful whether he would even have accepted it in theory.

Although Stephanopoulos' government lasted until the end of 1966, the King's action by itself probably sealed the fate of the monarchy. Papandreou declared an 'implacable struggle' against what he considered an abuse of the constitution. His militant supporters and some unwelcome allies (including the communists) campaigned vigorously in public meetings and demonstrations, many of which became violent. They clamoured for a General Election, which Papandreou was confident he would win. But he also faced a dilemma. The trial of the officers implicated in Aspida proceeded, and the name of his son Andreas was repeatedly mentioned. Being a member of parliament, Andreas Papandreou was immune from prosecution; but that immunity would lapse as soon as Parliament was dissolved. George Papandreou therefore sought the agreement of his opponents that parliamentary immunity should be extended to cover the election period. This was only one of the questions affecting the next election which were hotly disputed: another was, as always, the system of voting to be used. These and other disagreements led to the resignation first of Stephanopoulos' government and then of the 'service' government which followed it with a mandate to conduct elections. The King next took a very unusual course early in April 1967. He appointed a political government under Kanellopoulos, formerly the leader of the opposition (ERE) which had no prospect of a majority in Parliament; and he at once granted a dissolution (which he had refused to Papandreou eighteen months earlier) proclaiming a General Election for 28 May. It was never held: instead came the Revolution of 21 April.

If the election had been held in May 1967, it would have been won either by the National Radical Union under Kanellopoulos or by the Centre Union under Papandreou. There was a widespread fear lest in either event (but more particularly if Papandreou won) violent disturbances might follow, leading to a breakdown of public order. It is impossible to say whether the fear was justified or exaggerated, but clearly it was wise to take precautions. Accordingly, the Chief of the General Staff, General Spandidakis, held a meeting of his senior generals to discuss a contingency plan. It was agreed that before formalizing it, he would seek the consent of the King. The meeting was followed within twenty-four hours by the Revolution. Presumably one of the generals had communicated the decision to the group of Colonels under Papadopoulos, who had been carefully plotting for some years. It is unlikely that the disloyal general was Spandidakis himself, although he became for a time a reluctant member of the revolutionary government. More probably it was Zoitakis, whom the Colonels rewarded with the Regency when

King Constantine revolted and fled. In any case, so far as firm evidence goes, this appears to be all the truth in the rumour of a 'Generals' Plot' which was overtaken by the 'Colonels' Plot'.

Was the Revolution then, as its propaganda claims, an 'historical necessity'? There was undoubtedly a critical situation in the evolution of parliamentary democracy in Greece. But the crisis was not inherent in the system. It was the product of temperamental indiscretions on the part of George Papandreou, compounded by errors of judgment on the part of the young King. The blame must be shared, on Papandreou's side, by his son and other leading politicians; and on the King's side, by his advisers and courtiers. Objectively, the Greek political system was not at fault. It should be noted that the trials arising from the Aspida conspiracy were conducted and brought to a conclusion during the political crisis. It cannot, therefore, be argued that the Revolution was necessary to ensure that justice was done; and although it is true that Andreas Papandreou was not brought to trial with the accused officers, it is equally true that even after the Revolution it proved impossible to make out a case against him. Although indicted, he was, therefore, released and allowed to leave the country.

So the Revolution did not save Greece from the left-wing conspiracy in the army any more than it saved Greece from communism. It probably, though not certainly, averted the election of a new government under George Papandreou; and it was alleged that he, and still more his son, were in league with the communists. This was a difficult charge to level against George Papandreou, who had fought the communists in December 1944 and refused to depend on their support for his minority government in December 1963. As for his son, Andreas, it can only be said that allegations about what he would have done if he had succeeded his father, and even the assumption that he would have succeeded his father, are purely speculative. As an excuse for abolishing parliamentary democracy, such speculations are feeble and unworthy. So indeed are the arguments that Greece was in a state of disorder and turmoil. If violent demonstrations, riots, strikes and explosions in the streets are to be made a ground for the abolition of democracy, then the time could be judged ripe in 1971 for the army to take over the government of the United Kingdom.

As a matter of fact, Greek propagandists have come very close to hinting just that. But one has only to contemplate the argument on one's own doorstep to see the glaring fallacy of it. The solution to problems of order and stability lies in strengthening democracy, not in abolishing it. The merit of constitutional democracy is that when a government goes astray (as perhaps Papandreou's did in 1965), the constitution provides a built-in mechanism by which the people can obtain a remedy. The defect of a revolutionary dictatorship is that it contains no such mechanism, except another revolution followed by another dictatorship.

The present government of Greece claims, of course, that it is neither a dictatorship nor a police state. The Colonels are no longer Colonels but civilians. They assert that they are on the way to restoring democracy in the true sense. Readers of this book can judge for themselves whether their claim is justified. All that can be said with confidence now is that they appeared to start in exactly the opposite direction, and that their journey was not demonstrably necessary.

London, October 1971   *C. M. Woodhouse*

NOTES

1   KHOUTAS, Stylianos Th., *I Ethniki Antistasis ton Ellinon, 1941–1945* (The National Resistance of the Greeks, 1941–1945), Athens 1961, p. 19.
2   KANELLOPOULOS, P., *Ta khronia tou megalou polemou, 1939–1944* (The Years of the Great War, 1939–1944), Athens 1964, pp. 199–208; PAPANDREOU, G., *I Apeleftherosis tis Ellados* (The Liberation of Greece), Athens 1948, pp. 26–45.
3   *Ethniki Antistasis*, no. 145, Ioannina, August 1971.
4   STAVRIDIS, E. A., *Ta paraskinia tou KKE* (Behind the scenes of the KKE), Athens 1953, p. 547.
5   ZAKHARIADIS, N., *Deka khronia palis* (Ten Years of Struggle), Nicosia 1950, pp. 9–10.
6   ZAKHARIADIS, op. cit., pp. 30–33.
7   DEDIJER, V., *Tito Speaks*, London 1953, p. 331; DJILAS, M., *Conversations with Stalin*, London 1962, pp. 164–165.
8   ZAKHARIADIS, op. cit., pp. 28–29.
9   *Rizospastis*, 1 April 1946.
10 DAKIN, Douglas, *British and American Philhellenes*, Thessaloniki 1959, p. 214.

CHAPTER TWO

Politics and the Army
in Post-War Greece

INTRODUCTION

In the morning of 21 April 1967 the people of Greece discovered that during the night the army,* in a swift, well-planned *coup*, had overthrown the conservative government of Panayiotis Kanellopoulos and in its place established a military regime. Thus Greece overnight acquired the dubious distinction of being the first West European country to fall under dictatorial rule since the troubled thirties. The press and informed opinion outside Greece reacted in predictable fashion: surprise and shock at the turn of events in Athens, and concern for the fate of political prisoners, were followed by accusing fingers pointed at the triumvirate that emerged as the leading figures of the *coup d'état* – Colonels Papadopoulos and Makarezos and Brigadier Pattakos, the epithet 'fascist' often being employed to describe the type of regime they established. Eventually, foreign opinion polarized into two general categories. In the first category fell those who believed that democracy in Greece was somehow monstrously raped by the 'Colonels', and in the second those who felt that the Greeks got precisely what they deserved; they had never known how to handle democratic institutions and political liberties anyway. Some journalists attempted to reach beneath the surface and try to analyse the causes of

* The terms 'army' and 'armed forces' are used interchangeably throughout this essay. However, the 1967 *coup d'état* in Greece was exclusively an army undertaking, with the navy and air force playing a limited role only after 21 April 1967.

17

this military intervention in Greek politics. Generally, however, much of what has been written has failed to place this particular event in the broader context of civil–military relations in post-war Greece. In other words, the questions why an army that is considered 'professionalized', serving a nation that has existed as an independent entity for a century and a half in its modern form, and coming from a population that is (*a*) ethnically homogeneous, (*b*) literate, (*c*) 'politicized', and (*d*) at the 'take-off' stage of economic development, should take the grave, if not fateful, step of open political intervention have never been fully explored. This essay will attempt to correct that discrepancy.

MILITARY PROFESSIONALISM AND POLITICAL INTERVENTION

Everywhere in the world, in capitalist societies and in socialist ones, in the Western and Eastern blocs of nations, in primitive and in industrialized societies, armies play a political role. What distinguishes the army of one nation from that of another is the degree or extent of its political involvement. An army has to be viewed as an interest-group – one among many such groups in society. In many regards, armies are like farmers, industrial workers, or shopkeepers: they have special interests to advance or protect. Naturally, they always attempt to win policy-makers and the general public over to their point of view. In other words, armies are competing with many other social, economic, and professional groups for the usually scarce resources that must be allocated by political leaders.

Armies differ from other groups in society in four very significant ways. First, their rigidly hierarchical organization makes them formidable opponents in the competition for power and influence. Second, their virtual monopoly on the means of violence and repression is a valuable asset. Third, the distinctive appearance of soldiers (wearing of uniforms, etc.) gives an army the important advantage of visibility. Finally, the army's role as representative and defender of the 'national interest' gives it added weight in the contest for the allocation of national resources. If an army operates, as the armed forces of Greece do, a nation-wide radio and television network – with all the opportunities for public opinion manipulation that these media offer – its bargaining position becomes even more explicit. With all the advantages that armies have over other groups in society, one is justified in wondering, as S. E. Finer does, not why they intervene in politics but why they do not do so more often.[1]

Why does the degree of intervention differ from one society to the next? Why is civilian control of the military possible in nation A but not in nation B? Samuel P. Huntington believes that civil supremacy over the military can be best maintained by a thorough professionalization of the latter. He has written: 'A highly professional officer corps stands ready to carry out the wishes of any civilian group which secures legitimate authority within the state.'[2] On the other hand, Finer feels that professionalism alone is not a good safeguard against military involvement in politics. In fact, he states that military professionalism 'often thrusts the military into a collision with the civil authorities'.[3] He maintains that an explicit belief by the military in the principle of civil supremacy is the necessary ingredient of effective civil–military relations. Moreover, Finer has established an interesting theory about military intervention related to the level of a society's 'political culture'. He states: 'The levels to which the military press their intervention are related to the *level of political culture* of their society.'[4] Another researcher, M. D. Feld, suggests that social and political factors, not military professionalism, elucidate modern civil–military relationships. He believes that political stability is a prerequisite to, not a consequence of, the creation of a professional, 'apolitical' officer corps.[5] After surveying recent trends he comes to a pessimistic conclusion about the prospects of civil supremacy over the military, especially in new nations. This is because most nations today follow what he calls 'secularist goals', that is policies intended to improve general living standards. His argument rests on the following hypothesis: 'Since the military policy of a secular society has as its objective the creation of an apolitical armed force and the social policy of the professional soldier has as its objective the creation of an apolitical society, sustained and equal partnership between the two is impossible.'[6]

As far as Greece is concerned, the hypotheses of Finer and Feld seem to have greater validity than Huntington's. The Greek officer corps is a thoroughly professional organization, according to the criteria of professionalism established by Huntington.[7] Its professionalism, however, did not prevent it from using force to seize control of the government in 1967. Greece's 'level of political culture' and the 'secularization' of Greek society in the post-war period, that is to say factors other than military professionalism, accounted for the army's actions in 1967. We shall discuss these factors, and others peculiar only to Greece, shortly. Before we turn to that, however, we must consider the essential elements of civil–military relations in Greece.

POLITICS AND THE SOLDIER IN GREECE

Republicans and Monarchists, Communism and Nationalism   The principal and most enduring source of political division in the history of modern Greece has been over the question of whether Greece should be a Republic or a Monarchy. There have been repeated conflicts, and military interventions, in support of or in opposition to either point of view and the issue is clearly not yet settled. One of the reasons why the conflict persists is that the Monarchy is a political transplant, grafted upon the Greek body politic by the Great Powers following the Greek War of Independence. The powers felt that a Monarch would be able (*a*) to bring some degree of agreement among the quarrelling factions controlled by the various leaders of the struggle against Ottoman Turkey, and (*b*) to keep Greece on good terms with them. This was not necessarily what most Greeks wanted; the Monarchy, therefore, has failed to develop deep roots in modern Greece.

The army has always played a crucial role in the continuing dispute between Republicans and Royalists, most of the time before 1936 manifesting Republican sentiments. It was instrumental, for example, in the abolition of the absolute Monarchy of Otho, the first King of Greece, who was eventually forced to abdicate in 1862. In 1909 younger army officers with Republican inclinations organized a genuine revolution. That event has left a lasting imprint on the political history of modern Greece while, at the same time, altering the political role of the army through reforms imposed upon its organization, and especially the recruitment and training of officers.[8]

The political significance of the 1909 revolution is connected with the career of Eleftherios Venizelos, under whose leadership Greece expanded in size after the Balkan Wars of 1912–13, and played a prominent role, for a small nation on the periphery of Europe, in the international politics of the period. The importance of 1909 to the army cannot be exaggerated. It could be argued, for one thing, that the professionalization of the military in Greece, and its *raison d'être* – the defence of extensive frontiers – were a direct result of that particular event. At the same time, the shift in officer recruitment patterns, from the commercial and land-owning aristocracy to the middle classes and the peasantry, altered the political perspectives of the army leadership in a profound way. It is noteworthy that before 1909 army interventions in politics did not result in direct army rule. Rather, politicians were backed by officer groups, the officers themselves performing the function of arbiter rather than ruler. Army interventions in politics since 1909 have generally tended to involve officers in direct political roles. This substantiates Janowitz's thesis that the recruitment of officers from the aristocracy contributed to making the military profession generally conservative and disdainful of active politics. He states: 'As the military in the West became a middle-class profession, one consequence was that the profession was opened to more direct political involvement.'[9]

The conflict between Republicans and Monarchists, both inside the army and out, assumed new dimensions during and soon after the occupation of Greece by the Germans in World War II. Because the communists and their sympathizers had traditionally been the most vocal opponents of the Monarchy, and in 1944-45 seemed on the verge of gaining control of Greece, anti-communists of all hues and orientations found in the Monarchy a convenient symbol around which to rally their forces. (Naturally, the palace obliged; all three of its post-war occupants cheerfully assumed the role of anti-communist-in-chief.) In short, the historic Republican–Monarchist schism became aggravated after being imbued with the emotional ingredients of the conflicting cold-war ideologies. As far as the army itself is concerned, this change had the following consequences. First, it was simply purged of all officers with known Republican leanings. Second, those selected for officer training after 1944 had to survive the rigorous test of nationalism which was assumed to mean (*a*) loyalty to the King, and (*b*) steadfast opposition to communism and anyone having anything to do with it.

The subsequent experience of the December 1944 uprising in Athens, and the 1946-49 civil war – the bloodiest fratricide in the history of modern Greece – have left an indelible impression on all Greeks and especially army officers. Those who organized the 1967 *coup d'état* had fought against the communist insurgents and had personally experienced the effects of that terrible conflict, while younger officers were old enough in the late forties to have formed distinct impressions of the anti-guerilla struggle. These impressions were reinforced by large doses of anti-communist indoctrination in military schools. It is in the light of the civil war experience that the strong nationalism of the officer corps in contemporary Greece must be examined. And it is a form of messianic, populistic nationalism that has characterized the post-1967 regime in Greece.

NATO: The Fusion of Interests The army's successful prosecution of the war against the communist insurgents gave it renewed *esprit* and a generally positive public image. But it could not hope to continue enjoying a privileged status as far as the allocation of resources was concerned. The monumental task of economic and social reconstruction after a costly war, a brutal occupation, and almost four years of uninterrupted civil strife had to be given priority. The prospect of substantial reductions in the size of an army never appeals to career officers. In Greece, a good case could be made for the retention of a large standing army. While the internal danger had subsided, an external one remained. Greece, after all, had common borders with three communist states, two of which, Albania and Bulgaria, continued to be perceptibly belligerent. The 'external factor' – a critical one in any analysis of modern Greek politics – came to the rescue. For while the localized conflict in Greece was being concluded, the wider one between East and West – the cold war – had intensified. The formation of NATO could not have occurred at a more propitious moment.

The NATO alliance offered the nationalist forces in Greece, the army included, an enormous boost. Although Greece was outside the North Atlantic area, its participation in NATO was considered desirable from a strategic point of view. Because virtually all nationalist politicians felt it was in the Greek national interest to join the alliance, and because the communists and other forces on the left had not yet fully re-emerged on the post-civil war political scene, there was scarcely any debate in the critical early stages of the negotiations for Greek participation in NATO. Nearly everyone, it seems, was convinced that Greece's alliance with the West was inevitable. In the armed forces, the benefits to Greece of a Western alliance led by the United States were given enormous importance for two reasons: it guaranteed that (*a*) Greek national interests would be protected and supported by an alliance built around the great power of the United States, and (*b*) a sizable standing army could be retained and the process of its modernization would continue.

In short, the effect of NATO was to unite the geopolitical interests of the Greek nation with the corporate and professional interests of its armed forces. It is easy to understand, then, why for an overwhelming majority of career officers the NATO alliance is the closest thing to a sacred bond, and why anyone who would dare question Greece's role in it is regarded either as a communist or a fellow-traveller. So long as those questioning the value of NATO came from the extreme left (e.g. the pro-communist EDA party) and therefore stood little chance of gaining control of the government, the army was satisfied to remain in the background. But it perceived as a salient threat the attitude of a non-communist personality with a growing popular appeal, such as Andreas Papandreou, who repeatedly suggested that Greece might well profit from a 'Gaullist'-inspired stance toward NATO and United States patronage. One of the factors contributing to the 1967 intervention was the suspicion that a Papandreou victory at the polls would inevitably push Greece toward a 'neutralist' foreign policy.

The Political System of 'Clientage' and the Army Social scientists have found it intellectually rewarding to develop classifications for political and social phenomena and institutions. When considering political parties it may be profitable to place them into three general types or categories: the *ideological* type, in which radical parties of both the left and the right might be placed; the *programmatic* one, which is typically found in Western Europe and North America; and the *personality* party, which is a peculiar feature of new nations and some older but still 'transitional' societies. The characteristic quality of the third type of party is that it is formed around the demagogic virtues of a charismatic figure. Historically, Greek political parties, with the exception of the Communist Party of Greece (KKE) and its post-war successor, the United Democratic Left (EDA), have been of the last, or personality, type. In effect, the inability of 'nationalist' political parties to develop either ideological or programmatic foundations has been one of the chief institutional weaknesses in modern Greek politics. And it is the principal reason why the Greek parliamentary system has always been notoriously unstable. The by-product of this deficiency has been the 'clientage' system, whereby the relationship between voter and parliamentary deputy is determined by their mutual interests and not by an attachment to party ideals or pro-grammes. As Keith R. Legg writes, 'the personal political relationship remains the most crucial factor in Greek electoral politics.'[10]

It is quite possible under this system for a deputy with a faithful 'clientèle' to change political party association at will without really affecting his re-election prospects. The 'clientage' system can be useful to both patron and client. The patron knows that he can rely on a stable base of political support while the client has a personal contact in the nation's legislature, useful in cases that may necessitate intervention with the cumbersome and unresponsive bureaucracy. The political power, and therefore the importance of the individual deputy to the party leader, is determined by the number of votes the former can deliver at election time. In Greece, the clientage system has traditionally been the principal factor determining cabinet appointments.

What does all this have to do with the army? A great deal. First, the

army has always resented the effects of the clientage system on matters
that armies everywhere regard as prerogatives of the organization –
promotions, transfers, and assignments, for example. It is well known
that in the Greek armed forces transfers and assignments, if not so much
promotions, were often influenced by political considerations. This did
not involve only officers but enlisted personnel as well.

Second, many officers disapproved of the way voting was carried out
in the military. It was commonly charged after some elections that whole
units were marched to the polls after having been given thinly disguised
instructions by their officers on how to vote and for whom. At the same
time, a system of supervision was devised which had the effect of harassing
those who disregarded the instructions.[11] It is easy to see why such
practices would alienate some career officers; they must have realized that
such operations do not remain secret for very long and when they are
discovered they bring dishonour and disrepute upon the armed services
and their officers.

Finally, deliberate endeavours were made by political leaders to develop
clientage networks within the military upon which they could rely if and
when the more traditional sources of political support were exhausted.
Legg suggests, for example, that Constantine Karamanlis, leader of the
National Radical Union (ERE) party and Prime Minister from 1955 until
1963, was able to utilize his support within the army and clientage
connections in paramilitary organizations such as the Battalions of
National Security (TEA) and the police – especially in rural areas – to win
the elections in 1961.[12] Naturally, many officers – even some from among
those supporting Karamanlis – resented the use of the army as a political
instrument. It seems they were not prepared to do very much about it,
however, until another party, George Papandreou's Centre Union (EK),
won control of the government and in its turn tried to establish its own
clientage links within the army. This leads us to a discussion of politically
motivated officers' organizations.

The formation of secret societies within the Greek military has a long
tradition. It was such a society, for instance, that spearheaded the Revolution of 1909. And it appears that the leading members of the group
responsible for the success of the 1967 *coup* belonged to such a semi-
clandestine society, in this case known by the acronym IDEA whose
letters stand for *Ieros Desmos Ellinon Axiomatikon* (Sacred Bond of Greek
Officers). According to the generally well-informed American journalist
C. L. Sulzberger, IDEA was organized soon after the liberation of Greece
from Nazi rule by an officer who eventually, in 1956, became Army Chief

of Staff. At one time all Lieutenant-Generals (the highest rank in the Greek army) were or had been members of IDEA. The purposes of this organization were three: (*a*) anti-communism; (*b*) loyalty to the King; (*c*) support for conservative 'nationalist' political leaders. One of those who enjoyed the support of IDEA was Karamanlis.[13] During the early years of Karamanlis' rule, it seems to have fallen into inactivity. This inactivity did not last long.

Following the elections of 1958, from which the pro-communist EDA emerged as the leading opposition party with 78 deputies in the 300-member parliament, some officers became concerned (*a*) that communism was still a major threat in Greece, and (*b*) that politicians were either unwilling or incapable of doing anything to meet the renewed communist challenge. IDEA was revitalized with Colonel George Papadopoulos as one of its more prominent members.[14]

An officers' society known as ASPIDA (shield) became the *cause célèbre* of the political turmoil that broke out in the summer of 1965. This group of officers was organized by junior 'left-wing' army men allegedly to guarantee army support for the aims and purposes of the Centre Union (EK) party in general and Andreas Papandreou in particular. There has been a good deal of confusion and ambiguity about ASPIDA but one thing is clear; such an organization did exist within the army. What its actual purposes were has not yet been made absolutely clear. One theory has it that its members were chiefly disenchanted with the slow pace of promotions, low pay, and declining status of officership in a peacetime society concerned principally with 'secularist' goals, to use Feld's terminology, and were interested in improving the general condition of the military profession. If this were the case, their choice of Andreas Papandreou as a political mentor would seem natural: he was the rising star of Centre-Left politics. Another possibility is that ASPIDA was composed of officers who strongly disapproved of the use of the army as an instrument of conservative anti-communism and right-wing party politics.

The existence within the military establishment of conspiratorial officer cliques – no matter what their motives – signified a general breakdown in civilian supervision and control, a dangerous decline in discipline, and widespread factionalism within the officer corps. The King's constitutional role as commander-in-chief, in an active sense, not a passive one as is the case with the Queen in Britain, was intended to insulate the armed forces from partisan politics and thereby neutralize interventionist tendencies in the officer corps. This was predicated, however, on the assumption that the Monarchy would refrain from active political in-

volvement. Needless to say, that assumption was all too vividly disproved
by events.

Swords and Ploughshares An important aspect of the Greek army's
political influence derives from its role as a factor in the economic and
social development of Greece. Since the early days of the post-war
period, the Greek armed forces have been involved in a wide variety of
reconstruction and development projects. For example, taking advantage
of the fact of universal military training, they have contributed toward
the virtual elimination of the stigma of illiteracy among men under the
age of forty by forcing illiterate recruits to attend special schools where
reading, writing, and simple mathematics are taught. More importantly,
however, the Greek armed forces serve – as armies in all developing
countries do according to Janowitz – 'as a training ground for technical
and administrative skills'.[15] For instance, by building and maintaining
infrastructure projects such as roads and bridges the Greek army trains
a large number of young men to operate, maintain, and repair heavy
construction equipment, skills that can prove beneficial to them and to
society at large upon their return to civilian life. And the list of skills
learned in the armed forces that can be useful in civilian life is a very
long one.

By far the most impressive non-military work done by the armed
forces of Greece is in the general area of public works and housing. To
co-ordinate this type of activity a special unit was created in 1957 within
the Department of Defence – *Stratiotiki Yperesia Ergon Anasyngrotiseos*
(Military Reconstruction Projects Service). In the twelve-year period
between 1957 and 1969 this service was allocated well over one billion
drachmas – 1 billion 191 million, to be exact – (30 dr= $1 US), for a large
number of public works and housing projects. Two specific examples
are sufficient to make the point. In July 1968, an Air Force construction
unit was assigned the task of erecting several structures at the newly-
created University of Patras. With the use of pre-fabricated materials,
and military equipment and personnel exclusively, the task was completed a year later. In the fiscal year 1969 alone, military construction
teams installed 937 pre-fabricated housing units in ten different areas of
Greece, at a total cost of 70 million drachmas. These projects are to
accommodate families whose homes were destroyed by earthquakes.[16]

The social and economic roles of the Greek armed forces, only a few
examples of which have been given above, have important political
implications. Such visible non-military functions give the army –
especially the army of a developing nation – a self-perception and a

public image as an instrument of progress and modernization. The self-perception can lead professional soldiers to misjudge and over-estimate the importance of the army to the nation's development. Thus, they may decide to intervene when they feel that the political leadership does not give it due consideration in the allocation of resources or sufficient credit for its development accomplishments. At the same time, a positive public image can be turned into a political asset either in the struggle for resource allocation or after a direct political intervention.

FACTORS CONTRIBUTING TO THE 1967 INTERVENTION

It is possible to isolate five reasons why the military have intervened in twentieth-century Greek politics. Military interventions have resulted from: (1) conflicts between Republican and Monarchist factions within the army; (2) a humiliating defeat suffered by the army and blamed on the politicians; (3) the existence of a vacuum created by sustained political crises; (4) an ostensible attachment of the army to the principles of social justice and modernization; and (5) a communist threat (real or imagined). Reasons 3, 4, and 5 have been repeatedly given in justification of the April 1967 *coup d'état*. Together they constitute the political factors behind the 1967 intervention. Additionally, there is another factor, the psychological one, which we shall discuss in some detail.

Political Factors: Crisis and Fear The ingredients of the prolonged political crisis under which Greece laboured from July 1965 until April 1967 have been discussed in another part of this volume (see Chapter One). Suffice it to say for the purposes of this analysis, the inability or unwillingness of the major political leaders and the King to resolve their differences and arrive at an early compromise paved the way for the relatively easy success of the Colonels' *coup*. The crisis exposed the deep roots of the malaise afflicting the traditional sectors of the Greek political world and gave a strong impetus to anti-political forces within the military and the general public. Moreover, it gave rise to a dormant spirit of messianism within the officer corps which, once aroused, has always proved difficult to contain or reverse.

Ostensibly, the July 1965 crisis was caused by a dispute between the Prime Minister, George Papandreou, and King Constantine over who should become Minister of Defence at a time when an investigation into the ASPIDA affair was about to begin, rumours and allegations having been made that the Prime Minister's son Andreas was the political leader of the ASPIDA group. What the actual reasons might have been is probably irrelevant.[17] The fact remains that, as Sulzberger writes, 'the King eased the elder Papandreou out of office and installed a succession of weak governments in an effort to *disintegrate* the Papandreist Centre Union majority in Parliament'[18] (my italics). In effect, the King installed three successive governments – all from factions of the Centre Union – which, due to their political weakness and clearly transitional character, were unable to accomplish anything constructive. Greek political life during the eighteen months between July 1965 and April 1967 remained in that unenviable state of suspended animation the French so aptly call *immobilisme*. It is disgust with *immobilisme* and blatant political manipulation, more than anything else, that accounts for the unaccustomed apathy with which the Greek public responded to the army's destruction of the country's parliamentary institutions.

Public reaction to Papandreou's dismissal was swift and extremely vocal. Protests and demonstrations of all kinds kept the crisis atmosphere in full force. In the end this had the effects of (*a*) dangerously polarizing political attitudes, (*b*) forging the deputies remaining faithful to Papandreou into a potentially powerful political force, and (*c*) making the nature of the regime once again an important political issue.

That the King was able to employ 'salami tactics' to create three successive governments from the Centre – always with the unanimous support of the ERE opposition – was yet another clear symptom of the malignancy from which Greek parliamentary life was suffering. And while some politicians were actively collaborating with the King and his advisers to circumvent the system of majority rule, civilian control over the military completely disappeared. A political vacuum was created which, as had happened before in Greece and elsewhere, the army almost instinctively moved in to fill.

One of the reasons most often given to justify the army's political intervention in 1967 is that it was in response to a communist threat. Was there such a threat in 1967? The detached analyst must give a negative answer. Neither the post-1967 government nor independent investigators have been able to produce convincing evidence of a genuine communist threat. To continue insisting that communism constituted a political or military threat in Greece twenty years after its defeat and outlawing, and after constant splits and sectarian struggles within the left, helps to destroy the case for intervention that could be sustained on less ideological grounds.

Having said this, we must consider a qualification. Account must be taken of the fact that some military officers sincerely believed, and many more were looking for an excuse to believe, that communism was still a major threat to the political stability and pro-Western orientation of Greece. Such fears and beliefs were being daily reinforced by the right-wing press, sections of which kept insisting virtually up until the outbreak of the April *coup*, that Greece was on the threshold of another December (1944) uprising.[19] Many officers – because of the civil war experience and their own deep anti-communist convictions – uncritically accepted these irresponsible press warnings. In other words, the threat of communism was *perceived* as salient. As is well known, perception of a threat is as potent a factor contributing to behaviour as the actual existence of such a threat.

The Psychological Factor   Any society that experiences a sustained political crisis is likely to develop serious morale problems. In some societies political turmoil may become institutionalized to some degree. In that situation, the everyday life of the citizen may not be too closely affected by governmental crises inasmuch as the machinery of the state remains largely immune to changes in the government. The state apparatus under these conditions acts as a buffer, insulating the individual from the ever-changing political leadership. A case can be made that such a development has occurred in post-war Italy, and in France during the period of the Fourth Republic. In both societies the state apparatus continued to function more or less smoothly despite constant turnovers in the government. This has not been the case in Greece. An administrative bureaucracy that could remain outside the central arena of partisan politics, and could therefore function independently of the government of the day, has never been allowed to evolve. In short, the blurring of boundaries between government and state made it impossible for unforeseen changes or crises in the former to be cushioned by stable institutions in the latter.

Historically, the results of prolonged political crises in Greece have been economic dislocation, social disorientation, and administrative breakdown or paralysis. These are conditions that the army – imbued with the ideals of discipline, order, hierarchy, and sacrifice – is apt to view with considerable alarm. Besides, professional soldiers tend to exaggerate the effects of political crises to such a degree that the psychological preconditions for direct political intervention may well be built upon flimsy or insufficient evidence, mere rumours, or imaginary threats.

The 1965–67 crisis contained all the elements that give rise to frustration and anxiety, and therefore increase the interventionist disposition of the

military. What was required under these circumstances was some degree
of continuous civilian supervision over the armed forces or, lacking that,
strong royal influence in the officer corps, in conjunction with an absolute
attachment all round to democratic institutions and procedures. By 1967
the feuding politicians were in no position to supervise the armed forces
while the King's influence obviously did not extend to those who
organized and carried out the April *coup*. More importantly, by their
actions the King and a majority in Parliament had repeatedly shown a
disgraceful disregard for democratic rules. In so doing, both King and
Parliament sacrificed their claim to legitimacy on the altar of short-term
political expediency.

Another aspect of the psychological factor involved the prestige or
social position of the officer corps. It is undeniable that by 1967 the
prestige of the officer in Greece had declined dramatically. Factors contributing to this decline were: (*a*) almost twenty years of peace and rising
prosperity, and (*b*) the association in many people's minds of professional
soldiers with right-wing party politics. (Professional soldiers openly
complained to the writer that after 1961 it became increasingly difficult
to appear in public in uniform without facing the possibility of verbal
abuse. On occasion, even young children would go up to an officer in
uniform, shout 'Fascist' at him and run away playfully.) And despite the
loyal support it received from the army, the Karamanlis regime had
shown very little concern for the material well-being of the officer class.
This obviously contributed to an expansion of the inherent anti-political
mood of professional soldiers; it was compounded by a sense of betrayal
when Karamanlis decided to withdraw from active politics following the
1963 elections. Add to all of the above the perception of a communist
threat and you have all the major psychological foundations for military
intervention in politics.

THE COUPMAKERS: A SOCIOLOGICAL PORTRAIT

In his book about the political role of the military in Egypt, P. J. Vatikiotis
finds particular significance in the fact that 'Of the eleven men who
composed the founding committee of the Free Officers group in late
1949, eight entered the Academy in 1936.'[20] It is noteworthy that of the
twelve men who were instrumental in planning and finally putting into
effect the April 1967 *coup* in Greece, seven were members of the Military
Academy class of 1943, while four graduated with the class of 1940, and

TABLE I

Leaders of the 1967 Coup d'Etat

Name	Military Academy Class	Rank in 1967	Branch	Position in Government*
Karydas, K.	1939	Col.	Armour	Secretary General, Ministry of Public Works
Kotselis, P.	1940	Col.	Inf.	Secretary General, Ministry of Public Order
Ladas, I.	1940	Col.	Inf.	Secretary General, Ministry of Interior
Makarezos, N.	1940	Col.	Art.	Minister of Co-ordination
Papadopoulos, G.[3]	1940	Col.	Art.	Prime Minister, Minister of Defence and Foreign Affairs
Balopoulos, M.	1943	Lt-Col.	Art.	Secretary General, National Tourist Organization
Ioannidis, D.[1]	1943	Lt-Col.	Inf.	Commander, Military Police
Lekkas, A.	1943	Lt-Col.	Inf.	Secretary General, Ministry of Industry
Mexis, A.	1943	Lt-Col.	Inf.	Secretary General, Ministry of Social Welfare
Papadopoulos, K.[3]	1943	Lt-Col.	Inf.	Secretary General, Ministry to Prime Minister
Roufogalis, M.[1]	1943	Lt-Col.	Art.	Chief of Staff, Central Intelligence Agency (KYP)
Stamatelopoulos, D.[2]	1943	Lt-Col.	Inf.	Secretary General, Ministry of Transportation

[1] Still on active duty. All the others listed above (with the exception of Lekkas who did not resign until 1970) resigned their commissions in late 1967.

[2] Left the government in early 1968. As a columnist in the afternoon daily *Vradyni* Stamatelopoulos has become a critic of the Papadopoulos regime – a sort of loyal, if sometimes caustic, opposition.

[3] Brothers.

* *Editors' Note:* These positions were held as of summer 1971. Since then in a government reshuffle (August 1971), George Papadopoulos abolished all posts of General Secretaries of Ministries as well as the Ministry of Co-ordination. N. Makarezos became second Deputy Premier, while several General Secretaries of Ministries filled the newly created posts of Deputy Ministers – Governors of Greece's major Provinces. It is interesting to note that a few of these General Secretaries (such as Lekkas and Kotselis) were removed from all government posts, thus revealing a serious split within the group of coupmakers.

one with the class of 1939. Of some significance is the fact that the class of 1943 (seven of whom as Lieutenant-Colonels in 1967 were among the leaders of the *coup*) experienced the bitter-sweet sensation of mutiny and insubordination as young cadets in April 1941 when they were ordered not only to surrender to the invading Germans but to act as policemen as well – to make certain that the population of Athens did not offend the Germans in the initial stages of the occupation. This order the corps of cadets found unacceptable, and in a meeting unanimously decided to disobey their superiors. This they did, and in commandeered vehicles and small vessels they reached Crete in time to take part in the bloody battle for the island, giving a very good account of themselves while suffering a large number of casualties. Many of those who survived fought against the Axis powers, either in the Middle East with the forces of the Greek government in exile or with the 'nationalist' resistance inside Greece.

There are many striking similarities between the Egyptian Free Officers and the Greek Colonels who spearheaded the 1967 intervention. Vatikiotis notes, for example, that the original organizers of the Free Officers group had similar childhood and military experiences. Most 'were of humble origin – from all parts of Egypt. Their fathers and grandfathers were peasant farmers, small landowners, or minor officials in the Delta or Upper Egypt provinces.'[21] According to their own statements and proclamations, all of the officers listed in Table I were of humble origin (they seem to take pride in and to emphasize that fact) coming from the peasantry or lower middle class, from villages or small towns: only one of them (Balopoulos) was born in Athens. As the sons of peasant farmers, schoolteachers, or petty government functionaries, they had almost identical childhood experiences. Their education in village primary and provincial secondary schools must have been a source of hardship and sacrifice for their families. Their formal education was undoubtedly augmented by first-hand experience of the harsh realities of Greek rural life during the economic crisis of the 1930s. One can safely assume that the choice of a military career was not, for many of them, so much a matter of personal preference but of simple family economics – tuition in the Military Academy was free.

All of them reached the impressionable formative years of their life and entered the Military Academy during the Metaxas dictatorship. One must suppose that the Metaxas regime, with its heavy emphasis on strict law and order, its rigid anti-communism, its anti-political bias and slogans and visions about the creation of a 'Third Greek Civilization', left a deep impression on the young minds of the future Colonels. In the statements and public posturing of some since 1967, one cannot fail to notice a certain admiration and nostalgia for the late thirties. This, however, should not leave the reader with the impression that all of the officers listed in Table I are mindless authoritarians. As a group they are probably intellectually superior to the average Greek army officer. Nicholas Makarezos and George Papadopoulos, for example, graduated near the head of their class in 1940, as numbers three and four respectively. Some on the list are known to have studied non-military subjects (philosophy, history, politics, psychology) on their own, a few spent time abroad, either on military assignments or in army-connected schools. Of the twelve, Makarezos stands out intellectually. He has degrees in Economics and Political Science, and has served as a Professor at the Military Academy. He is the only one with quasi-diplomatic experience, having served as Military Attaché to the Greek Embassy in Bonn.

Perhaps the experience with the greatest psychological impact upon these officers was the 1946–49 civil war in which they all took part on the nationalist side. It is undeniably true that in terms of sheer viciousness and brutality no other conflict is as savage as a civil war. And when a civil war is invested with the almost religious fanaticism of the conflicting ideologies of communism and nationalism – as was the case in Greece – the social and political wounds it opens up, the hatreds it gives rise to, and the bitterness it creates stagger the imagination. Reconciliation after such a conflict becomes very difficult, if not altogether impossible. It is the civil-war experience, as was noted earlier, that accounts for the near-pathological anti-communism and messianic nationalism of the pro-tagonists of the 1967 *coup d'état* in Greece. That experience produced in most of them a psychological condition which might be best described as a saviour or messiah complex, with a critical bearing on all their actions.

The humble origins of these officers make them suspicious and disdainful of any elite – whether political, economic, intellectual, or even military – and explains the strain of populism in their post-67 programmes, policies, and rhetoric. Their intense nationalism – by its very nature – contains within it submerged elements of xenophobia that might very easily surface and be put to use when and if the right situation presents itself.

The membership of many, if not all, in IDEA (there is positive evidence that five of the twelve were IDEA members; two or three more were probable members, with a strong possibility that the entire list of twelve belonged to that organization) betrays a propensity for right-wing political activism, disregard for legitimate authority, and impatience with the bureaucratic rules and procedures of the military organization. In effect, most of the twelve men in Table I were politicians in uniform rather than simple soldiers faithfully serving the country's interests, as their post-67 rhetoric would suggest. Nothing substantiates this better than the fact that they managed to cling to power in the face of serious obstacles – domestic opposition, in the form of a near-total boycott by the old politicians, the attempted royal counter-*coup*, and continuous external pressures and protests.

San Bernardino, California, July 1971   *George Zaharopoulos*

NOTES

1 FINER, S. E., *The Man on Horseback*, London 1962, p. 5.
2 HUNTINGTON, Samuel P., *The Soldier and the State*, Cambridge, Mass., 1957, p. 84.
3 FINER, op. cit., p. 25.
4 Ibid., p. 87.
5 FELD, M. D., 'Professionalism, Nationalism, and the Alienation of Military', in Jacques Van Doorn, ed. *Armed Forces and Society*, The Hague 1968, p. 68.
6 Ibid., p. 68.
7 Huntington's criteria of professionalism are *expertise*, *responsibility*, and *corporateness*. See op. cit., pp. 8–18.
8 For a specific listing of changes in army organization and recruitment after 1909 see *Istoria tis Organoseos tou Ellinikou Stratou 1821–1954* (History of the Organization of the Greek Army 1821–1954), Athens: Army General Staff Historical Section, 1957, pp. 86–102.
9 JANOWITZ, Morris, *The Military in the Political Development of New Nations*, Chicago 1964, p. 57.
10 LEGG, Keith R., *Politics in Modern Greece*, Stanford 1969, p. 162.
11 LEGG states: 'In some cases, especially in 1956 and 1961, soldiers were apparently encouraged to select ERE ballots by the higher leadership.' Ibid., p. 218. Statistics for the military and civil service vote for elections between 1950 and 1964 indicate that extensive pressure was applied upon soldiers and civil servants to vote for the right-wing ERE at the expense of both the Centre and the Left. For example: in 1956, ERE received 47·4% of the national vote but 76·4% of the military and civil-service vote. In 1961, it received 50·8% of the national total but 78·9% of the military and civil service vote. In 1964, the ERE national total was reduced to 35·3% while 48·3% of the military and civil servants gave it their vote.

The overall size of the military and civil-service vote is also significant. In 1956 it constituted 4·7% of the total, and in 1961 4·4%. Two years later, however, in 1963, it was only 1·8% and in 1964 1·9%. See Table 8.6 in Legg, op. cit., p. 219.

12 Ibid., pp. 139–140.

13 SULZBERGER, C. L., 'Greece Under the Colonels', *Foreign Affairs*, Vol. 48, No. 2, Jan. 1970, p. 303. Sulzberger is probably the most knowledgeable, if not always the most unbiased, foreign journalist writing about Greece. Among his contacts have been the Royal family and all political leaders in the post-war period.

14 This account is in Savvas Konstantopoulos' *Stratos kai Politiki* (Army and Politics), Athens: 1970, pp. 31–32, 74–79. The author is editor and publisher of *Eleftheros Kosmos*, an Athens daily which has given its full editorial support to the aims and purposes of the post-67 regime. See also Sulzberger, loc cit., p. 304.

15 JANOWITZ, op. cit., p. 75.

16 SYKEA, *Apologismos 1969*, pp. 15–16.

17 The reader may be interested in Andreas Papandreou's own account of the causes of the 1965 crisis. This is to be found in his *Democracy at Gunpoint: The Greek Front*, Garden City, New York 1970. Of particular interest to the student of recent Greek affairs are the letters exchanged between George Papandreou and King Constantine in July 1965 (pp. 158–175).

18 SULZBERGER, loc. cit., p. 302.

19 Articles and editorials in the prestigious conservative daily *Kathimerini* written between 1965 and 1967 provide good examples of such fear-mongering. It is one of the many ironies and contradictions surrounding this case that Helen Vlachos, the owner of *Kathimerini* and another newspaper, was the only one to refuse publication of her newspapers under the censorship imposed by the military regime in Greece, and has since shown an uncompromising opposition to it.

20 VATIKIOTIS, P. J., *The Egyptian Army in Politics: Pattern for New Nations?*, Bloomington, Indiana, 1961, p. 45.

21 Ibid., p. 46.

CHAPTER THREE

The Ideology of
the 'Revolution of 21 April 1967'

'The phoenix rising from its flames is the emblem invariably
adopted by the Greeks.' F. S. N. DOUGLAS, *An Essay on
Certain Points of Resemblance between the Ancient and Modern
Greeks* (1813).

To attempt to define a coherent ideology underlying the actions of the
Greek military regime is a somewhat futile exercise for the very good
reason that such an ideology simply does not exist. What does exist is a
pseudo-ideology or, more accurately, a number of pseudo-ideologies
which the Colonels, or rather their ideologues, have hastily thrown
together as the regime has steadily retreated from its initial justification
for the *coup*. This was essentially a negative justification: that the army
had intervened on a strictly temporary basis to forestall an imminent
communist take-over of the government, and to put an end to the conditions of 'anarchy and chaos' to which the politicians had reduced
Greece. Later, in an effort to rationalize and legitimize the regime's
growing permanence, a classic *golpe de estado* on the South American
pattern became the 'April Revolution', which, moreover, was an
'historic necessity', essential if the Greeks were to be re-educated politically
and in the process rendered 'social' beings, and if the necessary preconditions for the 'New Democracy' were to be created. Traditional
liberal democracy, in the regime's view, is in a state of irreversible decline,
and this 'New Democracy' will be the political system of the future not
only in Greece, but throughout the Western World, where parliamentary
democracy is now a 'sick man'.[1]

This ideological bankruptcy should come as no surprise when one
considers some of the most important motivating factors that lay behind
the army's intervention: fear, personal resentment, anti-communism and

a vague and inarticulate sense of mission, of what S. E. Finer has termed
the 'manifest destiny of the soldiers'.[2] This was a feeling that the army
alone was truly attached to the traditional values of 'Helleno-Christian
civilization' as against those of Pan-Slav communism, and that it alone
was capable of interpreting the will of the nation, a vague metaphysical
entity far superior to the fallible will of the electorate as it might be
expressed in free elections. 'The army,' according to First Deputy Prime
Minister Pattakos, has most fully enshrined 'sacred love towards the
Motherland, belief in Christ, devotion to the institution of the family . . .
the love and sacrifice which Christ taught on the cross.'[3]

The first hint as to the new regime's ideological orientation occurred
on the evening of the *coup* in the broadcast to the nation by the regime's
ornamental civilian Prime Minister Kollias, who delivered a text that
can safely be presumed to have been prepared in advance by the leading
conspirators. This first communiqué, which in Edward Luttwak's typo-
logy could be described as 'messianic',[4] made it clear that the putschists
were essentially adhering to the classic formula of nationalism and
'clearing up the mess' so familiar in Latin America, the Middle East and,
more recently, in Africa.

Kollias declared that 'for long we have been witnesses to a crime which
has been committed against society as a whole and our nation. The
shameless and wretched horse-trading of the parties, the decay of a great
part of the press, the methodical onslaught against all institutions . . . the
paralysis of the state machine, the complete lack of understanding of the
burning problems of our youth . . . moral decline, confusion and uncertainty, secret and open co-operation with wreckers, and finally the cease-
less inflammatory declarations of conscienceless demagogues have
destroyed the calm of the country, creating a climate of anarchy and
chaos, of hatred and division and have led us to the brink of national
catastrophe. There remained no other means of salvation than the intervention of our army. [This necessitates unconstitutional measures] but
the salvation of the Motherland is the highest law. . . .'

'We belong to no political party,' Kollias continued, 'and we do not
intend to give advantage to any political group at the expense of another.
We do not belong to the economic oligarchy. . . . We belong to the class
of toil. And we stand by the side of our poor brothers. . . . We seek to
abolish corruption . . . and to create a healthy basis for the rapid return
of the country to true orthodox parliamentary life. We proclaim brotherhood. From this moment there do not exist rightists, centrists or leftists.
There exist only Greeks who believe in Greece. . . . When the Greeks are

united they create miracles. . . . We will march forward on the path of duty to the Motherland and of Virtue. Towards radical change. Towards prosperity and progress. Our basic objective is social justice. The just distribution of the national income. The moral and material improvement of society as a whole and especially of the peasants and workers and of the poorer classes. . . .'[5]

Kollias' speech, apart from its stereotyped references to the need to clear up the mess left by the politicians (which show a striking similarity to General Metaxas' proclamations after his assumption of dictatorial powers in August 1936) is significant on two accounts. First, there is no direct reference to the imminent threat of a communist takeover, which played such a large part in the regime's early propaganda. Second, it contained, in addition to its denunciation of the anarchy created by the politicians, suggestions of a populist orientation on the part of the new regime.

The great bulk of those rounded up on the night of the *coup* were communists, and the regime quickly claimed to have found a number of arms caches and seventy three-ton truck-loads of weapons and bogus uniforms which the communists, it was alleged, were planning to use when George Papandreou opened his electoral campaign at a mass rally planned for 23 April in Thessaloniki. Despite promises made by Papadopoulos himself (I, p. 13),* none of this evidence was ever produced.[6] Nonetheless, the regime initially emphasized that the country had only narrowly escaped from a communist takeover of government, such as had occurred in Prague in March 1948. A bulky illustrated booklet, published in English by the Panhellenic Confederation of Reserve Officers, and entitled *Why did the Revolution of 21 April take place?*, declared that before the *coup* the communists had controlled 'the beds of public hospitals, the licences of trifle-sellers, even the frozen chickens'.[7] Officers' houses, it was claimed elsewhere, had been marked with an indelible yellow dye in preparation for the hour of the communist uprising.[8]

Yet it also began to be emphasized that communism had never been widespread in Greece, although the regime doggedly and unsuccessfully argued for two years before the European Commission of Human Rights of the Council of Europe that Greece in April 1967 had been facing 'a public emergency threatening the life of the Greek nation'. Within a week of the *coup* Papadopoulos declared that Greeks 'cannot believe in com-

* References in parentheses in this essay are to volumes of Papadopoulos' *To Pistevo Mas.*

munism' (I, p. 15). Later he said that communism has never really taken root in Greece because it was incompatible with the 'Helleno-Christian spirit' (IV, p. 86). While in a remarkable speech of 6 March 1969 he declared that 'We do not face any danger, coming from whatever side. The country's armed forces and security forces, exploiting the vast support which our people provides to their organs, have succeeded so that the situation today (is) to be described as completely secure. . . . We had but a few communists in our country. . . .'[9]

Apart from the cancellation of peasant indebtedness, which in any case benefited only the better-off peasants, and a number of other measures such as making entry to the taxi-driving and baking trades easier, the early hints of populism were never fulfilled (see Chapter Six). Any moves in this direction, even if they had been seriously intended, were ruled out by the regime's overriding need not to alarm the country's business establishment with measures aimed at a more equitable distribution of the national income, and thus upset the country's somewhat precarious economic balance. The regime's economic development policy, according to Col N. Makarezos, Minister of Co-ordination until the drastic government reshuffle in late August 1971 and subsequently Second Deputy Prime Minister, is 'inspired throughout by the principles of free enterprise and is based on private initiative'.[10] Yet Makarezos has elsewhere claimed that the 'revolution' is 'applying a policy of social transformations aimed at economic elevation of the lower-income groups'.[11]

And indeed the regime has maintained at least some of its populist rhetoric, even though it has remained only rhetoric. The most authoritative statement of the regime's ideology to date, George Georgalas' *Ideologia tis Epanastaseos* (Ideology of the Revolution) stresses the point made in Kollias' initial speech that the putschists are the children of '*working people*', descended neither 'from the aristocracy, nor from the plutocracy, nor from any kind of closed caste'. As children of lower middle-class or peasant families, 'they know the taste of sweat. They know the travail of working people. They are flesh of its flesh.' And this, he maintains, has placed its stamp on the whole course of the 'Revolution' (p. 7). Moreover, other apologists for the regime have also maintained that it has a populist orientation. Rodger Davies, Deputy Assistant Secretary of State for Near Eastern and South Asian Affairs, testifying before a US Senate sub-committee in June 1970, claimed that the regime is 'country oriented' and that it has undertaken certain reform measures of an egalitarian nature 'which have been welcomed in rural communities'. But the only one which he was able to specify was 'the abolishment of church fees by which the wealthy could get first-class funerals and the poor would have to make do with whatever the minimum service was'.[12]

At the same time, the regime has specifically denied a Nasserist orientation.[13] Moreover, it has consistently denied that it has any kind of class orientation. Within two months of the *coup* Papadopoulos was declaring that 'the Revolution of 21 April was not a movement of individuals, or groups or social classes. It was a national uprising' (I, p. 52). It has been stressed elsewhere that the 'Revolution' is a 'synthesis of all the creative powers of Hellenism' aiming at the harmonious co-operation of all classes 'with agreement and concord among all citizens'.[14]

But if the early hints of populism have shown no signs of fulfilment, the regime has run true to the form of other military dictatorships in enacting a number of measures reflecting the limited intellectual horizons and thoroughgoing anti-communist and ultra-nationalistic conditioning of most Greek army officers. Among the regime's earliest acts was a decree closing the frontiers to mini-skirted, bearded or long-haired foreigners.[15] This was hastily rescinded in the interests of Greece's vital tourist trade. But in other decrees, schoolchildren (and their teachers) were obliged to attend church on Sundays, *spasimo* or the old Greek custom of smashing plates in *tavernas* was banned, all Greeks were required to stand at attention during the playing of the National Anthem, an index of prohibited books (which included a Greek–Bulgarian dictionary) was issued, and the music of Theodorakis was banned because of its 'anti-ethnic' content.

Inevitably, much concern was shown to protect Greek youth from 'Western neo-anarchism'. M. Sideratos, formerly undersecretary in the Ministry to the Prime Minister, has distinguished four strands in this 'neo-anarchism': the 'anarchist party', 'social anarchism', 'personal anarchism' and 'anarcho-communism'. He draws a spine-chilling picture of life in such great Babylons of criminality and decay as Chicago and Hamburg and of the universities of Europe and America corrupted by marijuana, LSD, 'free love, intemperate sexuality . . . sexual crimes, pornography, blue films, homosexuality and hippyism'.[16] This despising of the supposed decadence and irreligion of the West has deep roots in the history of modern Greek thought. In the early 1800s, for instance, the widely respected monk Athanasios Parios urged Greek parents not to send their children to the West for education lest they succumb to atheism, or worse still, popery.

Perhaps the most accurate touchstone of the socio-cultural views of the less sophisticated, but for this reason the most typical, officers is Col Ioannis

Ladas. Ladas first came into prominence in the summer of 1968 when, as secretary-general of the Ministry of Public Order, he personally beat up the author of an article in the weekly magazine *Eikones*, together with its editor, Panayiotis Lambrias, for having the temerity to suggest in an article on homosexuality that many of the worthies of ancient Greece had been homosexual. When the BBC's Greek service reported the incident, Ladas ascribed this to solidarity among homosexuals. Shortly afterwards Ladas was transferred to the secretary-generalship of the Ministry of the Interior, still a sensitive post, but one in which he would be more closely under the surveillance of the Minister, Pattakos. In the major reshuffle of August 1971, Ladas became Undersecretary-Governor of Thessaly.

Ladas' removal to the Ministry of the Interior did not prevent further outbursts from the Colonel, who maintained interesting links with the minuscule '4 August Party', founded in August 1965, and named after the date on which General Metaxas established his dictatorship in 1936. The leader of this party is Takis Plevris, who is also Ladas' private secretary. The party's overtly anti-semitic and racist journal *Tetarti Avgoustou* periodically acts as a forum for Ladas' views.

These are essentially characterized by ultra-chauvinism, bigotry and philistinism. In a speech before a group of Greek-Americans he asked, 'What is *Greece*?' To which he replied that 'Greece is a mission. And this mission consists of civilization.' 'Foreigners,' he continued, 'confess and acknowledge Greek superiority,' and he quoted Nietzsche to the effect that the Greeks have discovered everything. 'Human civilization was wholly fashioned by our race. Even the enemies of Greece recognize that civilization is an exclusively Greek creation.' The decline of Greece from ancient times was not due to 'organic' reasons, for 'the Greek race is full of life and strength'. Rather 'it was due to the fact that we were deprived of those worthy to govern us'. This prompted the army to intervene so that 'Greece could continue to radiate civilization in all directions'.[17]

Nor has Ladas hesitated to pronounce on broader cultural issues. When speaking at the laying of the foundation stone of an arts centre in Xanthi in September 1970, he declared that 'art must extol the moral ideals of society'. The poet whose work contains 'obscenity, cowardice, decline and pessimism', writes 'in a negative way'. His ideal is the poet who 'uses his talent to extol bravery, love, friendship, to praise heroism and virtue, and on the whole to support, from the artistic viewpoint, the ideals of society'. Correctly deployed, arts and letters can 'mould civilized characters with such a national and patriotic conscience that the criminal acts of the past should not be repeated, as happened with the foreign-led Red Satans – the communists – during the war and subsequent rebellion'.[18]

Long hair and hippies have also been the subject of his pronouncements. Those with long hair 'represent the degenerate phenomenon of hippyism'. Long hair is the 'hirsute flag of their nihilism', deliberately chosen to contrast with the close-cropped hair of the military. Hippies are, 'as is known', from all points of view 'anti-social elements, drug-addicts, sex-maniacs, thieves, etc. It is only natural that they should be enemies of the army and of the ideals which the military way of life serves.'[19]

The existence of such views within the Greek army should not occasion too much surprise, for, even before the *coup* the army had its own index of prohibited books, which included the works of Ernest Renan and Victor Hugo.[20] Moreover, their training as army officers scarcely gave them a sophisticated insight into the problems of modern politics. Communist infiltration tactics in the army, for instance, were studied on the basis of a pamphlet originally published by the Greek Communist Party as long ago as 1935. This was reprinted under the title *Communist Propaganda in the Armed Forces* (and marked 'confidential') by the Army General Staff in September 1967.

This unsubtle view of the world is also well reflected in the utterances of the First Deputy Prime Minister, Brigadier Pattakos, a member of the religious brotherhood *Zoi*, an organization with interesting links with the regime. In June 1968 Pattakos recalled the rallying cries used by the Greeks at crucial moments in their history, ranging from the defiant 'Come and get them' of the Spartans at Thermopylae when the Persians demanded that they lay down their arms, to the '*Ochi*' ('No') of General Metaxas when presented with the Italian ultimatum on 28 October 1940. The slogan which would forever be associated with the 'April Revolution', declared Pattakos, would be 'Halt or I shoot.'[21]

If men such as Ladas and Pattakos reflect most authentically the attitudes of the rank and file of the regime's supporters within the army, other and more sophisticated rationales have been advanced to justify the 'Revolution' and the regime's subsequent policies by Papadopoulos himself and by the regime's two principal civilian ideologues, Theophylaktos Papakonstantinou and George Georgalas. These men are both ex-communists, much to the chagrin of the regime's more committed supporters. Witness, for example, the bitter attacks by Col Stamatelopoulos, an influential member of the original junta, in the daily newspaper *Vradyni* on the appointment of Georgalas as the regime's chief spokesman. In this connection a third ex-communist should also be mentioned,

Savvas Konstantopoulos, editor of the pro-regime newspaper *Eleftheros Kosmos* (Free World), founded some six months before the *coup*. In the early months of the regime Konstantopoulos appeared to be assuming the role of principal theoretician of the 'Revolution', but his influence appears to have waned of late. Relations between the former comrades Papakonstantinou and Konstantopoulos do not appear to be of the most fraternal nature, judging by the attacks by the latter against Papakonstantinou while he was Minister of Education. Some indication of the regime's thinking can also be found in the journal *Theseis kai Ideai* which contains 'theoretical' articles written by members of the regime and their supporters.

Much of what passes for the regime's official ideology can only be described as verbiage. Col Makarezos, for instance, has claimed that 'the Revolution places *man* in the position of the infrastructural cornerstone of the community, relying on his qualities and capabilities to further all the social processes' and that, 'for the Greek, moral and spiritual values "supervalue" override mere "value" '.[22] Georgalas has put himself forward as the diagnostician of the 'decline of the consumer society'. His book of the same title was published in Athens in 1970 in the same series as Eldridge Cleaver's *Soul on Ice*. In this he urges a new role for social welfare, whose function, he believes, is no longer to provide employment or housing but is rather 'the application of lengthy psycho-therapeutic programmes'.[23] Papadopoulos himself has a gift for the pretentious and obscure, expressed in clumsy Greek: 'Philosophize. Philosophize as Greeks on behalf of mankind and develop your mental activity in the field in which the world-wide effort of the society of mankind must follow. . . .' (I, p. 195).[24]

But behind all this verbiage, one can isolate, if not a coherent ideology, then certain persistent themes, which throw light on the regime's thinking, although by analysing these there is a risk of attributing to the regime a body of thought more coherent and structured than it actually is. Papadopoulos' own thinking is conveniently made available in the six (as of August 1971) substantial volumes of *To Pistevo Mas* which are distributed free to all interested parties. The preface to the first volume, published in April 1968, declared *To Pistevo Mas* to be 'essential reading for young and old . . . [which should] not only be read but be carefully and minutely studied by all Greeks of whatever class'.

In these volumes Papadopoulos ranges over a wide variety of topics from 'absolutism' to 'Mahatma Ghandi', from 'Utopia' to 'Napoleon'. But what concerns us here are his political views. As we have seen,

Papadopoulos fairly quickly abandoned the pretence that there had been a serious communist threat at the time of the *coup*, and switched his emphasis to depicting a society in total decline. 'We had arrived at a situation of anarchism in this country of Helleno-Christian civilization. We had become estranged from all ideals, from every Christian institution, from every written and unwritten law, not as social beings, but as beings motivated only by instinct. We lived not in society but in a jungle' (I, p. 36). In an interview with Sir Hugh Greene in August 1970, he diagnosed the weakness of pre-*coup* Greece in less emotional terms: economic backwardness, the 'unacceptable backwardness' of the social services, lack of necessary foundations for rapid economic and social development, the poor condition of education, and finally the general inadequacy of the administration of the state machine (VI, p. 157). For the 'Revolution' to fail, he has claimed, would be 'a catastrophe for Hellenism' (I, p. 38), to return to the 'sinful past' (VI, p. 123) of the democracy of the April 20th type would be 'an ethnic crime' (IV, p. 58).

In Greece army officers have always been 'with a full spirit of self-sacrifice guides of the nation' (VI, p. 44) but the 'Revolution' was not 'a Revolution of the Army, or of only a part of the people, it was the revolution of the entire Greek people' (I, p. 36). For, as Papadopoulos announced to the people of Larissa in January 1968, 'We do not have enemies. There is only one enemy. Ourselves' (I, p. 107). Through the 'Revolution', 'the people has been liberated from itself, that is to say, it has been saved from the egotistical mentality' (I, p. 43). This need for the Greeks 'to cleanse ourselves' (I, p. 185) is a key element in Papadopoulos' thinking: 'the people who compose Greek society must again become social beings' (I, p. 74). An end must be made to the 'Blow you, Jack, I'm all right' mentality (IV, p. 205), a disciplined way of life must be imposed, as opposed to the anarchism of the jungle (VI, p. 122).

How then are the Greeks to be purged of 'the worm of egocentricity'? (I, p. 151). Education and the Church are the 'basic foundations for cleansing our life', Papadopoulos told Billy James Hargis, leader of the Christian Anti-Communist Crusade of Tulsa, Oklahoma (I, p. 126). Education is to be based on 'the ideals of Helleno-Christian civilization',[25] which are also, it is held, the ideals of the Western World. These ideals, an attempt to synthesize the essentially contradictory values of ancient Greece and of Byzantium, are proclaimed more often than they are defined by members of the regime.[26] Georgalas has suggested that the 'objectives' of Helleno-Christian civilization are 'the free man in harmonious co-existence with himself and with his fellow beings'.[27]

A major constituent of 'Helleno-Christian civilization' is an obsession with Greece's historical heritage. Papadopoulos and his colleagues certainly suffer in full measure from what the novelist George Theotokas once diagnosed as *progonoplexia*, or ancestoritis, a condition which has so distorted the cultural, and indeed the political, development of modern Greece. The Greeks are the 'elect of God' (II, p. 184),[28] Greece, under the 'Revolution', will once again be an example to other nations as it was in the time of Plato and Aristotle (IV, p. 58). Papadopoulos himself acknowledges the influence of the political thinking of Polybius and Plato (VI, p. 159). Much as Juan Perón liked to link Peronism with the achievements of San Martin, so Papadopoulos has sought to link the 'Revolution' of 1967 with Greece's struggle for independence which began in 1821. 'Under the guidance of [the Revolution] the Nation is moving forward to fulfilment of the aspirations of the generation of fighters of 1821. . . .' (VI, p. 87).

Observers have frequently noted the religious overtones in so much of the regime's propaganda. Brigadier Pattakos has claimed that 'Our programme will above all be built on the Christian virtues. We want to fashion a New Man . . . he must have the strength to do Absolute Good.'[29] Col Ladas similarly declared that the 'Revolution' seeks to make 'the love, the virtue, the honesty, the solidarity, the mutual help . . . which Christ taught, a national reality'.[30] And Papadopoulos himself launched the slogan of *Ellas Ellinon Christianon* (Greece of the Christian Greeks) which is everywhere to be seen in Greece, and is the slogan by which Greece once again is constituted 'a pole of ideological spiritual attraction'.[31]

Greece must once again become a country of the Christian spirit, the command 'Love thy neighbour as thyself' must once again prevail (I, p. 155). In addition to Christian virtue, education is also necessary so that the citizen can 'appreciate his rights, duties, obligations and consequently, with a full sense of responsibility, can regulate matters of common interest through the procedure of the vote' (I, p. 81), in other words to prepare for the 'New Democracy', for after all 'the Greek people revolted . . . to safeguard their democratic freedoms' (I, p. 131).

Papadopoulos makes frequent reference to the 'New Democracy' (a term employed earlier by Rafael Leonidas Trujillo), but his analysis of what precisely this consists in is not wholly explicit. The most complete analysis so far of the 'objective aims' of the Revolution and of the nature of the 'New Democracy' occurs in Georgalas' *Ideologia tis Epanastaseos*, and will be discussed later.

Although Greece has always 'constituted the exception that proves the rule' (VI, p. 29), the 'New Democracy' is definitely for export and is the answer to the 'Western neo-anarchism', [32] 'despotic and anarchist democracy',[33] 'chaotic conditions' and 'socialist misfortune'[34] prevailing in other countries of the Western World, who have much to learn from an essentially 'humanist Revolution' (Makarezos) which is able to guarantee freedom of expression 'without extraneous irritants like strikes and demonstrations'.[35] As Papadopoulos stated on the eve of Greece's withdrawal from the Council of Europe, the regime had been struggling 'to show the correct way to the members of the Council' (VI, p. 28), a number of whom had been seeking to 'impose their own form of socialist government on other states, which, while believing in democracy, do not accept the Marxist form of it'.[36] If only the rest of the world will listen, 'the star of Greece will shine during these difficult moments of mankind, to the benefit of all the inhabitants of the world. . . .' (IV, p. 226).

As we have seen, a persistent theme in Papadopoulos' political oratory, as indeed in that of the pre-war Metaxas dictatorship, has been the need to re-educate the Greeks politically and to instil in them a more profound sense of civic responsibility. In April 1970, he announced the publication of *Politiki Agogi* (Political Education, or Civics). This had been written by Theofylaktos Papakonstantinou, sometime Minister of Education in the regime, and whom Papadopoulos described as 'a sociologist and historian'. Such a book, Papadopoulos claimed, had never before appeared in Greece and 'universal public praise' was due to its author, who for reasons of 'moral order' stressed in the preface that he would not make so much as a single drachma out of the book. The Greeks, said Papadopoulos, now had at their disposal 'all the knowledge necessary to acquire the possibility of becoming responsible Greek citizens'. He regretted that it was not possible to offer the book in translation 'to our foreign friends'. For only if they truly comprehended this book and then concluded that it was inspired 'by any other ideal than the Greek ideal of personal liberty and of true Greek democracy, then and only then should they believe the sirens who claim that present-day Greece is not struggling to create the necessary preconditions for true democracy'. Those who questioned the regime's sincerity in this matter should seek 'the way of the psychiatrist' (VI, p. 99).

To help foreigners comprehend the import of this volume, an English-language synopsis was distributed by the Directorate of Press and Information of the Ministry to the Prime Minister. This claimed that Papakonstantinou's book had already become the bestseller of the year, in addition to being distributed free 'to all educators, civil-service personnel, members of the judiciary, officers and non-commissioned officers of the Armed Forces, officers and men of the police forces, prefects (nomarchs) and local government representatives, members of the clergy at all levels, university and college students, leaders of trade union and co-operative movements, athletic and boy-scout organizations, public and community professional libraries, and various scientific associations'. An abridged version of Papakonstantinou's text (ed. D. V. Tountopoulos) was also distributed to school children and used as a school textbook.

The book, in the words of the synopsis, comprised a 'methodical, clear and up-to-date compendium of the entire body of knowledge which comprises political education', a field in which the Greek people had previously been 'totally unenlightened'. For the Greek had lacked 'civic conscience', and this lack of political training was the 'deeper cause of modern Greece's permanently unsettled and turbulent history'. The author, 'an active opponent of all forms of totalitarianism', was given 'a completely free hand to write as his conscience dictated . . . guided only by the present-day facts of political science and Greek reality'. The ideological principles it expresses are 'an irrefutable reply to the critical attacks directed against the Greek regime'. 'Which of the world's dictatorships or totalitarian states,' the pamphlet asked, is so 'fervent in its advocacy of democratic government and ruthless in its condemnation of totalitarianism?'

Unquestionably then his book has approval at the highest level. But what light does it throw on the ideological orientation of the regime? The answer is, very little. Much of the text is taken up with an analysis of liberal democracy. He extols the democratic freedoms, such as freedom of speech, freedom of the press and freedom of association, and contrasts these with the situation in modern totalitarian states where an all-powerful secret police force, operating at the behest of a small ruling clique, operates through the use of terror and without regard for the rights of citizens (p. 56).[37] He also prints in full the texts of a number of key political documents such as Pericles' Funeral Oration (this had actually been prohibited for use in schools by General Metaxas), the Charter of the United Nations, and the NATO treaty (including its preamble). Much of Papakonstantinou's analysis of these matters is wholly unexceptionable, and merely highlights the semantic difficulties involved in the regime's understanding of terms such as 'democracy', 'liberal', 'popular', 'parliamentary', 'freedom', etc. This is not always the case, however. In discussing the Cyprus question, for instance, he claims that the British subjected hundreds of Cypriots to 'bestial tortures'. But he explains

Greece's withdrawal from the Council of Europe only by reference to the Council's 'one-sided anti-Greek stance' (pp. 479, 525).

But Papakonstantinou's text is of little assistance in trying to elucidate the ideology of the 'Revolution'. This, he maintains, was an 'historical necessity', a national, political, and social phenomenon with the following aims: national independence, assurance of internal peace, the cleansing of public life, rapid economic development for the benefit of all social classes, the lessening of social tensions, assistance for the weaker elements in society, the raising of the cultural level of the people, the more efficient working of the state machine, and reconciliation between the state and the citizen. The central objective of the Revolution, he adds, is to thrust Greece from a state of backwardness, into being a modern, democratic and powerful state (pp. 223–4). But he is distinctly chary of attempting to formulate a coherent ideology and instead contents himself with reprinting Kollias' original speech and lengthy but scarcely revealing extracts from a speech of Papadopoulos.

Where Papakonstantinou hesitated to tread, George Georgalas plunged in unhesitatingly a year later with his *Ideologia tis Epanastaseos* (Ideology of the Revolution). This was published in April 1971 and given much the same distribution as Papakonstantinou's earlier work. Georgalas became the regime's chief spokesman in the autumn of 1970. This was for him the high point of a chequered political career which had included a considerable period as a communist refugee in Hungary during the Rákosi era. Remarkably, this did not prove an obstacle to his later ambitions and fairly soon after his return to Greece in 1957 he became editor of an army journal entitled *Sovietologia* (Soviet Studies), and in the reshuffle of August 1971 was appointed Undersecretary-Governor of Crete.

His *Ideologia tis Epanastaseos* is dedicated 'to those who dreamed of and prepared the Revolution, and above all those who will inherit it'. The *coup*, he argues, was not a *coup* at all but a 'revolution', for in a revolution the protagonists are not merely a minority seizing power for its own sake but, on the contrary, they express 'the wishes, desires, strivings, and dreams of broad masses' and are able to give expression to 'a widespread disposition to radical, fundamental change'. The 'April Revolution' in fact came as a fulfilment of the 'aspirations of the Race' (p. 5).

It is, moreover, Georgalas insists, a true revolution despite the fact that it envisages no changes in the prevailing social and economic system, or in the traditional values that have prevailed in Greece. Where it is truly revolutionary, he maintains, is in the political sector, for the 'revolution' has completely destroyed the old political establishment. It has swept away 'the old parties, the electoral fiefs, the political oligarchies, the mentality, the inter-relations and the organizations of our political world'. The ground has been cleared so that the political future may be completely reshaped (p. 6).

Not only has the army saved the country from 'chaos and red totalitarianism' but it has a deeper objective, that of national rebirth (p. 8). This national rebirth embraces the now familiar areas of economic development, the creation of a modern state system, the renewal of education, the creation of a more balanced, harmonious society, without great contradictions. The regime does not claim to seek social equality, for this can never exist, but seeks to avoid cleavages that could lead to violent confrontations. This will be achieved by a fairer distribution of the national income among the different classes of society and between the different regions of the country. For, Georgalas continues, the regime does not believe in class struggle but in class co-operation (p. 8). Finally, the regime aims to create the necessary presuppositions for a more healthy political life, in fact for the 'New Democracy', which will of course be based on the Constitution of 1968.

Before proceeding to discuss the specific characteristics of the 'New Democracy', Georgalas examines the nature of freedom. There is no such thing as total freedom, he says, only freedom under the law. 'We, however, are proceeding further,' he continues, 'for we wish to create the *social* man which our age needs. We do not wish to abrogate the person as a personal and unique value, who has within him the spark of God. Each one of us is an entire world and must remain so. The personality must be sacred and inviolable. But, however, in our age and especially in our Greece, we must shun narrow egoism. The individual must stretch out to the whole. He must be "socialized" in the good meaning of the word. Common ideas, common objectives, common visions must unite us. For only in this way can nations survive' (pp. 59–60).

The meaning of freedom is not static, he continues; it differs from age to age and from country to country. In the same way there is no single type of democracy, there are variations in different ages, societies and countries. 'Old democracy' remains oriented to the 'older perceptions of freedom'. 'New democracy' incorporates the new concept of freedom, which is subdivided into the categories of economic, social, intellectual, and political freedom (p. 60).

Certain freedoms existed in 'pre-revolutionary' Greece. These will be preserved and under no circumstances will personal property or individual initiative, or what is generally termed the 'bourgeois' (*astikon*) system be tampered with. Rather it will be cleansed and thus enabled to survive. Moreover, these existing economic freedoms will be enlarged. The regime believes in the right of a man to work for a just wage. To achieve this ideal the economy must be developed (p. 60). To accelerate economic development the regime will create a special 'opening' for technocrats and the young (p. 6). Elsewhere Georgalas has claimed that the average age of ministers is forty-five, and, as part of this opening to the young, has urged students to increase their contacts with the armed forces.[38] Such have been the achievements of the regime, he told students of the University of Jannina in April 1971, that it might seem as if the regime had been in power for forty rather than four years.[39] Despite these rapid economic advances, however, he declared in October 1970 that there could be no possibility of elections until the national income had risen from $800 per head to $1100, which was not expected to occur until 1973.[40]

Social freedom, continues Georgalas, is the absence of obstacles to man's ascent. There is no room for closed 'castes' of the privileged. Everyone should be able to ascend the 'social hierarchy' according to his ability. Such possibilities were limited before the 'Revolution', but now 'Social Democracy' will become a complete reality. Intellectual freedom will be broadened to include all Greeks and not merely 'closed coteries' (p. 61).

Finally, there remains political freedom. 'This existed only on paper. From time to time we were called to the ballot to choose those we wanted to rule over us. But who chose whom we elected? . . . They were brought before us by the dark forces who manipulate public opinion. . . . There are few who believe that this constituted political freedom.' In contrast, he claims, the present regime seeks to give substance to political freedom. 'We want a *true Democracy*. For this reason we are taking a series of measures so that a true "Demos", the totality of free citizens, may prevail. The law and the Constitution of 1968 will ensure that there are no more personal parties. Political fiefs and political dynasties will be no more. We wish to create parties based on principle. And they will be created. There will be parties with *internal democracy*. . . . There will be leaders who will be marked out democratically. . . . Moreover we wish to create a responsible press, *free* but not *immune*, and not the instrument of a few people . . . we wish finally to create informed citizens. . . . [All this] will transform [democracy] in accordance with up-to-date criteria and will metamorphose it from old to new Democracy' (pp. 62–63).

The ideology of the 'Revolution', Georgalas insists, is a dialectic, not a dogmatic ideology, for it entails commitment to ideals not dogma, indeed anti-dogmatism is of authentic Hellenic ancestry (p. 16.) The ideals of Helleno-Christian civilization cannot be regarded as dogma. Moreover, the ethos of the regime is anti-dictatorial and anti-totalitarian (p. 38). Those who resist the 'Revolution' represent the forces of reaction (pp. 5–6). The 'April Revolution' is the 'Great Synthesis', it is the 'catholic effort of Hellenism to solve the problem of its rebirth' (p. 9). If the 'Revolution' succeeds, as it must, then 'we Greeks once again will lead the world' (p. 7).

Such then, in outline, are some of the principal strands of what passes for the regime's 'ideology'. The regime's principal spokesmen and theoreticians have deliberately been allowed to speak as much as possible for themselves, although in trying to tabulate their thinking in a reasonably intelligible form, there is, as has already been observed, a danger of making the regime's ideology sound more coherent than it in fact is. For the speeches of those empowered to theorize on ideological matters contain numerous inconsistencies, ambiguities and downright obscurities.

How then is the regime's 'ideology', or rather its ideologies, to be categorized? This is a difficult task for there are a number of strands to the regime's political beliefs, ranging from the naive simplism of the regime's attempt to legislate into being an 'Helleno-Christian Revolution', through the populist rhetoric of many of the regime's pronouncements, to the outright fascism of the fringe '4 August Party'.

Observers have described the regime's ideology as populist or, more often, as fascist. The populist thesis has greater plausibility than the fascist one, although as I have tried to show, the regime's populist rhetoric has largely been belied by its practice (see also Chapter Six). The label 'fascist' deserves examination, however, as it is frequently employed apropos the Greek military regime, principally but by no means exclusively in left-wing circles.

But it is a label that cannot be made to stick, unless the term 'fascist' is used in the wholly indiscriminate way, as a general term of abuse, that has now become the fashion. What precisely constitutes fascism is of course notoriously difficult to define.[41] Certainly the Greek regime manifests a number of characteristics in common with regimes that have been accepted as fascist. Among these are anti-communism, militarism, the banning of political parties and trades unions, ultra-nationalism,[42] the attack on traditional elites, even occasional hints of racialism[43] and of the

Führerprinzip (Papadopoulos is frequently referred to by his subordinates as the 'Leader of the Revolution').

Yet the regime cannot be regarded as fascist either of the left or right, populist or pro-establishment varieties. It has been suggested that the regime is deliberately trying to build up the youth organization *Alkimoi* (The Strong Ones, an organization of pre-*coup* foundation which competes directly with the Boy Scouts) into a body resembling Metaxas' pre-war EON (National Organization of Youth), which in turn was consciously modelled on the Hitler Jugend and the Giovani Italiane. Membership of the *Alkimoi*, however, even if strongly encouraged, is not compulsory as it was in Metaxas' organization, and overall membership remains small, although much larger than in pre-*coup* days. Again a sinister significance has been attached to the avowedly fascist '4 August Party', founded two years before the *coup* to perpetuate what it considers to be the ideals of the Metaxas dictatorship. This group is a negligible factor, however, for it has a very small membership, and little attention would be accorded to it but for its close links with one of the leading members of the junta, Col Ladas. However, the fact that two of the fourteen candidates nominated in the Athens district by 79 electors for membership of the regime's advisory 'mini-parliament' in 1970 were editors of the party's journal *Tetarti Avgoustou*[44] may be a straw in the wind.

More to the point, the regime's ultra-nationalism, like its populism, is much more a matter of rhetoric than of practice, and is essentially intended for domestic consumption. Witness the regime's hasty compliance with Turkish demands in Cyprus in November 1967 and the tacit abandonment of Greek claims to 'Northern Epirus' (the regions of Southern Albania with a Greek minority population) in return for closer relations with Tirana (see Chapter Ten). Certainly the present regime appears to have no inclination to indulge in war or threats of war to achieve its irredentist aims. Its nationalism, in short, cannot be categorized as 'aggressive'. Nor does the regime manifest the economic nationalism of the classical fascist regime. There has been no attempt to direct big capital in the national interest, and the regime shows itself more than willing to allow key industries to remain under foreign control and allows foreign firms generous terms for the export of profits on their investment (see Chapter Five). Even the attack on the traditional elites is limited to the old *politikos kosmos*, or political world, while the economic oligarchy in the country is not only untouched but positively pampered. Note, for example, the special and highly favourable conditions granted to shipowners registering their fleets under the Greek flag.

Moreover, the regime shows none of the radicalism which many fascist movements, at least in their early stages, have manifested. The Italian fascist manifesto of 1919, for instance, included a heavy capital levy and the confiscation of ecclesiastical property, while the Nazi programme of 1920 included the abolition of unearned income and the nationalization of trusts.[45] Nothing remotely similar has been proposed by the Colonels. Indeed they openly admit to wishing to maintain the traditional economic order. The regime has shown no sign of the truly revolutionary appeal that prompted the underground Hungarian Communist Party to urge support for *Nyilas-keresztes* (Arrow Cross) candidates in the Hungarian elections of 1939,[46] or of the radical 'Christian' fascism of the Romanian *Garda da Fier*. The regime, despite a ninety-two per cent vote in favour of the 1968 Constitution, lacks any mass backing, and has not, unlike Perón in Argentina who also came to power by *coup d'état*, tried to build up an *ex post facto* mass following or party, which is such an important instrument of government in true fascist regimes. As Nerio Minuzzo has pointed out, the Greek *coup* does not reflect mass aspirations, it came about 'not from instinct, but from calculation'.[47] Nor does the regime, despite its scorn for the democratic countries of the West, attack in principle the whole concept of parliamentary democracy, as did the traditional fascist regimes. Rather it claims to be dedicated to the concept in a 'modernized' form.

Nerio Minuzzo, following the terminology of Maurice Duverger, has described the regime as a pseudo-fascist paternalist dictatorship.[48] This is probably the most apposite descriptive label, for the regime has more in common with the traditional autocracies of the Near East and South America than with pre-war fascist regimes. There are obvious parallels, too, with what has been described as the 'clerical-military semi-fascism'[49] of Franco's Spain, although the Greek Colonels have no such power base as Franco had in the Falange.

Much of what passes for the regime's ideology is *sui generis*, but the historian of modern Greece nevertheless has the sensation of having heard much of it before. Considering the similarity in world view between the Colonels and General Metaxas, and that most of the protagonists of the *coup* grew to maturity and at least entered the Military Academy when Metaxas was at the height of his power (see Chapter Two, Table I), the leaders of the *coup* make surprisingly few explicit references to the ideological principles of Metaxasism which, in so far as they exist, are so close to their own (as indeed were some of his policies, as for instance his moratorium on peasant debts).[50] The contrast with their Turkish colleagues, who in the *coup* of 1960 claimed to be acting as the guardians of the sacred principles of Kemalism, is striking.

Metaxas, for instance, fully shared the Colonels' obsession with the purported selfish individualism of the Greeks. Speaking on the third anniversary of his 1936 seizure of power, he declared the necessity of 'the sublimation of our appetites, of our passions and of our overweening egoism before the totality of the national interest . . . then we shall be a people . . . that is truly free, otherwise, under the false cover of freedom, anarchy and indiscipline will rule over us. . . .'[51] He shared the same loathing of the *politikos kosmos*, the same obsessive anti-communism, the same belief in a synthesis of the values of the ancient world (in Metaxas' case particularly those of Sparta) with those of Christianity, the same messianic nationalism. 'Rise up,' he once declared, 'O youth of Greece. For you there is no other reality than the Greek Motherland, only in her can you rediscover yourselves.'[52] The same fear of 'atheism, materialism, naked violence and immorality'. The same desire to be all things to all men. The National Government 'belongs equally to everyone, that is to the poor and the rich, to the strong and the weak, to the great and the small'.[53] The same absolute identification of the regime with the nation, of the regime's objectives with national ideals.[54] The same lack of any sense of the absurd, although the leaders of the *coup* have yet to rival Metaxas' formal proclamation of himself as *Protos Agrotis* (First Peasant) and *Protos Ergatis* (First Worker) in 1937.[55] There are, of course, important contrasts between the regimes of Metaxas and the Colonels, but the parallels are none the less highly suggestive.

It is not the least of the many ironies surrounding the present regime that while so much of its propaganda is devoted to stressing that there can be no looking back, that Greece has made an irreversible break with the past in April 1967, and despite the fact that Brigadier Pattakos has declared that history does not repeat itself,[56] so much of its rhetoric and ideology, in fact, closely resembles that of Metaxas' pre-war dictatorship. General Metaxas set himself the goal of rendering the Greeks 'social beings'. Thirty years later Col Papadopoulos and his colleagues have similarly felt it incumbent on themselves to work to eradicate the 'worm of egocentricity' from the Greeks. Georgalas has claimed in his capacity as the regime's principal ideologist that 'We are tomorrow'.[57] He might with greater precision have proclaimed that 'We are yesterday'.

London, September 1971   *Richard Clogg*

NOTES

1 *Theseis kai Ideai* (Theses and Ideas), Feb. 1970, p. 45.
2 *The Man on Horseback. The Role of the Military in Politics*, London 1962, p. 32.
3 *Theseis kai Ideai*, July 1968, p. 6.
4 *Coup d'Etat: a practical handbook*, Greenwich, Conn., 1969, p. 175.
5 PAPAKONSTANTINOU, Theofylaktos, *Politiki Agogi* (Civics), Athens 1970, pp. 224–226.
6 Six volumes of Papadopoulos' collected speeches have so far been published (August 1971), under the title *To Pistevo Mas* (Our Creed).
7 p. 40. This extraordinary publication was apparently soon withdrawn, but was still available from the Press Division of the Ministry to the Prime Minister in the summer of 1968.
8 *Andreas Georgiou Papandreou*, published by the 'Piraeus Union of Young Scientists', Athens, July 1967, p. 46.
9 Council of Europe, European Commission of Human Rights, *The Greek Case. Report of the Commission*, vol. 1, pt. 1, Strasbourg 1969, p. 107.
10 Preface. *The Revolution of 21st April builds a New Greece*, Ministry of Co-ordination. Public Relations Service, Athens 1970.
11 Official translation, *Greece on the Way to Development*, Athens 1969, p. 11.
12 *Hearings before the Subcommittee on United States Security Agreements and Commitments Abroad of the Committee on Foreign Relations, United States Senate*, Ninety-first Congress, Second Session, pt. 7, June 9 and 11, Washington 1970, p. 1829.
13 M. Sideratos, Undersecretary to the Ministry to the Prime Minister in an interview in *Lo Specchio*, (18 Feb. 1968) quoted in *Testimonianze italiane sulla nuova situazione in Grecia*, Greek Embassy, Rome 1968.
14 *Stratiotika Nea* (Army News), 25 Nov. 1970.
15 General Pangalos, military dictator of Greece in 1925–26, had set a precedent by decreeing that women's skirts should not rise more than fourteen inches off the ground. Dictatorial regimes often seem obsessed by points of sartorial detail. Some years ago in Bulgaria trousers that could not be removed while the wearer still had his shoes on were forbidden.
16 *Theseis kai Ideai*, Feb. 1970, p. 2; cf. March 1970, p. 5.
17 *Apoyevmatini*, 6 Aug. 1968.
18 *The Times*, 17 Sept. 1970.
19 *Eleftheros Kosmos*, 26 Feb. 1971.
20 MEYNAUD, J., *Les Forces politiques en Grèce*, Lausanne 1965, p. 345.
21 Anon., *Vérité sur la Grèce*, Lausanne 1970, p. 142.
22 Official translation. *Greece on the Way of Development*, p. 3.
23 *I krisis tis katanalotikis koinonias*, Athens 1971, p. 156.

24 Quoted in *Vérité sur la Grèce*, p. 137.

25 Article 1, Decree Law 129, *Efimeris tis Kyverniseos* (Government Gazette), 25 Sept. 1967.

26 A proposed law that would have obliged all journalists, irrespective of nationality, working for foreign news media in Greece, to adhere to 'Hellenic Christian tradition' in their reporting of the news was subsequently rescinded. *Los Angeles Times*, 14, 19 Aug. 1971. See also Chapter Four.

27 *Eleftheros Kosmos*, 14 Apr. 1971.

28 Quoted in *Vérité sur la Grèce*, p. 140.

29 *Der Spiegel*, 15 May 1967. Quoted in Ansgar Skriver, *Soldaten gegen Demokraten. Militärdiktatur in Griechenland*, Köln/Berlin 1968, p. 148.

30 *Der Spiegel*, 30 Sept. 1968.

31 Pattakos, *Theseis kai Ideai*, July 1968, p. 5. The slogan is repeated on all possible occasions in accordance with the precepts of Col Constantine Vryonis of the Army Department of Military Justice in his *Manual for Cadres of National Propaganda* published in 1968. Vryonis recommends 'incessant dogmatic repetition of the national idea, opinion or belief in the press in the form of a slogan. Gradually . . . the people become familiar with it. In the end the national idea becomes their faith', quoted in the *Greek Observer*, 11–12, 1970, p. 11.

32 *Theseis kai Ideai*, Feb. 1970, p. 2.

33 Speech by Foreign Minister Pipinelis, 22 July 1968.

34 *Greece and the Commission of Human Rights. Reply of the Greek Government to the Report of the Commission of Human Rights of the Council of Europe.* Ministry to the Prime Minister, Press and Information Department, Athens, April 1970, p. 18.

35 *Greece, Land of Congress.* General Direction of Press and Information, Ministry to the Prime Minister, Athens 1969. This type of argument is clearly well received in some quarters. Representative James A. Burke (Dem., Mass.) argued against a House of Representatives vote to withold military aid to Greece partly on the grounds that the regime 'governs a crime-free society that America cannot match', *San Francisco Chronicle*, 4 Aug. 1971.

36 *Note verbale* sent by the Permanent Greek Representative to the President of the Council of Europe (12 Dec. 1969) printed in *Theseis kai Ideai*, Feb. 1970, p. 59.

37 His own statistical tables, however, show an increase of 51% in government expenditures in Greece on matters of state security between 1967 and 1970. As to whether the Colonels' Greece constitutes a 'police state' see the pertinent remarks of Brian Chapman, *The Police State*, London 1970, pp. 129–135. Professor Chapman is of course right in concluding that the present regime is not strictly a police state but a military autocracy, for

the security police remain wholly subordinated to the military leadership. One might, however, well categorize the present situation as a 'military police state', given the ascendancy of the military police ESA (*Elliniki Stratiotiki Astynomia*), which has increasingly taken over the task of hunting down and interrogating enemies of the 'Revolution'.

38　*Nea Politeia*, 3 Apr. 1971.

39　*Eleftheros Kosmos*, 4 Apr. 1971.

40　*The Times*, 20 Oct. 1970.

41　For a helpful discussion of fascism see the symposium, edited by S. J. Woolf, *The Nature of Fascism*, New York 1969.

42　Erwin Koch's statement that the 'Revolution' in Greece has nothing to do with nationalism or chauvinism is inexplicable, *Griechenland im Umbruch*, Frankfurt am Main, 1970, p. 154. Koch's description of Margaret Papandreou as 'the Bulgarian communist' (p. 117) is a sufficient indication of the general tone of the book.

43　e.g. 'All Greek history has been characterized by a mortal struggle against the Asiatic spirit,' Georgalas, *Ideologia tis Epanastaseos*, p. 44. The *Tetarti Avgoustou* group, of course, is openly racialist and anti-semitic. In the July 1968 issue it claimed that 13 out of 16 members of the European Commission of Human Rights, whose report proved highly critical of the regime, were Jews. A pamphlet written by an army chaplain, Archimandrite Kharalambos Vasilopoulos, entitled 'The Conspiracy of the Jehovah's Witnesses', contains a number of markedly anti-semitic passages. It was printed on the armed forces press for distribution to military units in Greece, *New York Times*, 30 May 1970, quoted in *News of Greece*, vol. 3, no. 3 1970.

44　*The Times*, 30 Nov. 1970.

45　WOOLF, op. cit., p. 127.

46　CARSTEN, F. L., *The Rise of Fascism*, London 1967, p. 178.

47　*Quando arrivano i colonnelli. Rapporto dalla Grecia*, Milan 1970, p. 44.

48　MINUZZO, op. cit., p. 43.

49　ANDRESKI, S. L., 'Some sociological considerations on fascism and class' in Woolf, op. cit., p. 99.

50　An exception to this general rule is the newspaper *Estia*, which frequently lauds the Metaxas regime. A long-established, extremely conservative and small circulation paper, *Estia* generally supports the regime, but does not reflect the views of those close to it.

51　METAXAS, I., *To prosopiko tou imerologio* (I. Metaxas' Personal Diary), iv (1933–1941), ed., Phaedon Vranas, Athens 1960, pp. 760–761.

52　Anon., *O Kommounismos stin Ellada* (Communism in Greece), National Society, Athens 1937, p. 133.

53　Ibid., p. 203.

54　Cf. A. Weidenmann, *Junges Griechenland*, Stuttgart 1940, p. 84. Sideratos in

a radio talk entitled 'Rumourmongers and Rumours' identified the
'Revolution' and the 'National Government' 'in the last analysis' with
Greece herself. *Oi psithyristai kai oi psithyroi*, General Directorate of the
Press, Athens 1968, p. 5. Weidenmann saw Metaxas' dictatorship on
4 August 1936 in Nietzschean terms, 'es ist der Triumph des Starken über
das Schwächliche . . .', p. 48.

55 DAPHNIS, G., *I Ellas metaxy dyo polemon, 1923–40* (Greece between the
Wars), ii, Athens 1955, p. 470.

56 *Theseis kai Ideai*, July 1968, p. 5.

57 *Ideologia tis Epanastaseos*, p. 5.

CHAPTER FOUR

The Colonels and the Press

On the morning of Friday 21 April 1967 the majority of Athenians woke up without realizing that they had slept right through from democracy to dictatorship. The extraordinary rapidity of the military take-over, as well as its comparative silence – there had been very little shooting – had allowed it to pass almost unnoticed.

It was the radio and the early morning news broadcasts that revealed the situation, first by being half an hour late (in itself a frightening occurrence) and then by speaking in harsh new military tones, and issuing a stream of orders followed by threats and very few explanations. No one was to leave his house; circulation was strictly forbidden; every civilian wandering on the streets could be shot; the reason for these 'precautions' was that an imminent danger to the nation had arisen during the night, and that 'King Constantine and the Kanellopoulos government had asked the Army to intervene. . . .' The *coup d'état* was on, and no civilian could do anything about it.

In our present modernized age, it is as terrifyingly simple as that. Suddenly your own familiar radio transforms itself into a hostile object barking orders from an unknown source. There is no way to ask questions, to demand explanations, there is no dialogue, no communication, no possibility of calling for anyone's help. The telephone, of course, is dead. There is nothing to do but wait. With so many nightmares hovering on the horizon, any voice can one day bluff you into submission. Think. . . . If you hear from your radio a cold decisive voice telling you that there has been a terrible accident involving a nuclear bomb, and that your only hope of survival is to stay at home behind closed doors and windows and wait for instructions, what can you possibly do except obey? And maybe allow a clever group of military men to proceed easily into complete occupation of every nerve-centre in the city, ministries and embassies, banks, universities, newspapers?

Inside the offices of *Kathimerini* we also sat and waited, but we were among the Athenians who knew a little more of what was happening, for we had been up all night following what was going on. Many of the editors were ready to leave for home when the first calls came, asking what was happening; why so many tanks were around; why officers were stopping cars, ordering pedestrians about, taking over from the police. No one had any answers and the sudden climate of tension kept everyone in the office, and also brought back many of the staff who had already left. About two o'clock in the morning the first eye-witness stories of arrests and violence were brought back by our city reporters, many of whom had been to police stations and could testify that the Athenian police were completely ignorant and innocent of whatever was going on, and were just as concerned about the situation as we were. Later the news came that Prime Minister Panayiotis Kanellopoulos had been forcibly abducted from his home, that most members of the government had been arrested as well as many politicians of the opposition. Just after three, the telephone was cut, armoured cars came and blocked our street, their machine-guns covering our entrance doors, and after that we found ourselves completely isolated.

Trapped inside the building, we could not guess much until a few hours later when the radio started up. After that we did a lot of speculating, and most of it proved to be disastrously right. Of course we knew that the anonymous voices were lying to the Greek people, pretending that the government had asked them to take over, as they, whoever *they* were, had arrested the Prime Minister and rounded up the government. And it was difficult to imagine the existence of an 'imminent communist take-over', another repeated lie, of which no one in Athens, no member of the government or even of the police, had any inkling. We knew that the danger was imaginary, the documents they claimed that King Constantine had signed were fakes, and that the whole operation was a gigantic treachery – but we, like the King, the government and the police, had no voice to counteract it. And the tragic hoax, spread by the radio, had reached every house in Athens, every town and village in Greece. And millions found it easy to believe. It is true that very little else betrayed the real situation during the first days. On 22 April communications were already restored, and what with people rushing to their jobs, or doing their weekend shopping, the streets of Athens on these clear spring days looked very much as they always did. A few tanks remained, and some armoured cars, but they were peacefully parked around some public buildings, and did not look in the least aggressive.

That some six thousand men and women had been brutally dragged from their beds and were now being herded into prisons and concentration camps was an invisible tragedy, and the change in the high-level government posts interested only the top political and military hierarchy. If it had not been for the radio at first and the newspapers in the following days, the knowledge that something disastrous had happened would have taken much longer to emerge.

The impression of foreboding and doom made by the vociferous broadcasts was reinforced by the look of the first *après-coup* newspapers. They repeated all the myths, exaggerated all the dangers that supposedly were looming over the Greek nation, and emphasized the 'bravery' of the saviours, the irresponsibility of the previous government, and the general corruption of all politicians. And, in a pattern that was to become painfully familiar, they were at the same time insisting that these irresponsible and corrupt men had patriotically called the Army to take over.

That the newspapers had been reduced by a fierce censorship to complete slavery was evident from the simple fact that all nine of them, three morning and six afternoon papers, looked absolutely *identical*. Not only were they publishing the same official announcements and hand-outs, but also, word for word, the same leading articles, the same commentaries, and the same front-page headlines. It was not a question of not being allowed to publish certain news, information, opinions, but what was much worse, of being obliged to publish everything sent by the newly formed military Press Service. They had to comply with this force-feeding of the public with poisonous lies and propaganda, print screaming calumnies against respectable politicians, and help immensely to solidify the edifice of deception built by the military junta.

Of the newspapers that appeared, only two of them, the morning *Eleftheros Kosmos*, and the afternoon *Estia*, both of the extreme right, were genuinely in support of the regime. The morning *Akropolis* and the afternoon *Apoyevmatini* and *Vradyni*, all conservative but also very pro-royalist and pro-Karamanlis, did not surprise their readers by their submission, while the remaining four, *Athinaiki* and *Vima* in the morning, and *Ethnos* and *Nea* in the afternoon, which had only a few days before been violently democratic and passionately pro-Papandreou, gave their readers a most unwelcome shock.

Five newspapers disappeared from the Athenian scene during that dramatic weekend. To nobody's surprise the two extreme left-wing papers, *Avghi* and *Demokratiki Allaghi* had been banned, and the non-appearance of the liberal *Eleftheria* was explicable on political grounds.

What came as a real surprise to the Greek public was that there was no *Kathimerini* in the morning and no *Messimvrini* in the afternoon. In the view of many, these two conservative and *par excellence* establishment newspapers should have been the most likely to accept the 'reality' of the situation, and conform peacefully to censorship. That they did not accept it, and refused to take part in the great brain-washing exercise that the military had started through the other newspapers, was one of the few snubs offered to the regime during this critical settling-in period.

One of the classic reference books, the venerable *Annual Register of World Events*, now in its 212th year of publication, describes the Greek *coup* in this way: 'In April 1967, a group of middle-rank officers, putting in operation a contingency plan drawn up by NATO, seized power in a bloodless *coup d'état*. The first actions of the government were by turns popular, savage and ridiculous.'

And, one must add, incredibly stupid. The men in power had no need to be savage, for the simple reason that at first, as the *Annual Register* rightly observes, they were, in a way, popular. One of the reasons for this popularity was that they were Greek officers, and until 1967 Greece had never suffered from her own Army. The enemy had always been either a foreigner or a foreign-inspired communist. The Army had been the protector, the friend and the victim. The word 'colonel' had not the evil sound it has now, all over the world, thanks to the junta. When these unknown officers appeared, the first information given to the Greek public was that they were of humble origin, boys of poor parents, and this suggested seriousness and honesty. Another reason that they were momentarily acceptable was that they represented a fundamental change. And change, as we all know, even change from peace to war, often brings a sense of elation to people who feel themselves inextricably chained to an unsatisfying kind of existence, and who hope that any new situation will give them, if not a better way of life, at least a different one.

An atmosphere of indulgence, a feeling of 'let them show what they can do', surrounded the military, and many a citizen conditioned to blame the out-going politicians for all his problems, whether rising prices, taxes or family worries, offered the benefit of the doubt to the new team that had taken over. So that they could have done with impunity, during the first months in power, all that they had promised to do, at least with regard to the Greek press. They could have lifted censorship, maintained a moderate control of the press, and allowed the newspapers to regain part of their personality. They did not do this. On the contrary, they proceeded to satisfy their newly found sense of importance by filling the newspapers with what they believed to be words of historical importance and political wisdom. The ramblings of both Papadopoulos and Pattakos, the two principal orators, were duly taken down and published verbatim, covering whole pages with moronic repetitions and nonsensical monologues of a kind rarely heard outside a psychiatric ward. In this way, without realizing it, they satisfied their worst enemies and opened the eyes of many would-be friends.

Meanwhile, what was happening to the Greek newspapers? Well, their readers, after the initial shock of horror and indignation (even the public which was not especially hostile to the junta could not reconcile itself to the uniformity), adjusted to the situation and accepted the need to buy at least one. It was the period when the Athenian went to the kiosk and asked, 'Give me a newspaper, I don't care which one.' Generally it was only to see what was on, to read the sports pages, solve the crossword puzzle, read the serials. The news that really interested the Greek public came through the foreign radio stations, from the BBC, from Radio Paris, from Deutsche Welle, all of which had programmes in Greek, and also from the foreign newspapers, which, surprisingly enough, were freely sold in Athens. Circulations which had dropped dramatically for a period of about two months rallied up to a point. As time passed, an understanding grew between the public and the press, both wretched victims of the same situation, and the readers veered instinctively toward the newspapers that reminded them of the past, and which they knew would, if they could, be as pro-Karamanlis or as pro-Papandreou as they ever were, even if at present they were obliged to repeat daily that they rejected the past and loved the present. There were, at the end of 1967, eight newspapers circulating in Athens (the centre-left *Athinaiki* had folded a few days after the *coup*) and most of them were slowly regaining their old positions, leaving the two last places, the seventh and eighth, to the two genuinely pro-junta papers, *Eleftheros Kosmos* and *Estia*.

This was a cause for consternation among the military and made them decide to publish a semi-official newspaper, a real 'Helleno-Christian' mouthpiece, which they hoped every Greek could be pressured to buy, one way or another. And on 16 September 1968 *Nea Politeia* emerged, a morning daily looking very much like *Eleftheros Kosmos*, just as dull and old-fashioned in lay-out, with the same sprawling leading articles printed in 14-point bold covering half the front page. For a very short time it looked as though it was going to be a success. It had more inside news, and as it was directly connected with Prime Minister Papadopoulos' younger brother, it was a safe bit of printed paper to tuck into your pocket when visiting government offices, police stations or friends in prison. Particularly so as police terror was at its height, with the coming referendum for the new Constitution shaping up as a tragic, Soviet-type election farce. The whole operation was openly, shamelessly rigged, with the slogan 'Vote Yes' not only covering the newspapers, which were never allowed even to utter the possibility of voting 'No', but traced in colour in the sky, painted in gigantic letters on the hills, defacing with banners, posters and inscriptions the whole of poor Greece. 'The first entirely free, completely democratic elections in Greek history . . .' Pattakos was declaring vehemently to groups of gaping foreign correspondents, who had never seen anything like it, not even behind the Iron Curtain.

Not that they had not expected it, well informed as they were by the press of their own countries. For another unexpected result of the inane censorship that had been inflicted on the Greek press was that, as the Greek newspapers were not allowed to publish anything at all, every Greek who wanted something said – tragic, impressive or strange; dramatic, revealing or just plain funny – tried to contact the foreign press. And the most important newspapers in the free world, realizing the plight of their Greek colleagues muzzled to asphyxiation, came wholeheartedly to the rescue. Journalists silenced in Greece were given more than friendly treatment in foreign newspapers; news forbidden even to be whispered inside the country was splashed on the front pages; anecdotes ridiculing top junta officials were reported with relish in diary columns; every bit of news was given special treatment, every development, good or bad, was commented upon.

As this possibility seeped into the minds of anti-regime Greeks, the 'Foreign Press Operation' was put into motion, and singly or in groups, they made the collection of news and information and the communication of it to the newspapers of the free world one of their most important activities. In fact it was genuine resistance work, and very dangerous at that, as most of the stories had to be smuggled out of prisons and handed to people who could safely get them out of Greece. It was by this escape route that the first torture stories came out. Incredibly brave people who had been tortured, who were still in jail and well knew the consequences of every act of resistance, confided *handwritten and signed* descriptions of what they had been through, and proved that as long as they were alive they could not be completely silenced. It was in the *Guardian* of 21

October 1967 that the Bouboulinas Police Station was first mentioned, and with this horrifying description the Greek regime suddenly took on a sombre appearance. There were fewer jokes but more stories, more descriptions, more protests and more documents coming out of Greece. The word had been given. The Greeks had only one ally – the press of the free world.

So the battle of the communications media started. Its first major victory was in the summer of 1968 when the disclosure of the famous 'Fraser Report' occurred, which disrupted a thriving public relations business. One of the confidential reports sent by its director, Maurice Fraser, directly to Prime Minister George Papadopoulos somehow found its way out of Greece and landed on the desk of the editor of the *Sunday Times*. It was a beautiful document, relating how many articles had been slipped into newspapers; how many influential people he had contacted and persuaded; how an English member of parliament had agreed to work for his firm, and so on – describing activities in Germany and Sweden and future plans for activity throughout Europe. Published in every European country, it created newspaper history, especially so as there had been an injunction to stop its publication which the *Sunday Times* fought in court and won.

The whole Fraser network, which had cost some hundreds of thousands of dollars, collapsed; the splendid offices in London and other European cities closed down; Maurice Fraser resigned from the Public Relations Association, and little has been heard of him since. And members of European parliaments have decided to avoid junta Greeks bearing presents and invitations.

The situation of the Greek press remained virtually the same until the autumn of 1969. It is true that the government had announced time and again that it would lift censorship, sometimes even that it had already lifted censorship, but in reality only the Ministers of the Press and the chiefs of the Press Service changed and very little else. There were again nine newspapers circulating in Athens, as *Simerina*, the afternoon edition of *Eleftheros Kosmos*, came out in the summer of 1971 and added one more pro-junta newspaper to the three already going. These nine newspapers sold approximately 450,000 issues daily, of which the four pro-junta ones together did not even reach the 40,000 mark.

And again it was for no discernible reason, except a negative one. Up to October 1969, when preventive censorship was lifted, the newspapers all carried more or less the same material, and all were obediently pro-government, devoid of the slightest criticism. They published what they were told to publish, and did not publish what they were told not to. It was just that the four pro-junta newspapers were of their own accord more enthusiastic, making the five others seem less so. The problem, in reality, was not created by the press but by the reader. And the basic error on the part of the regime was to allow nine newspapers to be published in Athens, a number that gave the reader the opportunity of choice, of shunning the orthodox ones, the ones representing the forces of oppression, and of buying the victims.

When preventive censorship ceased, the situation for most editors became for a short time more agonizing than before. Because as yet the press law had not changed, and the only difference was that you had to apply it yourself, instead of relying on the censor. But still there was at the time some show of relaxation. It was quite clear that the Greek government was aware of the mounting criticism expressed in many European countries, and also of the danger of being expelled from the Council of Europe. Neither the military nor the Americans, all out to protect them now, wanted this to happen. So promises of future democratization were offered right and left, an official timetable was given to European governments in which dates were set for the lifting of martial law and the holding of elections; the International Red Cross was invited to come to Greece and freely visit the prisons and concentration camps; a new and more liberal press law was to be announced any day now, and the Greek press was to be freed from all its fetters.

Any day now, but not quite yet. What the Colonels wanted during that period was to succeed in this exercise in deceit, and avoid being branded as the brutes they were by the most civilized countries in the world. What, on the other hand, the opponents of the regime wanted was to see them ignominiously chased out, for the good of Greece and all concerned, especially that of Europe and the Council. But there had to be a counter-attack; the falsity of the promises had to be revealed, and the whole battle had to be fought through the columns of the foreign press.

And so it was, with extraordinary success. The crucial date was 12 December 1969, the day the Ministers of Foreign Affairs of the member countries of the Council of Europe would meet in Paris to decide upon the Greek question. That day the Greek Minister for Foreign Affairs, Panayiotis Pipinelis, would be giving the fight of his life, to win at least a postponement, and as he was an experienced diplomat he was quite likely to succeed. Already he was working towards this goal, and during the month of November he was often quoted in the foreign press for his declarations to the Greek people that freedom was just around the corner: 'I can assure the Greek people that the present government will advance towards the full implementation of the Constitution, and a return to democracy.' Pipinelis' words would have kept their credibility for a little while at least if, on 23 November, the first of the three carefully prepared time-bombs had not exploded. It was, appropriately, a copy of the briefing given by the same Pipinelis to a meeting of Greek ambassadors, discreetly invited to Switzerland, at Bad Schinznach on 26 August. There, talking freely and in complete confidence, he explained that there was no intention to return to democracy, he mocked the idea of representative government as seen in other 'so-called Western democracies, which are hypocritical and secret oligarchies without a sense of responsibility', and he finished by saying: 'I shall commit an indiscretion and tell you that, in any case, there is no question of elections. . . .'

First published in the *Observer*, and during the following week in every major newspaper in the world, the revelation of this briefing made a tremendous impression on the higher ranks of diplomatic Europe which had so far considered Pipinelis the one redeeming feature of the Greek government. His honesty was assaulted by the publication of this document (which was never denied), and many of his friends were bitterly disillusioned on realizing that he was in full harmony with the junta in deceiving the Greek people and the ministers of the Council of Europe. Many observers believe that this disclosure was responsible for the change of heart and vote of many European representatives.

The echoes of the Pipinelis story had barely died away when, one week later, the secret Report of the Human Rights Commission of the Council of Europe appeared in the press. The European governments of the member countries of the Council had already received the four volumes, 1,200 pages in all, in which the Greek government stood condemned for a variety of sins, ranging from deceiving the Greek people as to 'an imminent danger' which never existed to the torturing of their opponents. But as is usual with governments, they were treating it with extreme discretion and keeping it safely under cover. But once it was brought out, through channels never disclosed, all 1,200 pages of it carefully photocopied and their authenticity verified, its importance could not be denied. If governments tied by diplomatic niceties were forced to silence, newspapers had no such handicaps and the Report's revelations covered not columns but pages. The Report was based on investigations conducted over two years by a team of lawyers of international repute and had an

authority that could not be contested. Even the junta, reacting in blind
fury, could only accuse the foreign press of the crime of 'premature disclosure which could influence the meeting of Ministers'. For days every
major newspaper in the world tried to do exactly that, and carried the
story of the once secret Report on the Greek case, describing at length
the verified cases of torture applied to extort confession or information,
from which five of the victims had died. The weight of this huge body
of evidence, together with the horrifying details of the individual stories,
made a terrific impact on public opinion and counteracted the American
effort to persuade the European governments to postpone any unfavourable decision. World-wide opinion had been aroused and could not be
ignored, and human decency for once defeated diplomatic scruples.

After the revelation of Pipinelis' hypocrisy and the confirmation of the
junta's barbarity, came a third disturbing story about the Colonel's plan
to export dictatorship to neighbouring Italy, which also seemed a favourable field for this kind of regime. This time it was a photocopy of a top-
secret document sent to the Greek Embassy in Rome, marked 'Strictly
confidential. To be opened only by the Ambassador', which gave an
account of the actions and the expenditure of the Greek military in their
effort to organize a similar *coup* in Italy. It was authentic cloak-and-dagger
stuff, with coded names, mysterious initials, and peremptory orders for
full secrecy, especially in the meetings between the key figures of the
conspiracy and the ambassador himself. Because Greece was so much in
the news, even this extraordinary tale rated front-page treatment and
appeared in many national newspapers crowned with sensational headlines such as: 'Greek Premier plots *coup* in Italy . . . Ambassador in Junta
Conspiracy.'

If the Greek newspapers had enjoyed full freedom during this period
they could not have done any better. It is not too much to say that this
admirably orchestrated mobilization, started from inside Greece by
unknown and very brave volunteers who succeeded in providing these
scoops to their contacts abroad, was instrumental in demolishing the case
that the Greek regime had so carefully prepared. What happened afterwards is recent history. Pipinelis lost his last battle, Greece withdrew
before being expelled, and the Colonels, disregarding the intelligence of
the Greek people and of world opinion, resolved to call it a victory. The
Greek press was ordered to describe their panicky retreat as a major
triumph, a 'show of national pride and independence', and the city of
Athens had to celebrate it by putting out flags for three days.

In reality the 'victory' rankled, and the year 1970 started in an atmosphere of increased bitterness and a desire for retaliation against both the foreign and the Greek press. The crime of the latter, as we have said earlier, was that it managed somehow to communicate secretly with the public and attract readership by creating the impression of being in opposition without saying anything whatsoever against the government. With the new Press Law, which came into effect on 1 January 1970, the regime made a brave try to eliminate these offenders. As expected, the new law carried most of the restrictions of the previous one, was just as illiberal and as purposefully vague, and what was more, had as an 'extra' a unique article designed to punish a newspaper for the simple crime of being read. This came in the form of a new and very heavy import duty on newsprint, levied on the following scale:

Average daily circulation	Import duty
up to 25,000 copies	None
25,000 to 50,000 copies	50%
50,000 to 75,000 copies	75%
75,000 to 100,000 copies	90%
over 100,000 copies	95%

As all the anti-junta newspapers were over the 25,000 mark, and two of them over the 100,000, they found themselves so heavily penalized as to be nearly driven out of business. In order to survive they had to raise the price of each copy, always a desperate step for a Greek newspaper to take, especially if the rival newspapers using cheap newsprint could sell at a lower price. But again, after a short period of circulation slump, the newspapers had got most of their readers back, and what was more, and infuriating to the military, had found some loopholes in the new law and were voicing mild but recognizable anti-regime opinions.

A new era? Not really. Martial law remained in force, arrests without charge or explanation were daily occurrences, and behind the doors of various police stations 'interrogations' went on, discouraging any initiatives. But still, a sort of 'Prague Spring' was in the air, and the paper most affected by the new-found optimism and daring was the afternoon *Ethnos*, formerly a liberal, always respectable and generally unlucky newspaper, which had been struggling with financial difficulties for years and had many times been on the verge of closing down. Now it had started experimenting, taking small steps forward, criticizing – even mocking – the situation, suggesting reforms and possible evolutions. And for the first time in its sixty-odd years, it found itself leading the Greek press, fighting a battle recognized and admired by the public. As its circulation went up and up, caution gave way to a sort of recklessness, which to everyone in the know inevitably spelt disaster. And on 24 March 1970 the axe fell. The reason, or more accurately the pretext, for the confiscation of that day's issue was the publication of an interview given by the distinguished economist and former Centre Union Minister, John Zighdis, concerning Cyprus. The following text is the entire and by now historic interview which killed *Ethnos* and gave way to a new wave of arrests and terror:

> *What is your opinion of recent events in Cyprus and their possible consequences?*
>
> The tragic events of recent days prove that the Greeks in Cyprus are threatened by fratricidal division. The same facts prove that the sacred ties which bind them to Greece are put to a terrible test. In the disturbed international atmosphere the dangers which arise from this situation are visible to all.
>
> *Do you think that it would be more useful if the national question in Cyprus were faced by all the politicians in our country in a 'responsible and consistent' manner?*
>
> The Cypriot people fighting for liberty now more than ever need the affection, the presence and the counsel of Greece. And yet at this very moment counsel or threats are so irresponsibly formulated with regard to the abolition of their liberty. Such a thing is indeed unheard of.
>
> The affection that Cyprus needs is that of a 'politic' government which could offer it, in an inspired and effective way, a government which would have the full confidence of the Greek people. Such a government would have at its disposal greater authority for the support of the Cypriot struggle on an international plane.
>
> The return to democratic order is therefore necessary, so that within its framework a government of National Unity could be formed which would know how to confront critical situations. And this should be realized as soon as possible so that the threat of new national trials could be warded off.

Ethnos was charged with infringing the new Press Law, as the interview was 'liable to stimulate anxiety among the public'. Within days everyone connected with the interview was arrested: John Zighdis; John Kapsis, the journalist who carried out the interview; Constantine Ekonomides, the editor; and the three co-publishers of the newspaper, the brothers Achilles and Constantine Kyriazis, and Constantine Nikolopoulos. Tried before a military court on 31 March, they were all sentenced to heavy fines and terms of imprisonment ranging from one to five years. John Zighdis, a native of the island of Rhodes, who had experienced Mussolini's regime and had a deep hatred of dictatorship, declared in a spirited defence: 'This is a hasty measure designed to intimidate the press, me, the political world and every Greek. If you convict me, it will be the first time in history that an appeal for national unity has been considered as anti-national propaganda. . . .'

On 4 April, much to the distress of the Greek public, *Ethnos*, stricken by the heavy fines and the plight of its publishers, folded up. The International Press Institute, which from the very first days of the *coup* had been the organization most concerned with the plight of the Greek press and of Greek journalists, covered the whole story in its April–May 1970 *Press Bulletin*. In the introduction it said: 'This is not an internal Greek affair. It is a matter that concerns the press of the whole world. We must remember and recall unceasingly the names of the brave and admirable defenders of the freedom of the press, as well as those of their "judges". . . .'

The other Athenian newspapers got the message and groped for different ways to satisfy the Greek public's thirst for some form of opposition. During the last days of March and the first week of April, the 'Trial of the 34' gave them more than enough material as the depositions of the defendants, most of them highly respected Greeks, and the descriptions of the tortures to which they had been subjected made unforgettable reading. The regime for some inexplicable reason had for the first time allowed the Greek newspapers to publish the proceedings of a political trial, and the public was both appalled and deeply impressed. What had emerged was the quality, the dignity of the men in the dock, the high tone of their witnesses and lawyers – in contrast to the lamentable procession of the witnesses for the prosecution, minor employees and police informers. They accused the defendants in such a vulgar and incoherent fashion with such a variety of improbable villainies that even the judges were embarrassed. Once again, the newspapers that published the proceedings, without any comment, saw their circulation rise to new heights, while all four of the pro-junta newspapers remained mostly unsold, hanging forlornly outside the kiosks. The reason was simple. The Greek public, given a choice, would not buy a newspaper that called either Professor Karayorgas or Professor Mangakis a 'terrorist' and a 'criminal'.

From that time until this fifth year of the Colonels' regime the Greek press has been under visible or invisible censorship. The first, and certainly most oppressive, phase was the early one when, as the saying goes, 'everything that was not forbidden was obligatory'. Then preventive censorship ended, and what obligation to publish there was, and there still is, came through telephone calls, 'friendly' advice, and spoken or unspoken threats. But there is no doubt that during the year 1971 the newspapers, using another method, have regained much of their past personality. The secret is simply foreign news. Because of the danger in touching on even the most innocent subject dealing with economics, politics, or foreign policy if it is connected with Greece, the newspapers chose to dwell on foreign politics, foreign scandals, foreign economics, foreign elections, foreign disasters, foreign revolutions, even foreign serials and reviews of foreign books and foreign shows. And through the choice of this material, which cannot possibly be defined by any law, it is possible for each newspaper to acquire a political orientation. One subject alone, the war in Vietnam for example, is sufficient to stamp a newspaper as being extreme right, liberal, or of the left, by the simple expedient of publishing the article of one American columnist or another. There was no difficulty in recognizing if the My Lai drama, and the adventures of officers Calley and Medina were judged from the point of view of the right or the left. And as time passed, both editors and public – and of course the government – realized the possibilities of these indirect but very clear political assertions. There is no doubt in anyone's mind that the two Lambrakis papers, *Nea* and *Vima*, are back in their old centre-left slot: anti-American, anti-military, pro-black, pro-Angela Davis, indulgent towards permissiveness; while the four others, pro-junta and on the extreme right, with *Estia* in the lead, admire Spiro Agnew and Martha Mitchell, insist that Marxism has infiltrated every Western government and that the Pope is a communist. In between, the two newspapers of the Botsis brothers, *Akropolis* and *Apoyevmatini*, play a less definite game, and of late, for reasons of their own, seem to lean discreetly toward the junta. This has left to *Vradyni* the honour of being the most respected Athenian newspaper, the only one that shows signs of journalistic nerve, that is bold enough to try to speak up for the politicians, to hint at the plight of the political prisoners, and in general to travel in the dangerous waters in which the brave *Ethnos* had foundered. Naturally, its circulation is rising daily, and that of course is yet one more provocation.

That this choice given to the Athenians has taken on the character of a daily poll is the most infuriating and elusive of the many problems the regime has to face. Even the more sceptical observers have to accept that this unofficial voting, day after day, by hundreds of thousands of people, cannot be rigged in any way. It is impossible to believe that in the event of free elections the buyers would not automatically become voters, and just as only 10% now buy junta, that only so many would vote junta too. In a way, this has been a mixed blessing, because it has opened the eyes of the military to a political reality. More than anything else, this impossibility of attracting the silent majority has made them shun any idea of elections. To stay in power they know they have to keep gun in hand, and silence as much as possible the voices of the people they hate most on earth – the journalists. They detest both foreign and Greek journalists; they loathe the correspondents; they detest the publishers and the editors; they hate the cartoonists – they abhor each and every one of them. The most revealing blast of this all-consuming hate was the latest project of one more new law, concerning journalists this time, which emerged in August 1971, and which was simply a scheme to abolish the profession. It called on all journalists – even foreign correspondents working in Greece – to adhere to 'Helleno-Christian' principles. It initiated special 'loyalty' credentials that would have to be renewed every six months and signed by a committee appointed by the regime, and was on the whole so extraordinary and created such a reaction of mixed astonishment, worry and hilarity that it was promptly shelved, in the evident hope that it would also be quickly forgotten. Another set of laws concerning journalism appeared in October 1971 which, while in no way comparable to the first, still tried to regulate journalism by laying down a vague code of ethics, such as 'journalists should aim at avoiding inaccurate or malicious stories'. Considering that the services of the Ministry of the Press can interpret any story in any way they wish to, and that the martial law still in force allows the government to arrest anybody without any justification and treat him in any way it pleases, it is easy to realize that the press, like everyone else living in Greece, is always obliged to play along, take a few liberties when they are offered and to retreat into meek silence when the climate worsens.

It will be very difficult, when this whole dismal period has passed and the Greek newspapers really get their freedom and their voices back, to assess the role and the importance of those that were published during the dictatorship. It is certain that in many ways they helped the junta and that they had certain moments that had better be forgotten, just as they had others that will justly be respected and remembered. That they were most of the time considered to be hostile and were subject to every form of harassment was to their credit, even if it really stemmed from the inability of the military to accept the reality of the situation.

And that reality was that, more than the journalists, and the publishers, the real enemies were the readers – the elusive men and women of Greece who used the Greek press to say every morning and every evening that in their great majority they hated the present situation, and everyone connected with it. The simple fact of giving the silenced Greeks the opportunity of letting the world know this was a service of immense importance on the part of the Greek press.

London, October 1971   *Helen Vlachos*

CHAPTER FIVE

The Greek Economy since 1967

Spokesmen for the present Greek regime have stated that the country was threatened with economic chaos in April 1967, and that monetary stability and economic progress have been achieved by today's rulers. The first part of the argument is known to be untrue. Progress in the last five years, in terms of increase of national income and improvement of living standards, was founded on monetary stabilization in the early fifties and resulted from the development mechanisms set in motion and successfully reinforced in the decade 1957–1966; at the end of 1966, the gold and foreign-exchange reserves were exceptionally high. Under these conditions and impulses further economic advance was almost certain.[1]

On the other hand, the present rulers' claim to success in the management of economic affairs does not appear implausible to some sections of the population, particularly in urban centres, where the improvement of living standards was not discontinued after 1967. Many Greek and foreign businessmen – usually those more dependent on collaboration with the present authorities – tend to lay great stress on the importance of 'social calm', as opposed to 'social unrest' in Western democratic societies. It is important, however, to distinguish between views influenced by short-term business considerations and an objective assessment of performance in relation to past achievements and future prospects. The relevant questions are: is the process of growth, in acceleration until 1967, now gathering or losing strength? To what extent are constraints on growth now loosened or tightened? To what extent is the distribution of income improving in favour of major categories of the population?

Although the rise in spending and output in the last four years has proceeded at an annual rate approaching that of the 1963–66 four-year period, there is a widening discrepancy to the disadvantage of income from agriculture and some economically strong groups are receiving highly favourable treatment. Despite powerful credit and other stimulants, the average rate of growth of private fixed capital formation has remained since 1967 below the average of the period 1963–66, while the growth rate of industrial investment has been reduced by half. Three out of four major concessionary deals with intermediary operators for industrial projects, on which the regime relied to a great extent, have been abandoned, and another contract for the construction of a major highway has run into difficulties over the raising of the necessary funds.

The slowdown in the cumulative process of reinforcing industrial development has been accompanied by a serious deterioration in the balance of payments. The Greek economy was deprived of substantial foreign exchange resources as a result of international reaction to the *coup*. Thus (*a*) the cumulative net shortfall in receipts from tourism between 1967 and 1971, inclusive, is estimated at 200 million dollars, (*b*) capital resources of the order of 200 million dollars expected from the European Economic Community over a four- or five-year period were not made available. The total of 400 million dollars in these two categories of resources corresponds to the amount of high-cost short- or medium-term finance which has had to be secured by 'distress action' to cover a markedly increased current deficit in the balance of payments. Within five years, between the end of 1966 and the end of 1971, foreign indebtedness has more than doubled, to an estimated total in the order of 2,300 million dollars.

The suspension of fundamental constitutional rights and democratic procedures, and the resulting intimidation and arbitrary action, have gravely affected the civil service and educational institutions, thereby weakening two factors of major importance for progress.

The suspension of human rights and representative government has also undermined the international bargaining position of the country, particularly as regards most European governments and the European Economic Community (Common Market). The Agreement of Association between Greece and the Community has largely remained dormant since 1967. Long-term loans from the European Investment Bank, in part at subsidized rates of interest, have been discontinued, and so has 'agricultural harmonization' which would have consolidated equal treatment for Greek agricultural exports. Moreover, joint action and consultations on essential matters – such as the enlargement of the Community – have not taken place as provided in the Agreement of Association, and Greece's progress towards full membership has been stopped.

I THE POWER BASIS OF THE REGIME AND ECONOMIC POLICY

Almost five years after the *coup*, the regime rests on force, without evidence that it has gained the support of any appreciable portion of the population. The new rulers have made attempts to acquire popularity by displaying concern about the interests of the lower income groups – the farmers, the workers and the young. This was apparent in some of the regime's early and much-advertised actions, such as the cancellation of agricultural debts, the provision of low-cost housing for workers and free text-books for university students. In reality, similar decisions had been taken by previous governments, and others were being planned with greater caution and on a more rational basis: for instance, instead of an outright cancellation of agricultural debts, long extensions of repayment and reductions of interest and other charges had been granted, with due consideration to conditions for particular crops and local problems.

The regime has shown far more of its true nature in its dealings with the business community, whose co-operation it has regarded as essential. It has wooed this section of the population by means of anti-communist propaganda and its claim that the new rulers are the sole guarantors of law and order, and thereby of the rights of property and private enterprise. But the more effective wooing has been done by accepting proposals or requests by business groups or particular concerns in a spirit of loose *laissez-faire*. On the other hand, the dismissal of the elected boards of trade unions and agricultural co-operatives has eliminated any effective representation of the interests of workers and agricultural producers (see Chapter Six). At the same time purges and intimidation have disorganized governmental services and other public or semi-public bodies. These developments have resulted in a decisive weakening of considerations of public interest inspired by the deeper necessities of economic and social progress.

The regime considered itself duly authorized to prepare a five-year programme (1968–72) which was largely based on a draft programme (for 1966–70) elaborated on the instructions of previous governments – but this has not been acknowledged in public. The differences between the two texts are marginal but not wholly insignificant. Thus, in the regime's programme there is less emphasis on industrial investment, and more on investment in tourism, and a greater inflow of foreign capital is anticipated to balance external transactions. An important deviation of the new rulers from the economic conceptions of previous (democratic) governments is to be found in the former's reliance on business operators for initiating and carrying out organizational activities and investments of major importance. Thus, soon after the *coup* a contract was passed with a private foreign firm which was to provide extensive administrative services for the development of two Greek regions, including raising the necessary finance abroad. This was typical of the new rulers' belief that there should be no inhibitions about granting major or uncontrolled benefits to private firms in order to promote activities deemed, by some vague criterion or assessment, to be 'advantageous to the country'. The same approach is manifest in the substantial tax concessions granted to particular groups, as well as in the willingness to award public works contracts on the basis of direct negotiations with private parties rather than on that of competitive bids.

The lack of a popular base accounts for the regime's use of various political anaesthetics designed to divert public attention from fundamental national, constitutional and political issues. One of the anaesthetics is the stress on the enjoyment of consumer goods, especially in the cities where increasingly wide sections of the population are encouraged, to a considerable extent, by greater credit facilities, to move to patterns of expenditure characteristic of modern consumer societies. Sports and games – another obvious diversion – are also zealously promoted. Spending on football pools increased sevenfold between 1966 and 1970; and, for the first time, a casino has been allowed to operate in the vicinity of Athens.

The necessity of encouraging political apathy makes effective economic regulation very difficult. Immobility is apparent even in those fields selected by the regime for more drastic action, as for example in the reorganization of social security or the introduction of a new system of market and price control: the results were minor in the face of reaction from interested groups. This stagnation is also partly attributable to the failure of the regime to attract a sufficient number of first-rank, competent specialists: the barrier of passive resistance and non-collaboration presented by the majority of academics, scientists and technicians makes it virtually impossible for the new rulers to shape and carry out the coherent and imaginative policies required by a society reaching the upper levels of an intermediate stage of economic development and aiming at rapid further growth. Such policies should necessarily include the promotion of competition against monopolies or oligopolies, the establishment of public control over essential activities, mainly in basic utilities of key importance for economic growth, and the introduction of reforms aimed at strengthening social responsibility in private enterprise.

TABLE I

BASIC DEVELOPMENT INDICATORS

Average annual compound percentage rates of increase of magnitudes at constant 1958 prices, unless otherwise stated

	1957–66 (ten years)	1963–66 (four years)	1967–70 (four years)	1968–71 (four years) (estimated)
Gross National Product (at factor cost)	6·2	7·65	6·2	7·0
Agricultural income	3·1	4·2	2·6	1·9
Agricultural income at current prices	5·9	9·1	4·7	4·0
Urban income	7·1	8·7	7·15	8·2
Urban income at current prices	9·3	11·5	10·4	11·5
Industrial production (excl. public utilities)	..	11·2	8·0	10·0
Consumption				
Private	6·3	7·65	6·2	6·6
Private at current prices	8·1	10·4	7·1	7·7
Public	4·4	6·4	5·5	3·8
Public at current prices	9·2	13·9	13·1	12·0
Gross fixed capital formation				
Private	11·0	15·2	10·5	14·4
Private at current prices	13·8	17·2	14·1	16·8
Private excl. dwellings	12·5	17·0	12·4	15·1
Private in manufacturing	14·2	23·5	11·3	..
Private in dwellings	9·4	13·1	8·8	13·3
Public	11·6	7·9	12·4	13·4
Public at current prices	13·4	8·4	16·3	17·5
Aggregate current foreign exchange				
Earnings, at current prices	10·25	13·75	10·6	13·5
Earnings from exports, current prices	6·8	13·5	11·1	9·1
Payments* for imports, at current prices	9·5	15·8	10·2	14·0
Payments† for imports of capital goods, at current prices	19·6	18·2	14·6	18·3

Notes: * Plus supplier credits; † 1958–66.
Sources: Estimates on data from Ministry of Coordination, *National Accounts of Greece 1960–69*, Athens 1971; Bank of Greece, *Monthly Bulletins;* latest official announcements.

The view[2] that the policies of the regime are those applied or planned before the *coup* (quite apart from the contradiction between this and the charge of irresponsible economic management in the past), disregards the necessity of continued adjustment in public action at each phase of the process of development. The character, attitudes and policies of government under the present rulers are moving away from the type of state organization and the policies required for the healthy and vigorous transformation of the Greek society at its present stage. The lack of strong and coherent action designed with the participation or assent of true representatives of the farmers and workers, results in the apparent slowdown of agricultural growth, in the absence of new forms of industrial and financial organization and in the coexistence of increasingly grave labour shortages and emigration with underemployment and unemployment.

II Economic developments since 1967 compared to earlier periods

A comparison between the four-year periods 1967–70 or 1968–71 and the four-year period 1963–66 (Table 1) shows a marked decline of the average annual rates of growth in income from agriculture, in gross fixed capital formation in manufacturing industry and in export earnings. There has also been a substantial widening in the balance of payments deficit on current account.

The growth rates of real gross national or domestic product of Greece had been higher on the average, during the last twenty years, than the corresponding average rates for all OECD European countries and lower only than the Japanese rate. Since 1967, however, the size of these differences has changed to the disadvantage of Greece. Compared to that for all European OECD countries, the rate for Greece was 64% higher in 1963–66 and 32% higher in 1967–70. The rate for Greece was about 80% of the rate for Japan in 1963–66, and less than 50% in 1967–70. The change reflects a slow-down[3] in the process of narrowing the gap between Greece and the rich countries.

Slow-down in Agriculture

1 *Marked reduction of the rate of increase in output and income from agriculture*

The rising rate of growth of income at constant prices from agriculture, fisheries etc., as reflected in the higher rate for 1963–66 compared to the average for 1957–66, significantly declined in 1967–70 and in 1968–71 was less than half the 1963–66 rate. The target rate of 5·2% set in the 1968–72 programme is two and a half times the actual rate for 1968–71.

2 *Widening discrepancy between per capita income from agriculture and non-agricultural activities*

Despite continued mass emigration from the rural areas the rates of increase of per capita income from agriculture declined significantly after 1967, as shown in Table 2. The fall is clearly more pronounced in the rates at current prices, reflecting slower increases in agricultural prices.

TABLE 2

AVERAGE ANNUAL COMPOUND RATE OF INCREASE
IN PER CAPITA INCOMES

	Per capita income from agriculture		Per capita income from non-agricultural activities	
	Constant prices	*Current prices*	*Constant prices*	*Current prices*
1963–66 (four years)	6·0	11·0	6·6	9·3
1967–70 (four years)	4·5	6·0	5·3	8·4
1968–71 (four years)	3·8	6·0	6·3	9·6

Note: Aggregate income from agriculture, forestry and fishing and *other* aggregate income divided by respective population figures, obtained on the basis of the 1961 and 1971 censuses and linear extrapolations for intermediate years. Population in settlements of less (equal to or more) than 2,000 inhabitants taken as indicative of agricultural (urban) population.

The movement of income per capita certainly differed by crops and varying rates of emigration, with probably stagnant or slowly increasing per capita incomes from traditional crops such as tobacco, currants and sultanas and wheat. The rates of increase of per capita urban (non agricultural) income after 1967 were close to the 1963–66 rates and significantly higher than the rates of increase of per capita income from agriculture, implying a widening gap between the two income categories. The opposite, i.e. a more rapid rise of per capita income from agriculture, suggesting a narrowing of the gap, is apparent in 1963–66.

The decline since 1967, over a period of four or five years, of the rate of increase in agricultural product cannot be attributed[4] to unfavourable climatic conditions. It is certainly the result of a complex set of factors. There are, however, indications of reduced rather than increased state support for agricultural development: (a) subsidies from the budget to promote changes in the structure of crops, after major increases until 1966 and further rises in 1967 and 1968, declined[5] in 1969 and were reduced in 1970 to a level lower than that of 1966; (b) the share of investment for agricultural development in total central government investment declined from 28% to 24%. Although expenditure for large-scale reclamation or irrigation projects continued to rise, there was a decline[5] in essential supplementary spending to induce the necessary shifts and adjustments in production; (c) the cancellation of agricultural debts in 1968 was not associated with any systematic policy designed to promote agricultural modernization and growth; borrowers who had settled their obligations before the announcement of debt cancellation did not benefit from it; (d) the uncertainty with respect to the conditions under which a number of Greek agricultural products could be exported to European markets, after the suspension in 1967 of major parts of the Agreement of Association between Greece and the European Community. More generally the interruption of 'harmonization' of agricultural policies with the Community has been a serious setback to Greek agriculture. It is accepted that marked improvements in production, especially with continued mass emigration from the rural areas, could be secured only by major increases in the size and changes in the organization of agricultural holdings. The traditional procedure of plot re-allotment and consolidation had long proved too slow and inadequate.

The resumption in the last few years of mass emigration from the rural areas and the slow-down in agricultural production are becoming mutually determined processes, leading to agricultural stagnation. This is already pronounced in some of the main tobacco-producing areas in the north of Greece.

Slow-down in Industrial Investment

3 *The expansion of industrial production and exports realized by firms already established and fixed capital largely installed before 1967*

Most of the increase in recent years in industrial production and exports was associated with firms existing and investment decided on and for the greater part carried out, before 1967. About one-third of the increase of industrial production and about three-quarters of the rise in industrial exports resulted from four leading industries: chemical, basic metallurgical (aluminium, nickel and steel sheet), transport equipment (shipyards) and petroleum products. The increased activity in the leading industries is almost exclusively associated with ten firms, all established before 1967. Investment by these firms during the four-year period 1967–70, estimated on the basis of published information[6] of the Federation of Greek Industrialists, represented only about one-third of their total fixed assets at the end of 1970.

4 The rate of increase of private fixed capital formation in manufacturing halved after 1967

A slow-down or levelling off is apparent in the rise of fixed capital formation, and a pronounced decline has taken place in the rate of growth of investment in manufacturing, for which the 1968–71 rate (probably higher than the 11·3% rate for 1967–70) would still be about half the 23·5% rate for 1963–66. These differences largely reflect the impact of major industrial projects initiated before 1967 (some of which were completed or extended after 1967), and the absence of important new initiatives in the last five years. The decline in additions to industrial capacity must necessarily affect future expansion of industrial production and exports.

The slow-down of industrial investment is also reflected in the composition of investment. The share of private fixed capital formation in manufacturing out of total private fixed capital formation, declined from about 16% before 1967 to just over 14% in 1968–69 (for which statistics are available) and the fall should be compared with an increase to 18·5% aimed at for 1968–72 by the five-year programme.

5 Changes in relative earnings in the urban sector

Differences in the average annual rates of increase in money earnings between various categories of hired personnel were more pronounced after than before 1967, as can be seen from Table 3. The four-year average rates of increase showed significant declines between 1969–70 and 1968–71. The decline is particularly pronounced for minimum wages reflecting two increases in 1967 (13·5% as from 1 February 1967 and a further 6% as from 1 July 1967), accompanied by a considerably slower

TABLE 3

RELATIVE CHANGES IN MONEY EARNINGS

Average annual compound percentage rates of increase

	1963–66 (four years)	1967–70 (four years)	1968–71 (four years)
Civil Servants	9·0	7·5*	..
(Average about 105,000 in 1970)			
Military†	10·0	13·0*	..
Employees of Public Enterprises and Banks	8·8	4·7	..
(Average 47,000 in 1970)			
Hourly wages in industry	9·3	8·8	6·3
Weekly earnings in industry	8·8	9·6	8·6
Monthly salaries in industry	7·8	7·7	6·9
(Total hired personnel about 400,000 in 1970)			
Minimum wages (men)	8·0	8·4	5·1
Urban income‡	11·5	10·4	11·5

Notes: * Estimates for three years 1967–69, detailed statistics for 1970 not being available; † Estimates assuming no change in the size of regular military personnel; ‡ Aggregate at current prices.

Sources: Estimates based on data from *Statistical Yearbooks* and *Monthly Statistical Bulletins of Public Finance, Annual Reports* of Public Enterprises and Banks, *Statistical Yearbooks* and *Monthly Statistical Bulletins, Three-Monthly Bulletins* of the Ministry of Labour Statistical Service. Indices of wages, salaries and earnings based on a sample of industry establishments employing ten or more workers.

rise in subsequent years. These relationships probably suggest a slowdown in the increase in the relative remuneration of unskilled to skilled workers.

Employment in industrial establishments with ten workers or more, according to the official index, rose by average annual rates of 3·3% in 1963–66, 2% in 1967–70 and about 3% in 1968–71. If these movements were indicative of the whole urban sector, taken in conjunction with the slowdown in the rise of money earnings, they would suggest a falling rate of increase in total wage and salary earnings in relation to the rate of increase in aggregate urban income. Accordingly, and in view of the slow rise of income from dwellings, an accelerating rise in non-labour income from entrepreneurial and professional activities would appear likely, and this, of course, before taking into account differential tax treatment or other advantages. Although this statement refers to the whole private sector, for which the necessary detailed statistics are not available, it appears to be supported by a substantial rise in the rate of profit in a wide sample of several hundred relatively large industrial firms, as reported[7] for 1969.

Available statistics are inadequate for an estimate of the change in total urban employment. However, according to indications from the rise of the number of persons employed in industrial establishments (with ten workers or more) and in the civil service, public enterprises and major banks, the increase in total urban employment in absolute figures over the four years 1967–70 is not likely to have much exceeded one hundred thousand persons. Net emigration during the same period, nearing two hundred thousand, was probably about twice the estimated increase in urban employment. These orders of magnitude suggest that the substantial decline of unemployed registered at labour exchanges, and increasingly felt labour shortages, are a reflection less of a rise in employment at home than of the drain on Greek manpower resumed on a large scale since 1969.

Deterioration in the balance of payments

6 Marked slow-down in the growth of earnings from the export of goods

The rate of increase of *total* current foreign-exchange earnings for 1968–71 would probably be about equal to that of 1963–66. But the increase in export earnings has markedly slowed down, from an annual rate of 13·5% in 1963–66 to 11·1% in 1967–70 or 9·1% in 1968–71.[8] The increase in export earnings since 1967 was almost entirely due to the expansion of industrial exports initiated in the early sixties at an annual rate close to 15% and associated with the acceleration of industrial investment in the 1963–66 period. On the other hand the rate of increase in agricultural exports declined from about 11% in the 1963–66 four-year period to 7·15% in the 1967–70 four-year period, with stagnant or falling exports of traditional agricultural products such as tobacco, currants and cotton.

7 Sharp increase of current invisibles in 1971 narrowing the cumulative shortfall from previous years' earnings, with the overall annual current deficit remaining not far from 400 m. dollars

Current invisibles markedly increased in 1971, probably by about 33% for the whole year. The rise in earnings from tourism would be close to

55%, and that of shipping and emigrant remittances were expected to be of the order of 30–35%. These increases reflect to a considerable extent accelerated sales of foreign currencies induced by the international monetary uncertainties in the latter part of the year. But there is also perhaps a catching up following the declines or slow increases after 1967 (see Table 4), as a result of which the average annual rates of increase in the total and the main current invisibles are markedly below the corresponding target rates that were set by the regime.

Indeed, if one applies the rates of growth of the four-year period 1963–66 to the gross total, as well as to the particular current invisibles, the projections lead to estimates fairly close to the expected 1971 actual earnings. The estimated gross receipts on the 1963–66 rates of growth result in total earnings in 1971 close to 1,200 million dollars, which should not be significantly far from the actual 1971 level. This correspondence for 1971 is found also for the particular categories of invisibles.

TABLE 4

AVERAGE ANNUAL COMPOUND RATES OF INCREASE
OF GROSS CURRENT INVISIBLE EARNINGS

Gross earnings	1963–66 (four years)	1967–70 (four years)	1970–71* (one year)
Total	13·8	10·5	33·0
Tourism	18·1	8·0	55·0
Shipping	13·8	10·5	30·0
Emigrant	13·8	10·5	33·0

Note: * Estimated.
Source: Bank of Greece, *Monthly Statistical Bulletins.*

But the cumulative total of estimated earnings for the five years 1967–71 would exceed, by more than 400 million dollars, the cumulative actual earnings for the period. Three-quarters of this difference is due to lower receipts from tourism and the rest to a slower increase in shipping earnings. Even if one could attribute (and this is doubtful) the downward deviation from trend of shipping earnings to changes in international conditions and other non-exceptional factors, this interpretation would evidently not apply to the shortfall of receipts from tourism, in view of its large size. In fact, variations in international tourism or other factors inducing year-to-year fluctuations in receipts could not account[9] for a difference of 300 million dollars. In the past, deviations of receipts from tourism from trend values were corrected within two or three years, with their net total being less than 10% short of anticipated receipts over a period of bad and good years. Accordingly, at least 200 million dollars of the shortfall (the difference of 100 million dollars corresponding to more than 10% of expected receipts) should be attributed to a strong extra-ordinary influence, which is known to have been the international reaction to the suspension of democratic procedures in Greece. The figure of 200 million dollars represents a loss of foreign-exchange earnings to the economy, at least for the 1967–71 five-year period, which was not offset[10] by the major expansion in 1971.

Payments plus supplier credits for imports expanded in 1968–71 at 14·3% per annum compared to 15·8% in 1963–66. These movements correspond to an increase of the trade deficit from 745 million dollars in 1966 to an estimated level of the order of 1,300 million dollars in 1971 and a rise in the current account deficit from 266 million dollars in 1966 to about 400 million in 1970–71.

The movements of current foreign-exchange payments and earnings are substantially different from those planned by the regime, and the discrepancies cannot be accounted for by the deterioration in the terms of trade. The rate of increase in imports has not been lowered as planned and the rate of increase in exports has not been maintained as anticipated. The deficit on current account, instead of remaining practically unchanged (a 2% decline by 1972 is the forecast in the 1967–72 programme), will probably be larger by about 50% in 1970–71 as compared to 1966.

III   POLICIES AND PROBLEMS OF DEMAND EXPANSION: THE PUBLIC SECTOR

The dominant objective of the regime is to support a continued rise in demand with little regard to its composition or to its consequences. The main expansionist effect was achieved by an acceleration in the rise in public investment and a great increase in the overall deficit of the public sector. In the four-year period 1967–70 the average *annual* rate of expansion in central government spending was particularly pronounced for defence (21%), sport (estimated at more than 50%) and investment in small local projects (more than 50%) but much lower (10% or less) for public services such as education, health and social services.

On the other hand, the average annual rate of increase in private investment remained below the pre-1967 average despite a marked increase in the rate of bank credit expansion and concessionary deals to attract foreign investment.

1 *Increasing relative importance of the public sector in national expenditure; significant rise in overall public deficit*

Aggregate public expenditure at current prices (according to national account statistics) for consumption and investment in the three years 1967–69[11] was higher than in the preceding three years 1964–66 by about 50%; correspondingly the share of the public sector in gross national expenditure rose from 17·5 to 20%. The cumulative saving of the public sector (i.e. 'general government') increased between the two three-year periods by about 40%, with central government saving rising by about 35%. Accordingly, in the three-year period 1967–69 compared to the preceding 1964–66 three-year period, the cumulative deficit of the public sector, including expenditure for fixed capital formation, rose by about 55%.

The major part of the increase in the overall public deficit (always at current prices) represented the rise of the central government deficit caused largely by an annual expansion of fixed capital formation at current prices in the three years 1967–69 by more than 15% (or 16·5% in the four-year period 1967–70). The percentage of the surplus of the ordinary central government budget (covering current expenditure and public debt amortization) plus revenues from past investment on total central government investment declined significantly; a stable or increasing percentage would have been healthy and desirable, if the drive of private productive investment were sufficiently strong.

2 *Rise in total tax revenue; significant tax reductions and exemptions for some wealthy groups*

Total taxation, i.e. including local taxes and social security contributions, as a percentage of net national income rose from an average of less than 27% in 1964–66 to about 32% in 1967–69. The rise in central government revenue should be attributed mainly to the more rapid expansion of the urban sector and probably to increased liquidity. Threats of severe sanctions resulted in a once-for-all rise of tax revenue and an acceleration in the collection of tax debts. There was also a substantial increase in indirect tax revenues, as a result of which the change in the share of direct taxes in total tax revenues was not significant.

The rates of direct taxation as from the beginning of 1968 were reduced across the board and family allowances were increased. But for the assessment of the net redistributive effect of these changes, account should be taken of some important modifications in the taxation of certain categories of high incomes. The most important of these were: (a) the setting of a reduced maximum tax rate on income from dividends, implying a substantial limitation of progressive taxation on higher incomes from distributed profits; (b) the marked widening of tax allowances for investment accompanied by the elimination of preferential treatment in favour of investment outside the Athens area; and (c) the reduction of tax rates on income from shipping and the marked enlargement of tax exemptions to shipowners.

The third category of changes is worthy of particular attention. In 1968 taxes on larger ships engaged in international transportation were drastically reduced, with the progressive character of the rates eliminated and their dependence on freight rates and the type of chartering abolished.[12] The proceeds from the taxation of ships were reduced in 1969 and 1970 to about one-third of those of 1968, although the shipping tonnage registered under the Greek flag increased from about 8 million tons at the end of 1967 to more than 11 million tons at the end of 1969.[13] At the same time larger ships (3,000 gross tons and over) and passenger ships engaged in international transportation or tourist traffic were exempted from taxes on inheritance, donations and on the establishment of dowries. No other assets except state bonds enjoy such treatment.

3 *Rate of increase in expenditure for defence two or three times higher than rates of increase for education and health*

Developments in current public spending (shown in Table 5) are also indicative of the character and the policies of the regime. The annual rate of increase in expenditures for defence and public security in the three-year period 1967–69 was more than 21%, according to national accounts and budgetary statistics, corresponding to a significant rise in the national burden for defence.[14] The annual rates of increase in the same period for other categories of expenditure were 10% for education (or 7% for the Ministry of Education, according to budgetary statistics) and close to 7% for health and social services (or 8% for the combined Ministries of Social Services and Labour, according to budgetary statistics).

Changes in annual spending are also reflected in the variations in the respective shares in total current expenditure (also shown in Table 5). Between 1966 and 1969 there is a marked increase in the share for defence

TABLE 5

CHANGES IN ANNUAL CURRENT GOVERNMENT EXPENDITURE,
1967–69*

	Average annual (compound) rates of increase 1967–1969 (three years)	*Percentage share in total current expenditure*	
		1966	*1969*
Current expenditure of *general* government on goods and services *National Account Statistics*			
General administration	7·5	25·5	22·0
Educational services	10·0	14·0	13·0
Health and social services	7·0	11·0	9·5
Defence	21·5	32·0	40·0
'Ordinary' † expenditure of *Central* government *Budgetary Statistics*			
Civil ministries	12·5	77·5	73·5
Ministry of Education	7·0	12·5	10·0
Ministries of Social Services and Labour	8·0	9·5	8·0
Defence and public security	21·0	22·5	26·5

Notes: * Detailed statistics are available for 1969 but probably no significant changes occurred in 1970. Differences between the upper part ('General Government') and the lower part ('Central Government') of the Table reflect differences in concepts and classification as applied to the national accounts or budgetary presentations. 'General Government' in addition to 'Central Government and the Dodecanese' comprises local authorities and all public funds including social insurance funds. † In addition to some differences of classification 'ordinary' budgetary expenditure includes current expenditure and amortization of the public debt.

Sources: National Accounts of Greece, 1960–69, Athens 1971, Table 6; *Statistical Yearbook of Public Finance.*

and public security and a decline in the share of other current expenditure, including that of education and health.

4   *Major expansion in small local projects in central government investment*

Changes in the composition of public investment show (Table 6) a decline in the share of agriculture and manufacturing and an increase in the share of electricity and other public utilities in fixed capital formation by *general* government, according to national accounts statistics. The acceleration of investment by *central* government is to a considerable

TABLE 6

CHANGES OF ANNUAL EXPENDITURE IN GOVERNMENT
FIXED CAPITAL FORMATION, 1967–69*

	Average annual (compound) rates of increase	*Percentage share in total fixed capital formation*	
	Fixed capital formation by *general* government *National Account Statistics*		
	1967–69 (three years)	*1966*	*1969*
General government fixed capital formation	17·0	100·0	100·0
Agriculture, mining and manufacturing	10·0	17·0	14·0
Electricity, gas, etc.	29·5	25·5	34·5
Transport and communications	14·0	39·0	36·5
	Fixed capital formation by *Central* government *Budgetary Statistics*		
	1967–70 (four years)	*1966*	*1970*
Central government fixed capital formation	16·5	100·0	100·0
Agriculture, mining and manufacturing	12·0	31·0	26·5
Transport and communications	13·0	36·5	33·0
Various service activities	11·5	24·5	21·0
Prefects' small local projects and other	46·5	8·0	19·5

Notes: * See notes on Table 5. All percentages refer to magnitudes at current prices.
   Sources: National Accounts of Greece, 1960–69, Athens 1971; *Statistical Yearbook of Public Finance and Monthly Statistical Bulletins of Public Finance.*

extent associated with a marked expansion of small local projects, while investment in all other sectors proceeded at a significantly lower pace. The share of investment in agriculture and manufacturing declined from 31% in 1966 to 26·5% in 1970 with a corresponding increase in prefects' small local projects and others from 8% to 19·5%. Expenditure supplementary to major agricultural projects (land reclamation or irrigation) and for industrial infrastructure declined. Small local projects do have social importance, but their productive contribution is uncertain; they are useful, however, for propaganda purposes. Their effect in promoting local self-government is doubtful since local authorities, since 1967, have been appointed, not elected.

5   External finance for central government investment mainly by 'distress action' in the form of contractors' loans

About three-quarters of the growing overall deficit of the central government was financed by internal borrowing, as against half in 1963–66. About 75% of the treasury bills are purchased by commercial banks while bond issues are extensively supported by the banking system. In the two years 1969 and 1970, bank holdings of government bonds increased by about 1,900 million drachma against new issues of a total value of 4,200 million drachma. Such support continued in 1971 and was extended to bonds issued by public enterprises.[15]

The percentage covered by external finance is lower in 1967–70 as compared to the preceding four-year period and has taken place mainly through loans by contractors on State and Bank of Greece guarantee. The division between the various functions in construction and the financial arrangements constitutes a long-standing basic principle of healthy financial management and control. The type of 'distress' borrowing represented by contractors' loans, to which the regime has been forced to resort as a substitute for long-term development loans, has had two major disadvantages: (a) the terms of repayment[16] were hardly appropriate for infrastructure projects, from which the benefits could be expected only over a long period of years; (b) public works contracting on the basis of external loan proposals, and not on competitive bidding centred on the cost of construction, inevitably resulted in increased expenditure for the same amount of work; the excess cost is of the order of 20% to 30% according to some estimates. Not dissimilar, but of a special character, are the arrangements concluded with a foreign firm for the construction of a major highway in the north of Greece. The contractor, the American Macdonald Company, undertook the finance and supervision with the right of sub-contracting and equipment purchasing, while the contractor's fee was fixed as a percentage on the final cost of the project. Despite these provisions the contractor ran into difficulties in raising the necessary funds.

IV POLICIES AND PROBLEMS OF DEMAND EXPANSION: THE PRIVATE SECTOR

Incentives to private enterprise, in the form of tax exemptions and interest rate refunds, have increased substantially in recent years, in addition to a major expansion in bank credit to the private sector. However, the rates of growth in production and investment remained close to, or lower than, the corresponding rates before 1967. Some of these relationships are analysed in Tables 7 and 8.

TABLE 7

RATES OF INCREASE IN GROSS NATIONAL INCOME, INDUSTRIAL
PRODUCTION AND PRIVATE FIXED CAPITAL FORMATION COMPARED TO
RATES OF INCREASE IN BANK CREDIT

	Average annual compound rates of increase of			
	Gross national income	*Index of industrial production*	*Total bank credit to private sector*★	*Total private fixed capital formation (at current prices)*★
1963–66 (four years)	10·9†	11·2	14·1 (14·4)	17·2 (25·3)
1967–70 (four years)	8·7†	8·0	19·0 (19·1)	14·1 (12·6)
1969–70 (two years)	10·7	11·1	22·0 (20·3)	15·3 (15·5)

Notes: All rates estimated from the corresponding magnitudes at current prices, except for the index of industrial production. ★ Percentages in brackets refer specifically to manufacturing, i.e. the rates of increase of bank credit and of fixed capital formation in manufacturing. † The GNP price deflator for 1963–66, was 3% and 2·4% for 1967–70.

Sources: National Accounts of Greece, 1960–69, Athens 1971; Bank of Greece, *Monthly Statistical Bulletins* and official announcements.

1   *Increases in output and investment associated with much greater expansion in bank credit*

The average annual rate of expansion in total bank credit before 1967 (Table 7) was (*a*) about 30% *higher* than the corresponding rates of increase in gross national income, at current prices, and in the volume of industrial production, and (*b*) markedly *lower* than the corresponding rates of increase in private fixed capital formation at current prices. After 1967 (in the 1967–70 four-year and in the 1969–70 two-year periods) the average annual rate of expansion in total bank credit is (*a*) *more than double* the rate of increase in gross national income and in the volume of industrial production and (*b*) markedly *higher* than the corresponding rates of increase in private fixed capital formation.

These tendencies would indicate a much weaker inducement to invest after 1967, which was apparently not overcome by major increases in bank credit and other incentives.

2 Lower contribution of investors' own funds in fixed capital formation

An increasing part of fixed capital formation was financed by credit, which would imply a smaller percentage contribution by the domestic business community's own capital. This general conclusion is drawn from a comparison of the estimated percentage contribution to private fixed capital formation of long-term loans from the banking system (new loans or increases in outstanding balances), controlled capital inflows and

TABLE 8

DOMESTIC LONG-TERM BANK LOANS, FOREIGN CAPITAL (UNDER LAW 2687/1953)
AND SUPPLIER'S CREDITS IN RELATION TO GROSS AND NET PRIVATE
FIXED CAPITAL FORMATION

	Domestic long-term bank loans (A)	Capital inflow under Law 2687 (B)	External credits for the supply of capital goods (C)	Total external financing (D)=(B)+(C)	Total financing domestic and external (A)+(D)
			Percentages on gross private fixed capital formation		
	New loans	Gross inflow	New acceptances*	External financing	Total new financing
1963–66 (four years)	16·1	5·7	1·6	7·3	23·3
1967–70 (four years)	26·2	2·6	6·6	9·2	35·4
1969–70 (two years)	28·1	2·2	7·3	9·5	37·6

Percentages on gross private fixed capital formation (excluding dwellings)

	New loans (excluding dwellings)	Gross inflow	New acceptances*	External financing	Total new financing
1963–66 (four years)	21·8	9·5	2·8	12·3	34·1
1967–70 (four years)	28·3	4·2	10·9	15·1	43·4
1969–70 (two yesrs)	31·2	3·7	12·1	15·8	47·0

Percentages on net private fixed capital formation†

	Net increase in outstanding loans‡	Net inflow§	Net increase in outstanding credit¶	Net increase in external financing	Net increase in total financing
1963–66 (four years)	14·2	7·7	2·0	9·7	23·9
1967–70 (four years)	23·3	2·0	4·1	6·1	29·4
1969–70 (two years)	28·2	1·1	3·2	4·3	32·5

Notes: * Estimates.

    † Estimates for private capital depreciation.

    ‡ New loans minus repayments.

    § Gross inflow minus repatriation.

    ¶ New acceptances minus repayment of old acceptances.

    Sources: National Accounts of Greece 1960–69, Athens 1971, Table 14; Bank of Greece, *Annual Reports*; Bank of Greece, *Bulletin on Greece's external transactions.*

supplier credits (new acceptances or increases in outstanding balances). These percentages (shown in Table 8) were estimated correspondingly on gross and net private fixed capital formation as well as on gross private fixed capital formation excluding dwellings. All estimates point to the following changes: (*a*) the increase after 1967 of the percentage of total new financing on fixed capital formation is in all cases pronounced and continued; (*b*) the increase is due to the expansion of loans from domestic banks and supplier credits for imported capital goods; (*c*) there is a marked decline in the percentage contribution of the inflow of foreign capital, which is a form of external finance much healthier than supplier credits (these latter are generally considered to have the serious disadvantage of reduced possibilities of quality and price control in procurement);

(*d*) a more rapid expansion in bank credit than the corresponding formation of real assets implies an increasing relative indebtedness of the business sector. It should be noted in this connection that, despite the 1967 measures for the reactivation of the capital market, the amount of non-bank equity issues in 1967–70 was lower than in 1963–66.

The reduced participation of business funds in investment implies a less responsible assessment of the prospective results from the particular projects under construction and a further weakening of risk taking and of the private development drive, which has already shown signs of reduced strength after 1967. These tendencies are leading to a tightening of the financial constraints on growth.

3   *Monetary aspects: major expansion in overall liquidity associated with rapid increase in bank deposits*

The marked increase in bank credit was associated with a great rise in bank deposits, mainly in small saving deposits, most of which are withdrawable on demand. The substantial increase in bank deposits reflects a probable rise in saving associated with the expansion of urban income and an increasing preference for bank deposits against other assets; it also implies an activation of money holdings in the banking system leading to further increases in bank deposits and loans, within a recycling process.

A characteristic feature of monetary developments after 1967 is the rise in overall liquidity as measured by the ratio of the supply of total money (including only demand deposits) and 'quasi' money (all other deposits) to gross national product at current prices. This ratio increased from an average of about 43% to an average of about 52·5% in 1967–70, with a pronounced rise in recent years up to almost 58% in 1970. These changes reflect a major expansion in liquidity which is, however, accompanied by a considerably less rapid increase in production and investment and by a marked rise in the balance of payments current deficit. The association between a given rate of increase in private fixed capital formation and an increasingly rapid bank credit and liquidity expansion leads to a tightening of the monetary constraint on economic development.

The average annual compound rate of increase of the official consumer price index in the period 1967–71 (five years) is estimated at about 2%. The corresponding rates of increase are about 3% for the four-year period 1963–66 and about 2% for the ten-year period 1957–66. Accordingly, the increase in the price-level over long periods appears generally low and there is no foundation for the claim that monetary stability is an achievement of the last few years. Internal and external monetary equilibrium was attained in Greece in the early fifties and reinforced in the decade 1957–66 with the practical elimination in 1966 of the habit of gold sovereign hoarding, inherited from the period of enemy occupation. There is a considerable difference, however, between monetary stability with a balanced 'basic' position in the external accounts and the impression of overall stability with a large deficit in the 'basic' balance of payments covered by 'distress action', as analysed in section VI.

V CONCESSIONARY DEALS FOR FOREIGN INVESTMENT

A change in emphasis and approach towards foreign capital became apparent shortly after April 1967. The regime was less selective and more disposed to consider and extend concessions for foreign investment. Attractive terms were added to the arguments of 'efficiency' in the administration, and 'social calm', to counteract the uncertainties of a relationship with a type of government known to be scarcely acceptable to the Greek people. The new attitude was probably also influenced by the consideration that the establishment of operations and interests in Greece by major foreign concerns could secure much-needed public relations and political support on an international scale.

Approvals under Greece's 1953 special legislation, ensuring reinforced constitutional power to the guarantees for the servicing and repayment of foreign capital or the extension of other concessions, have considerably increased since 1967. According to official statements and statistics, in the four-year period 1967–70, excluding major deals for projects of a total value approaching 1,700 million dollars, aggregate 'approvals' were of the order of 700 million dollars, which is close to the corresponding aggregate during the thirteen-year period 1954–66, since the enactment of the 1953 legislation. However, actual inflows of capital under this category, estimated[17] at 298 million dollars (241 million dollars excluding the value of aircraft made available *on lease*, or 170 million dollars according to another estimate[18]), were considerably lower in 1967–70 than corresponding inflows in the four-year period 1963–66 estimated at 340 million dollars. The discrepancy between approvals and actual inflows in the four-year periods is too large to be accounted for by the time-lag between the conclusion and implementation of the respective projects. It probably reflects a tendency of foreign enterprises to obtain the special advantages for foreign investment with no firm intention of implementing the corresponding investments, a practice which was bound to increase uncertainty and hesitation by other would-be domestic or foreign investors. Moreover, the conclusion or negotiation of major contracts not with the final investors but with intermediary operators, in addition to other adverse effects, frequently leads to unspecified and not easily assessable advantages for particular enterprises or plants, thereby causing distortions in competition discouraging other business initiatives.

Four major foreign investment deals[19] of that type were concluded by the regime since 1967. Three of these have already been abandoned. The first, signed in May 1967 with an American firm, Litton Benelux, provided for administrative and co-ordinating activities, the preparation of studies and the conduct of negotiations, all leading to projects of an expected total value (according to official announcements) of about 840 million dollars in two major regions of Greece, Western Peloponnese and Crete. This contract indicated that the regime was disposed to rely on arrangements with foreign firms undertaking, at a fee and/or other remuneration or benefits, to seek and ensure foreign investment in Greece. This same deal extended permission to the contracting private firm for initiatives and regulatory action belonging, under normal conditions, to the responsibilities and competence of the State. It should be noted that the whole of the arrangements, as proposed by the firm concerned, were strongly criticized and generally rejected during a debate in the Greek Parliament in August 1966. The acceptance of this contract in principle by the post-April 1967 regime, with minor amendments in its main provisions, was indicative of the new approach to foreign investment and its conclusion has probably adversely influenced direct investment in the following years.

The main characteristics of these concessionary deals were the following.

First, the contracting private partner, a large international business operator in the three out of the four cases,[20] was an intermediary and not expected to be the principal direct investor or financier; he undertook to arrange with other interested parties and/or sources of capital the implementation of a group of projects. This basic feature had significant implications:

(*a*) the acceptance that private operators could be allowed to negotiate the country's credit internationally

(*b*) the provision of sufficient advantages and guarantees to ensure the success of the subsequent negotiations with the final investors or financiers

(*c*) long delays in these negotiations despite the initial advantages and guarantees, causing the suspension of new ventures or expansion by other interested firms.

Second, the complex character of these deals providing for a variety of services and projects, not always initially determined in detail, make the holding of international tenders for their award meaningless or difficult. Neither the cost of the projects nor the benefits accruing to the private contracting partners and their subcontractors or financiers could be accurately assessed and compared with alternative solutions. These difficulties were increased by the long-term relationship created by these contracts. Changes in prices, rates or other costs to the advantage of the private contracting partner could not be assessed or invoked for adjustments to the benefit of the country, while variations in conditions to the disadvantage of the contracting partner were bound to lead to disputes, delays and finally to the breakdown of the relationship.

The following is typical of the lack of coherence in these dealings. After the abandonment of a contract for a 60 million dollar complex of plants for the construction of various types of trucks and tractors, a new contract for a 6·7 million dollar passenger car production unit was recently concluded with two foreign firms contributing or arranging for an equity participation of less than 2 million dollars. This provides for a six-year right of exclusivity and for a twelve-year obligation on the Greek State not to enter into a similar arrangement. Meanwhile, another project for a heavy vehicle factory is under consideration.

It is clear that in these deals the anticipated public-relations effects are dominant. The need for integrated activities and international specialization either is not sufficiently appreciated or recedes under the pressure to conclude spectacular deals, even if these are associated with exclusive rights binding the country over long periods, and inevitably possess a speculative character. Under these conditions, projects with political and strategic overtones, such as the building of an aircraft spare part and repair plant for military and civilian aircraft, now sponsored by the American and French governments, appear to have a greater chance of being implemented – unless trapped in the difficulties of the foreign aid bill in the Congress of the United States.[21]

VI THE BALANCE OF PAYMENTS: THE CUMULATIVE SHORTFALL OF ABOUT
400 MILLION DOLLARS MATCHED BY 'DISTRESS ACTION'

As already explained (II, 7), of the total net shortfall of more than 400 million dollars in current invisibles during the five years 1967–71, at least 200 million dollars should be attributed to the setback of the expansion of tourist receipts following the international reaction to the interruption of democratic procedures in 1967. This setback contributed significantly to the widening of the deficit on current account, which in 1971 was expected to be not far from 400 million dollars, despite the exceptional rise in current invisibles.

The falling into abeyance of major parts of Greece's Agreement of Association with the European Community, after the suspension of human rights and civil liberties in 1967, deprived the Greek economy of capital resources of about 200 million dollars over the last four or five years, largely in the form of long-term development loans, in part at subsidized rates of interest.

The aggregate shortfall in these two categories of foreign exchange resources, of the order of 400 million dollars, is close to the cumulative total of short- and medium-term debts secured by 'distress action' in the four years 1967–70 to make possible the overall equilibrium in the balance of payments.

1   *A surplus reversed into a rapidly increasing deficit in the 'basic' balance of payments*

The 'basic' balance of payments, i.e. the deficit on current account after deduction of the net inflow of *long-term* capital, is generally considered as the critical magnitude for the evaluation of developments in external accounts. The 'basic' balance of payments of Greece (Table 9) changed from an average annual surplus of 14 million dollars in the period 1960–66 to an average annual deficit of 82 million dollars in the period 1967–70 or an average annual deficit of 120 million dollars in the period 1968–71. The estimated 'basic deficit' for 1971 would show a further increase over the 1968–71 annual average. These changes are clearly due to a marked expansion of the current deficit without a corresponding increase in the inflow of long-term capital.

The four-year cumulative total of the 'basic' deficit was 328 million dollars in the four-year period 1967–70 and would probably exceed 450 million dollars in the four-year period 1968–71, the further rise of this total by 120 million dollars (or almost 40%) indicating the trend.

2   *Declining share of 'approved' capital inflows*

Gross inflows of developmental capital on 'approvals' under Greece's 1953 special legislation represented more than one-third in the four years 1963–66, and much less than one-fifth in the four years 1967–70, of total gross capital inflows (or about 40% and 18%, respectively, if the

TABLE 9

THE BASIC BALANCE OF PAYMENTS POSITION
Annual averages (in million dollars)

	Current balance	Long-term capital	'Basic' balance
1960–66	−158	172	14
1967–70	−298	216*	−82
(1968–71)	(−350)†	(230)*†	(−120)†
(1971)	(−400)†	(240)†	(−160)†

Notes: * Includes since 1968 'contractors' loans' for state investment; † Estimates based on nine-month developments.
Sources: International Monetary Fund, *Annual Survey*, 1970, p. 101; Bank of Greece, *Monthly Statistical Bulletins*.

inflows are taken *net*). This sharp decline suggests a loosening in the relationship between inflow of capital and particular development projects (Table 10):

3 'Distress Action' to secure overall equilibrium

The extraordinary measures labelled as 'distress action', are the following (Table 10):

(*a*) large increases in supplier credits which are known to be among the least healthy forms of development finance (total indebtedness from supplier credits at the end of 1971 is expected to approach 600 million dollars, exceeding by about one-third the corresponding official reserves. The increase in supplier credits by 231 million dollars in the four years 1967–70 is double the corresponding increase in the four years 1963–66, representing more than 40% of the rise of payments for imports. Hence at least 80 million dollars are an excess rise in supplier credits, representing accordingly 'distress action')

(*b*) transfers from the gold sovereign domestic fund, held at the Bank of Greece for contingencies; these would probably exceed[22] 100 million dollars in 1967–70 compared to 22·4 million dollars in 1963–66

TABLE 10

ANALYSIS OF CAPITAL INFLOW
Cumulative totals in million dollars

	1963–66 (Four Years			1967–70 (Four Years)		
	Gross inflow	Outflow	Net inflow	Gross inflow	Outflow	Net inflow
I Private	686	−77	609	878	−161	711
1 Controlled* under Law 2687/53	340	−7	333	298†	−65	233
2 Commercial banks	68	−37	31	211	−50	161
3 Other business	37	−11	26	49	−24	25
4 Non business	241	−22	219	320	−28	292
II Public	163	−42	121	266	−152	114
1 State	123	−18	105	161	−103	58
2 Public institutions	40	−24	16	105	−49	56
III Supplier credits (Increase)	115	—	115	231	—	231
IV Accomodating	30	−8	22	262	−29	233
1 State	30‡	—	30	137§	—	137
2 Central Bank	—	−8	−8	125	−29	96
Grand Total	994	−127	867	1,637	−348	1,289

Notes: * Corrected by inclusion of particular items identified in the Notes attached to Table 42 of the Bank of Greece *Monthly Bulletin*, by addition of three-quarters of inflows effected by 'Other (private) enterprises' as recorded in the *Bulletin of Greece's External Transactions* published by the Bank of Greece; † Includes about $85 m. of inflows effected by Olympic Airways of which $47 m. represent the value of airplanes made available (in 1969) *on lease*; ‡ Five Year loan from the 'European Monetary Fund'; § Public works contractors' loans.

Sources: Based on data from Bank of Greece, *Bulletins of Greece's External Transactions* and *Monthly Statistical Bulletins*.

(c) contractors loans on State and Bank of Greece guarantee, of a total amount of 137 million dollars in the four-year period 1967–70, most of them repayable in five years at effective rates approaching 10%

(d) Bank of Greece loans of a gross total of 125 million dollars in 1967–70. A 30 million dollar loan in 1966 by the State from the European Monetary Fund would fall into this category.

'Accommodating' finance under (c) and (d) is a measure of the immediate balance of payments pressure; it amounted to 233 million dollars (net) in 1967–70 as against 22 million dollars in 1963–66. All arrangements under (a) to (d) reflect 'distress action'; they add up to 442 million dollars in 1967–70 compared to 44·3 million dollars in 1963–66. The extent to which 'distress action' is used for overall equilibrium is indicative of the size of the present balance of payments problem as well as of the constraints likely to become operative on future economic development.

4 'Window-dressing' in the form of short-term deposits in foreign exchange

The overall foreign-exchange position appeared during 1971 to have been favourably affected by a marked increase of about 150 million dollars of bank deposits in foreign exchange, most of them of a duration of less than one year. About a quarter of these deposits are on terms and guarantees of Greece's special legislation for foreign investment, and about one-third originate from Greek seamen and workers or are realized under a 'housing loan-deposit scheme'. A third category labelled 'other deposits' rapidly increasing since the beginning of 1970, are of a period of three to six months on negotiated rates of interest exceeding the corresponding uerodollar deposit rate. The Bank of Greece was authorized[23] to pay a commission as an added inducement to attract such deposits in a period in which this type of rapidly moving international short-term capital was not welcomed in many European coutnries. Within 1971, until the end of September, the increase in these 'other deposits' was of the order of 80 million dollars. At least part of that increase as well as the 60 million dollar medium-term 'accommodating' loan by the Bank of Greece should be considered as reflected in the 1971 rise in foreign exchange reserves.

In view of the large increase in the last few years of the current account deficit and the unsatisfied need for long-term development capital, as reflected in the rise of the 'basic' deficit, the importance attached to these 'other deposits' constitutes a measure of the reliance on 'window-dressing operations' to maintain an appearance of adequacy in the external position of the Greek economy.

5 *The relative position of gold and foreign-exchange reserves significantly worse compared to 1966, despite windfall increases in 1971*

The level of reserves should be compared to imports and foreign-exchange liabilities. The comparisons should be made both for *official* reserves, including the IMF gold tranche, as well as for *total* reserves, i.e. official reserves plus gold from the Bank of Greece domestic sovereign fund (Table 11).

Within five years total foreign indebtedness has more than doubled, to

TABLE 11

FOREIGN INDEBTEDNESS, IMPORT PAYMENTS AND FOREIGN EXCHANGE RESERVES
(Million dollars)

		1966	1970	1971*
A	Total foreign indebtedness† (End of December)	1,104	1,988	2,300
B	Total maturities within next twelve months plus certain short-term liabilities as of end of year‡	285	490	620
C	Imports: Annual (C_1)	1,149	1,696	1,900
	Monthly average (C_2)	96	141	158
D	Official§ reserves (End of December)	273	310	450
E	Total¶ reserves (Estimated) (End of December)	353	334	480
	Ratio of D to B	0·95	0·65	0·75
	Ratio of E to B	1·25	0·70	0·80
	Ratio of D to C_2	2·9	2·2	2·9
	Ratio of E to C_2	3·7	2·4	3·1

Notes: * Estimates † net balance of *identifiable* liabilities to the rest of the world, excl. *pre-war* debt; ‡ Incl. amortization, maturing and unsettled supplier credits and liabilities from seamen's and workers' deposits in foreign exchange (est. for 1971); § Incl. IMF gold tranche; ¶ Official reserves (D) increased by domestic gold sovereign fund.,

Sources: Estimates based on data from OECD, op. cit. Table 7; Bank of Greece, *Annual Report for 1968, Bulletins of Greece's External Accounts, Monthly Statistical Bulletins.*

an estimated total of 2,300 million dollars. Aggregate maturities within the next twelve months, plus liabilities from workers and seamen's deposits as of the end of year, more than doubled, and import payments increased by about 65%. The corresponding rise in end-of-year *official* reserves is estimated at about 60% and 40% in *total* reserves.

The ratio of expected reserves at the end of 1971 to short-term liabilities plus maturities within the next twelve months, although higher relatively to 1970, would be lower than in 1966 and the difference would be significant for total reserves. Similarly, although the ratio of reserves to imports would at the end of 1971 probably be higher than in 1970, and equal to that of 1966 for official reserves, it would be markedly lower for total reserves.

VII Conclusions

Greek economic experience since 1967 is associated with a grave loss of opportunities, resources and strength. The origin and character of the present regime make reliance on increasing profit inducements and concessionary deals inevitable. Under such impulses and arrangements economic development would suffer either from difficulties in securing rapid and abnormal profits – as has already appeared in the breakdown of almost all major foreign investment contracts concluded in recent years – or by wild rapid profit-seeking undertakings. But growth will proceed on the mechanisms already established and there will be an appearance of improvement in social conditions as long as mass emigration continues.

Despite the fallout of the tourist explosion and possible further increases in current invisibles, the balance of payments constraint will become increasingly pressing. However, the rise in spending and consumption may continue and a climate of euphoria may be maintained, as long as 'windfalls' and 'window-dressing' or other 'distress actions' postpone the moment of reckoning.

The long-term prospects of the Greek economy largely depend on the restoration of democratic procedures. For it is only on the strength of popular support and social acceptance that the conditions of economic and social progress can be secured in Greece. These should include: (*a*) social peace based on the rule of law in the form of democratically enacted legislation, as distinct from stillness enforced by intimidation and arbitrary action; (*b*) an increasingly wide and active participation in decision-making and in the fruits of progress of farmers and workers, trained specialists and technicians; (*c*) the political ability to undertake drastic action and essential reforms and to enter into lasting contractual arrangements; (*d*) an international position commanding respect and allowing effective negotiation and protection of vital Greek interests.

With such conditions, the long-term prospects of the Greek economy are bright. Political antagonism frequently became heated in the past but many causes of social strife, such as the racial or religious discrimination encountered in developed and under-developed countries, are absent in Greece. Poverty still exists in the rural areas, yet repeated land reforms since the early part of the century have almost eliminated large-scale land-ownership. Despite marked inequalities in wealth and income there has been continued improvement in social conditions over the last sixty years. With brief interruptions (about ten in almost 130 years) representative government from about the middle of the nineteenth century secured substantial democratic advances and significant progress in labour and social legislation in comparison with many Western countries. A profound attachment to the ideals of freedom is associated in the Greek people with a feeling of repulsion towards totalitarian practices of any kind.

These characteristics explain why an authoritarian regime has small chance of ever gaining popular support in Greece. These same features imply that only by the respect of the democratic principles in public life can real long-term social peace and permanent improvements in government be secured.

Within such a perspective, the principal source of Greek economic development would be the available, still underemployed and untapped human resources. Imagination and drive in business initiatives could become a constructive factor only within a wider international framework and in co-operation with a truly representative government. A rapid expansion and improvement of the educational system would release an increasing number of responsible experts, managers and State officials, who would become a leading force for progress in a Greek society playing its full part in the emerging European context.

Athens, October 1971   *John Pesmazoglu*

NOTES

1 On the state of the Greek economy at the beginning of 1967 see Bank of Greece *Annual Report* for 1966 published on 20 April 1967. No responsible statement has been made in recent years about a forthcoming economic collapse (as distinct from serious deterioration, especially in the balance of payments) and vague references to such opinions by representatives of the regime have no foundation. See 'Colonels Pay the Price', by Campbell Page, *Guardian*, 25 February 1971.

2 Mr R. P. Davies, Deputy Assistant Secretary of State, United States Department of State, referred to this view on 12 July in the Hearings before the Subcommittee on Europe of the Committee on Foreign Affairs of the United States House of Representatives; see *Greece, Spain and the Southern NATO Strategy*, US Government Printing Office, Washington 1971, p. 34.

3 This significant deterioration since 1967 is not mentioned in statements on the relative growth rates in recent years, as for example, in the testimony by Mr R. P. Davies, loc. cit., p. 33.

4 Cf. OECD, *Economic Surveys, Greece*, February 1971, pp. 31 and 33.

5 See *Statistical Yearbooks of Public Finance*, Table IX:21 for current expenditures of the Ministry of Agriculture and Table X:3 for breakdown of central government investment.

6 See *Ekonomikos Tachydromos*, Athens, 9 September 1971, pp. 31 ff.

7 Federation of Greek Industrialists, *Greek Industry in 1970*, Athens 1971, pp. 78 ff. The corresponding estimate for 1970 is not available.

8 An absolute decline in exports in 1971 (apparent in the statistics of the first nine months of the year) was largely due to a suspension of nickel exports.

9 The following were the percentage changes in tourist earnings in Greece and two neighbouring countries: Greece: 1967 −11%, 1968 −6%; Turkey: 1967 6%, 1968 56%; Yugoslavia: 1967 28%, 1968 25%, *L'Observateur de l'OCDE*, No. 42, October 1969, p. 35.

10 This, of course, does not exclude further catching up in future years.

11 Based on *National Accounts of Greece, 1960–69*, Athens 1971.

12 These amendments were introduced by Compulsory Law 465 of 1968 and Legislative Decree 509 of 1970. The contrast should be made with the taxation on small vessels up to 500 tons engaged in internal transportation which are taxable at a flat rate of 14 dr, or 35 dr in some cases, per ton of *gross* tonnage, with the rates on the larger ships in no case exceeding 12 dr per ton of *net* tonnage.

13 Moreover, the average rate of increase in foreign-exchange earnings from shipping in the four-year period 1967–70 was markedly below the average of the four-year period 1963–66 and caught up only in 1971. See above, III, 2.

14   The percentage of defence expenditure on gross national product in Greece
      increased from an average of 4·2 in the four years 1963–66 to 4·8 in the
      four years 1967–70 and 4·9 in 1970. Corresponding percentages in other
      NATO countries remained stable or declined in the three or four years before
      1970 with the exception of Belgium, The Netherlands and Norway in
      which there were small increases with the percentages remaining close to
      3 or between 3 and 4. The percentage for Italy was close to 2·8 in 1969–70
      and that for Turkey declined from 4·2 in 1969 to 3·7 in 1970. Among
      NATO countries percentages higher than or equal to that of Greece in 1970
      were encountered in USA (7·8), Portugal (6·5) and the United Kingdom
      (4·9). The average for all European NATO countries was about 3·5 in 1970.
      See The Institute of Strategic Studies, *The Military Balance*, 1971 and
      previous years.
15   The point is of significance in view of the presentation of the coverage of
      bond issues as manifestations of public confidence and political support to
      the regime. The intervention of the banking system in the bond markets
      was negligible in the past.
16   See section VI, 3.
17   See Table 10.
18   Cf. 'Survey on Greece', *The Financial Times*, 20 October 1971, p. 38.
19   The relatively large foreign investment contract for the construction of a
      highway in northern Greece (see III, 5) is not included, being associated
      with public investment, not with a private venture.
20   In one case the contracting party was a group of private persons under-
      taking a 60 million dollar project, which was abandoned about a year later.
21   See *Financial Times*, loc. cit., *International Herald Tribune*, 26 October 1971.
22   Estimates based on detailed presentations in the survey on Greece by OECD,
      op. cit., Table 7 and information from the Bank of Greece *Annual Report*
      for 1968.
23   Decisions of the Currency Committee at its sessions 1592, 9 February 1971
      and 1602, 14 April 1971

CHAPTER SIX

Workers and Peasants under the Military Dictatorship

Everything that has been written up to now on the Greek dictatorial regime is either related to its brutality, suppression of basic human rights, cultural backwardness and notorious incompetence, or to the historical and political circumstances that made possible its successful establishment. Surprisingly enough, very little has been written in the form of systematic analysis on the impact of the regime on the economic welfare of the various strata of the Greek population. A lot of generalizations have been advanced about the nature of the regime. To make such generalizations, it is essential to show how the interests of various social groups have been affected by the regime's policies. It is only with the help of this kind of analysis that one can find who this regime really stands for.

In 1971, the economically active population of Greece was estimated by the Greek National Statistical Service to be 3,732,468. Of these, 1,955,670 (i.e. 52·4%) were occupied in agriculture and related activities and 1,309,711 (or 35·1%) were workers employed in industry, services or the public administration. Manual workers employed in manufacturing activities comprised just 12·8% of the total economically active population. A very large proportion, therefore, of the Greek working class consists of white-collar workers or workers employed in the service sector. The rest of the economically active population (i.e. 12·5% of it) consists of industrialists, craftsmen, shopkeepers, merchants and managerial and professional people.

The figures above refer to the economically active population and when account is taken of the fact that heavy emigration from the agricultural areas has significantly changed the age structure of the population of the countryside, the share of the total population making a living out

of agriculture and other primary activities is reduced to slightly below
50%. Very roughly, therefore, one-half of the Greek population consists
of peasants and agricultural workers and one-third of workers (with
white-collar workers predominant). It is for this reason that this article
concentrates on these two major classes which comprise about 85% of the
Greek population.

In examining how the economic welfare of these two major classes
was affected during the recent period of military dictatorship, we shall
not exclusively concentrate on the money income (or income at constant
prices) concept of economic welfare. Attention will also be focused on
other factors which affect the level of people's economic welfare, such
as the provision of various social services, conditions of work, etc.

While Greece has been ruled by a group of military conspirators, her
national economy has continued to grow, although at a slower pace.
Under these circumstances our problem then is to examine how the
relative income position of the workers and the peasants evolved during
this period – relative, that is, with respect both to past rates of change
and to changes during the same period in the incomes of the other social
groups (property- and capital-owners, professional people, etc.). This does
not mean that instances of absolute decreases in money wage earnings
have not been recorded. During the first months after the *coup*, civil
servants and employees of public corporations had a number of supplementary sources of income cut under the pretext of a rationalization of
the wage structure. And extolling the virtues of hard work, the then
military General Secretaries of the government departments forced civil
servants to work overtime without proper compensation.

Over the period 1964–67 income from employment at current prices
increased by 42·6%. Over the period 1967–70 it increased by 30·0%.
Taking into account price increases, the corresponding rates of increase
at constant prices were 33·5% and 23·7%.

According to the policy laid down in the first five-year programme
published by the regime, wage increases should have been related to the
average rate of productivity increase in the non-agricultural sector.[1] The
recorded changes in wage earnings clearly indicate that they were
substantially lagging behind the increases in the productivity of the
non-agricultural sector. In fact, in some sectors recorded increases in
wages are just half the recorded increases in productivity.

In the first thirty months following the *coup* and until the publication
of Decree 186/1969 (see below), the military government authorized the
signing of a new National Collective Agreement granting an increase of

8% in 'basic' wage rates. It is estimated that about 40% of workers are involved in the National Collective Agreement. The wages of the rest are stipulated on the basis of Branch Collective Agreements. During the same period, the Permanent Labour Arbitration Court of Athens had issued four court decisions authorizing increases of not more than 8% in the money wages of several groups of workers.

In the period that followed the issue of Decree 186/1969 (which as we shall see below completely revised the collective bargaining procedure) wage increases never exceeded this 8% ceiling – a norm substantially below the realized increase in productivity.

Between December 1969 and December 1970, money wage earnings in manufacturing activities increased by 6·7%.[2] During 1970, the index of retail prices increased by 3·7%[3] leaving, therefore, an increase in real wage earnings of about 3·0%. Most likely this increase in real wage earnings is substantially lower, given the fact that the Greek index of retail prices is out-dated and does not any longer reflect the true picture of the level of prices in the country. The commodities that it includes, and the weights used in its construction, no longer reflect the consumption habits of the urban household.[4] Thus the increase in the real purchasing power of the industrial worker has been insignificant during the period of the dictatorship.

On the basis of the data available from the Greek National Accounts, one can further see that total money income from wages and salaries has increased annually since 1967 by 11%. If we take into account that employment was rising between three and four per cent annually, then this gives an increase of money wage earnings per employee of between seven and eight per cent annually. But income from profits and rents exhibited accelerating rates of growth: 4·0% between 1966 and 1967, 9·0% between 1967 and 1968 and 15·0% between 1968 and 1969.[5]

It will not serve any purpose to accumulate additional statistical evidence to show what can clearly be detected from the above record, namely that the money income of a wage earner was increasing during this period at a much slower pace than the income of a property- or capital-owner. The relative income position of the workers (relative that is to that of property-holders) has been deteriorating since 1967.

In countries where trade unions are relatively free to function and truly represent the interests of their members, the pursuit of such an incomes policy by the government which leads to the award of a sub-stantially larger share of the fruits of growth to the owners of capital and property in general, would have led to considerable industrial strife. The fact that this did not happen in Greece is due to the wholesale attack that the military government waged against the trade unions from the first days of the *coup* as well as to the fundamental changes in the procedure of collective bargaining introduced by the regime. In order to understand how the military government managed to keep wage increases below productivity increases and to deprive workers of a number of rights secured to them under the pre-*coup* legislation, it is essential to examine the Colonels' attitudes towards trade unions and collective bargaining in particular.

Despite the fact that Greece has never been an industrial nation, nevertheless its labour legislation before the *coup* was among the most progressive in Europe. Due to the impact of a group of enlightened liberal politicians, a series of legislative measures on hours of work, compensation in case of dismissal, strikes and conditions of work in general, were introduced in the course of the second and third decades of this century. These laws secured the position of the worker in industry and potentially protected him from any attempt at exploitation by primitive entrepreneurs. Of course, implementation of this legislation required the operation of an effective network of factory inspectors. This made the application of labour laws dependent on the political complexion of the government and more particularly the Minister of Labour of the day. Labour unions have also been under considerable government patronage, especially since the introduction of a law under the Metaxas dictatorship in 1936, under which union membership fees were collected by the government and then distributed to the various unions by the state. Through this device post-war governments exercised considerable control over the trade-union movement.

The union movement was also very fragmented, and this fragmentation was encouraged both by industrialists and by the government-sponsored union leaders (*ergatopateres*) who, given the system of voting in the General Confederation of the Greek Workers (GSEE – the body at the top of the trade-union hierarchy), always had good reason to create yet another docile union which could guarantee their re-election in the executive of the GSEE.

Nevertheless, within certain bounds, unions did possess a degree of bargaining power versus the employers. They were free to strike and, moreover, workers had the opportunity to start unions on the basis of voluntary contributions. Several militant unions, operating outside the GSEE, were very active in Greece just before the *coup*.[6]

Essentially, the regime's policy towards the unions has been to reduce –

almost to the point of extinction – their bargaining power and to transform them into branches of the state apparatus.

This forced transformation of the trade unions passed through several phases. In the initial phase, the military authorities seemed to be moving towards a total abolition of the then existing trade-union structure. Hundreds of active trade unionists were arrested and sent to concentration camps, especially those connected with the left-communist alliance of the United Democratic Left (EDA). One hundred and fifty-eight unions were dissolved by order of the military authorities on 4 May 1967 for alleged violation of their constitution. The charges were never proven because no appeal to the courts was allowed. The property of these unions was confiscated. Trade unionists who were not arrested had nevertheless lost their jobs on the instructions of the military authorities to the management of the enterprises in which they were employed. In fact, after the *coup* commissars of the military regime have been placed in most of the sizeable firms with the explicit aim of watching the activities of the workers.

The enactment of all these measures raised considerable protests from the international trade union movement because they constituted an outright violation of the International Labour Conventions No. 87 and No. 98 which had also been signed by Greece in 1961, and of the decision of 26 June 1952 of the ILO regarding the independence of the trade-union movement. Furthermore, the International Transport Workers Federation was threatening a boycott on Greek ships. Faced with such strong international reaction, the regime changed course and, accepting the necessity that it had to maintain the appearance of a trade-union movement, embarked upon a new policy of transforming the structure of the existing unions.

Their first preoccupation was to get rid of the elected executives of the non-dissolved unions. Various tactics were employed. Firstly, a committee, consisting of a military officer, a security officer and two well-disposed trade unionists, was appointed with the aim of persuading undesirable persons to submit their resignations. Their persuasion techniques, however, did not succeed and the regime dismissed, by direct orders of the various military commanders in August 1967, all elected members of the then existing trade-union executives who were considered undesirable. Their places were filled with people who promised allegiance to the regime. Under conditions of martial law, industrial action against such an interference in the running of the affairs of the unions was obviously impossible. Apart from these measures the regime had also ordered that no pamphlet, leaflet or any other document could be circularized by union executives without being approved by the military commander of the area. Finally in May 1969, the regime made special provisions in Decree 185/1969 to enable it to dismiss the leadership of the General Confederation of Greek Workers (GSEE) which up to that time had not been touched. This leadership consisted of extreme right-wing figures, wholly attached to the employers' interests. However, the regime wanted to get rid of those people who had any base whatsoever within the movement; instead it preferred to install in these positions people dependent on them. The frequent changes in the offices of Chairman and Secretary of the GSEE that have followed since 1969 suggest that the regime's intention is to have a labour leadership that is very weak and entirely dependent on them and with which it can deal more effectively.

All these arbitrary measures were also supplemented by the enactment of new legislation on industrial relations. The basic legislation in this field consists of (a) the provisions of the 1968 Constitution concerning freedom of association, (b) two decrees passed in 1969 and published in the government gazette on 10 May, regulating the functioning of the unions and the procedure of collective bargaining (Decrees Nos 185 and 186), and (c) Decree 890 published in the Government Gazette on 28 May 1971 on professional societies and associations.

An exhaustive analysis of the impact of this legislation on industrial relations cannot be given here. However, the essential aspects of these legislative measures will be sketched below in order to enable the reader to see how these measures substantially undermined the position of the trade unions *vis-à-vis* the employers and how, as a result of these measures, the unions have ceased to function as instruments for the protection of the interests of the workers.

Article 19 of the 1968 Constitution introduced restrictions on the right of association which did not exist under the previous (1952) Constitution of the Greek State. According to this article, 'any association of persons whose aim is, or whose activity is directed against, the preservation of the existing boundaries of the State, or against the existing regime, or against the existing social order, security of the State, or the political or personal liberties of the people, is prohibited. Such an association is dissolved by court decision'. This provision is so general and vague that an illiberal regime can easily use it to disband any union which does not toe the government's line. Most important, however, is the fact that this Constitution deprives all employees of the government, either central or local, all employees of nationalized industries as well as all employees of non-nationalized public utilities organized (according to the wording of the

Constitution) as 'legal entities of public law', of the right to unionize. Thus this provision immediately reduces a very large section of the Greek working class to a completely defenceless position towards their employers. Furthermore, the government can, by proclaiming an enterprise a 'legal entity of public law', increase this group of industrially defenceless workers even further. Apart from the civil servants and all local government employees, workers affected by this provision of having their right to unionize removed include post-office workers, hospital workers (nurses or other personnel), electricity workers, gas- and water-board workers, teachers in any state-financed educational institution, dockers and other port workers, and all workers in nationalized enterprises such as sugar refineries, oil refineries, etc.[7]

The employees of the above organizations, plus all personnel employed by them (a more general provision), are also deprived of their right to strike. But for the rest of the working class the right to strike is practically abolished with the introduction of a new provision contained in paragraph 5 of the aforementioned article 19 of the 1968 Constitution. According to this provision 'any strike motivated by political or other aims alien to the material and moral interests of the workers is prohibited'. Such a provision is so open to arbitrary interpretations that it gives a free hand to the government and the security authorities to characterize any strike that might annoy them as politically motivated or as not being in accordance with the true interests of the workers. The 1968 Constitution thus introduces the principle that the workers are incapable of interpreting their own interests and thus they need a paternalistic government agency to decide for them what their interests are and whether they should call a strike to defend them. It is not surprising that since May 1969 (when according to an official announcement the articles of the 1968 Constitution regarding freedom of association and assembly were formally reinstated) no strike action has been seriously contemplated by any union. It was only in the summer of 1970 that the employees of the Commercial Bank of Greece threatened to resort to strike action if their employer did not comply with the decision of the labour arbitration court granting them wage increases. In the course of a few days the executive, under government pressure, hastily issued a statement claiming that at no stage was strike action contemplated, and that the whole story was due to misunderstanding on the part of the press. The employer has not subsequently properly complied with the arbitration court's decision.

Further restrictions on the functioning of the unions were introduced by Decree 185. Article 9 of this decree stipulates that in order to be elected to any union post, a person must be in employment in the relevant enterprise during the six-year period before the day of the election. Thus, professional trade unionists are not recognized and moreover the chance of somebody being in a position to contest a union post is in the hands of his employer, who by dismissing him can jeopardize his chances of becoming eligible for election to a union post. Article 34 of the latest Decree, 890/1971, stipulates that an employer is obliged to grant leave of absence without remuneration of eight to sixty hours monthly to any worker holding a union post. It is not difficult to see that the employer will be prepared to grant the maximum of the hours allowed for union work only to those who are not prepared to challenge his policies on wages and other labour matters.

Clearly then, all these legislative provisions of the junta's laws on industrial relations aim at supplying the employer with ammunition adequate to enable him to manipulate and control the labour unions. From the point of view of industrial relations the Greece of the Colonels had undoubtedly become a true employers' paradise.

But as if all these restrictions were not enough, the system of collective bargaining was radically altered by Decree 186/1969. The basic change was to deprive the General Confederation of Greek Workers of the right to conclude a national collective agreement covering 'basic wage rates'. According to the previous legislation (Law 3239/1955) GSEE was responsible for negotiating a collective agreement covering basic wages of the country's employees, whereas branch federations or branch or local unions were responsible for conducting the negotiations for the determination of the wage rates covering the workers of their branch or locality. When the negotiations for a collective agreement on wages reached an impasse and the requested intervention of the Ministry of Labour could not bring about any result, the union or the GSEE had the right of appeal to the arbitration court of first instance and then to the arbitration court of second instance. The decision of the arbitration courts could be modified by the Ministers of Labour or Co-ordination if they considered it a violation of the policy of the government on incomes. With the enactment of Decree 186, the level of 'basic' wages will be determined by the government itself and not through negotiations between the employers' associations and the General Federation of Greek Workers. The only right accorded to GSEE is the elementary one of being heard by the government before the new level of basic wages is set.

According to the same decree, all labour contracts apply only to the members of the unions that negotiated them. Such a provision is particularly disadvantageous to the workers under the present climate of industrial relations. The wholesale attack against the unions created the belief that union membership could be considered as evidence of anti-regime feelings, and workers are reluctant to join them. This provision also enables the employer to discourage a worker from joining a union (e.g. with the threat of dismissal) and pay him at rates lower than those stipulated in the collective agreement. The threat of being dismissed can act as an effective weapon in an economy operating with considerable margins of unemployed or underemployed labour.

Labour contracts cannot be revised before the lapse of a twelve-month period – even if other factors have substantially changed in the meantime. In the past, branch or local collective agreements tended to follow the lead given by the National Collective Agreement through which 'basic' wage rates were determined. Now, with the 'basic' wage rates determined by the government itself, branch federations, branch unions or local unions are deprived of a major negotiating weapon.

The whole legislation on collective bargaining as determined by Decree 186 reflects the regime's paternalistic view that social conflicts can be solved by order rather than by negotiation. When the policies of those who give the order are biased towards serving the employers' interests, it is not difficult to predict what the future orders will be like.

This short analysis of the system of industrial relations instituted by the military regime does not give a full picture of the regime's attitudes towards workers. The military government has not only undermined labour's bargaining position with regard to wage determination. With a series of additional measures it deprived the workers of a number of rights that they had secured under previous legislation. Under Law 2112/1920 certain restrictions were imposed on the employer against arbitrarily dismissing a worker, and the right of an employee to receive compensation in case of dismissal was established. Under pressure from the employers' organizations, the military government included in its five-year plan[8] the following policy statement: '[It is the aim of the government's policy] to reduce the restrictions imposed on firms against dismissing redundant personnel and the compensation paid in case of dismissal. In the long run, provisions have to be made to reduce the compensation offered to workers and clerks who can find another suitable job.' Immediately after the publication of the text of the plan, the employers' organizations asked the government to issue the relevant decrees. Twenty-four labour unions, with appointed executives, felt that their compliance with the regime could not go that far. They launched strong protests and the Colonels, always sensitive to discontent which cannot be controlled, postponed the enactment of the planned Decree. The abolition of the provisions of the most fundamental law of Greek labour legislation, Law 2112/1920, still remains an explicit aim of the regime of 21 April.

The regime tried to make further concessions to employers by introducing new measures concerning regulation of hours of work. In 1969, they tried unsuccessfully to increase the hours of daily obligatory work of the building trades' workers from seven to eight. Reports of impending militant action by construction workers forced the Ministry of Labour to back down. However, in 1971 (August), the Consultative Committee created by the regime proposed a draft law 'on time limits concerning the hours of opening of shops and of work of their personnel' which reinstates the situation of the pre-war years in Greece, where the employer determined the number of hours that his shop stayed open according to his own whims and according to the stamina of his employees. Again, this is in accordance with explicit government policy. Back in 1969, the then Minister of Labour and the General Secretary of the same Ministry were reported in the press as adhering to the view that all regulations concerning hours of opening and closing of shops constitute 'policing of commerce' and that the government intended to relieve employers of these police measures. Furthermore, the regime abolished the law requiring, in accordance with the provisions of the international labour convention, legal authorization before the imposition of overtime work. By another act, overtime and productivity bonuses in the state-owned railways have been eliminated altogether.

The Ministry of Labour has also revised the regulations concerning safety at work and factory inspection. The terms of the new regulations impose practically no legal responsibility on the owner of the factory for breaches of the law regarding prevention of accidents, hygienic conditions at work, etc.[9] In a similar exercise, the Greek Ministry of Mercantile Marine introduced in 1970 a new 'Internal regulation of conditions of work on Greek ocean-going boats'. A basic feature of the new internal regulation (which was introduced without any consultation with the seamen) is that it obliges seamen to perform duties in the course of their normal work which were either paid at different rates on the basis of the previous regulation or were recognized as the duties of the port workers. Port authorities and maritime unions in many parts of the world are becoming increasingly aware in recent years of a serious negligence on the part of the Greek services of the Mercantile Marine Ministry in properly inspecting boats under the Greek flag. In 1970, 135 Greek seamen lost their lives in accidents involving the sinking of their ships mainly as a result either of fire, over-loading or worn-out equipment. And in accidents caused by unforeseen natural factors, the loss is magnified by the fact that the life-saving equipment provided is insufficient. Early in 1970, the President of the International Transport Workers Federation blamed violation of international maritime conventions for the high rate of casualties of ships of Greek ownership. Many times in the past few years port authorities in major ports all over the world have, after inspection, found that in many ships the rules for the safety and the well-being of the seamen working on them do not meet international standards. In November 1969, for example, the Hamburg port authorities stopped the sailing of the Greek owned M/S *Thios Costas*. This 10,000-ton liberty ship was sailing with faulty lifeboats whose launching system did not work, empty fire extinguishers, holds that were not watertight, filthy living quarters and lack of medicines and first-aid equipment. The crew of 30, sailing without a qualified radio officer, also complained of bad food conditions. In another case (out of many that have become known recently as a result of the increased vigilance of international trade unions) in March 1971, the tanker *Alkis*, known to be of Greek ownership, was found in Rotterdam to have two large holes on the deck plates, bow and stern. In the bow, where the outside and inside plates connect, the iron joining rods were badly bent in two places. In the course of the first quarter of 1971, this boat changed captains four times.

On top of this, monthly wages of Greek deckhands and firemen were pegged at £60 from March 1967 to January 1971. No wonder then that the Greek seamen leave the Greek boats in search of employment opportunities either aboard vessels of foreign ownership or as *Gastarbeiter* in Germany. Faced thus with a serious manpower shortage, the Greek shipowners resort to the employment of Asian or Arab workers whom they pay at appallingly low rates, incurring the wrath of various unions the world over, which are again threatening boycott action.

A discussion on the impact of the military regime's measures on the economic welfare of the Greek workers would be incomplete if it did not examine the regime's attempts to reorganize the Greek social security system. Twice to date, first in the summer of 1970 and later in the summer of 1971, the military government has tried (unsuccessfully) to introduce a new decree regulating the provision of medical care and the granting of pensions to workers and their families. Strong protests on the part of organized labour groups and an open revolt of the rank and file which could not be contained by the appointed or selected union leaderships, forced the regime to back down, but not to give up the hope of trying once again.

In Greece today there exist about 40 social security organizations operating in the fields of illness, temporary or permanent disability and old age. The largest – and the most inefficient – is the Social Security Foundation (IKA). The revenues of all these organizations derive (1969) 33% from the employers' contributions, 37% from the employees' own contributions, 24% from the state's contribution and 4% from the organization's own income from property. Compared with the social security systems of the six EEC countries,[10] Greek employers contribute a much lower percentage for the expenses of running their employees' social insurance schemes. In Italy, for example, the employers contribute 66% to the total expenses of running the social security system of the country, whereas in Luxembourg the corresponding figure is 39%. Yet one finds in the text of the five-year plan the following statement regarding the regime's social policies: 'the abolition of the complementary social insurance schemes and the creation of a new organization running under the responsibility and *at the cost* of the employees' . . . 'the amalgamation of all social insurance organizations providing basic insurance into bigger ones'.[11] It is thus the explicit aim of the military government to reorganize the social insurance system of the country by reducing the contributions of the employers – obviously as an attempt to improve the competitive position of the Greek industries. The interesting thing is that the reduction in the contributions of the employers is to be accompanied not by an increase in the contributions of the state but by an increase in the contributions of the workers themselves. One cannot fail again to detect a marked bias of the regime in favour of the employers' interests. As was mentioned earlier, the military government was forced to withdraw its plan for the reorganization of the social security scheme of the country in August 1971 and, indeed, the withdrawal was accompanied by the replacement of the Minister for Social Services. It must, however, be remembered that the basic direction of policy on this matter is clearly stated in the regime's five-year plan, and unless the workers are prepared to defy the regime by more vigorous means one would expect this policy to be finally implemented. Part of this policy certainly makes sense in terms of rationalizing the fragmented social security system of the country. But this should not be done at the expense of the workers.

The above review of the policy measures taken by the regime which directly affect the workers is not by any means exhaustive. Many other actions of the Colonels have directly or indirectly touched on the welfare of the Greek worker and his family. And the overwhelming majority of these measures adversely affect the Greek worker. Before the *coup*, study grants were available to workers' children through the labour exchanges. These grants are no longer available. The funds of the *Organismos Ergatikis Katoikias* (Organization for Working-Class Housing) were confiscated and are now directly used by the regime for its own programme of people's housing.

Nothing has been said up to now on employment policies. Given the growth of the country's economy, new jobs have been made available at a rate of three to four per cent annually. That this increase was insufficient to absorb the country's unemployed workers (estimated to be 200,000 in the urban areas alone) can be seen by an inspection of the statistics on emigration. The following figures give the net emigration in thousands from 1963 onwards.

1963	− 67·7	1967	+ 30·8
1964	− 63·8	1968	− 56·9
1965	− 54·9	1969	− 90·3
1966	− 23·3	1970	− 83·6

Those who migrate abroad do not necessarily come from the hidden labour reserves of the agricultural sector. Many of them come from the urban centres and are semi-skilled or even skilled workers. It is not so difficult to see the reasons that force them to emigrate in view of the previous discussion. In some cases the extent of emigration is such that serious shortages develop. In the summer of 1971, the Association of Greek Textile Manufacturers officially requested the government to lift the ban on immigration from Asia and Africa, so that they can resort to the employment of Pakistani workers in Greek textile plants. Such are the absurdities to which the regime's thoughtless policies lead.

In the remaining part of this paper we shall turn to the examination of the regime's policies that directly or indirectly affected the welfare of the Greek peasantry. Some gestures that the regime made initially led many people to believe that the Greek peasants have benefited from the policies of the military regime. Profiting from the implementation of a plan to further extend the social security provided for the country's peasantry which was prepared by the pre-*coup* government, the regime tried to project an image of the peasants' protector. That was undoubtedly a measure beneficial to the peasants, but it was really a natural growth of the social security scheme for the peasants initiated in the early nineteen-sixties.

Other measures in agriculture were already in preparation by government departments long before the *coup* took place. The abolition of the price-support policies for wheat, dried fruits and tobacco (which took place in early 1968) and its replacement by a system of minimum intervention prices coupled with income support was proposed as early as 1966 by the Centre for Economic Planning and Research,[12] and was about to become government policy. The essence of this new policy is that the government intervenes only if crop prices fall below a fixed minimum price. The peasant is simultaneously guaranteed a minimum income which he receives in the form of cash grants. Only peasants with a plot of land below 40 *stremata* are entitled to these cash grants. Basically, such a policy leads to a more rational allocation of resources in agriculture because it allows for a more systematic play of market forces. The peasants' position under this system may, however, be jeopardized if the marketing of the agricultural products is taking place under monopsonistic conditions. To see, therefore, how the regime tried to safeguard the peasants' position in a system where the market forces become dominant in determining crop prices we have to find out what measures, if any, have been taken to improve the competitiveness of the markets for agricultural products. It is here that the regime's record is extremely weak. Instead of improving the peasants' position by encouraging the role of the producers' co-operatives, the military authorities mounted the same wholesale attack against these institutions as they did against the trade unions. Instead of encouraging the participation of many buyers in the markets for agricultural produce, they are constantly granting exclusive buying rights over large areas of the country for specific products. The company of the Greek-American tycoon, Tom Papas, has secured the exclusive right to buy all tomatoes from producers in Western Greece. With the agricultural co-operatives in an extremely weak position, and with only a single buyer in the market, one does not have to have a specialized knowledge of economics to realize how the price will be determined in this monopsonistic situation. Other firms, dealing with the processing of agricultural products, have also managed to acquire similar rights. It might be argued here that such a measure gives the enterprise security over supply sources, and for this reason it will encourage the development of more agricultural product processing industries. This may be so, but the social consequences that are implied in this policy must be fully realized. Such a measure may serve the purpose for which it is intended without undermining the peasants' position if it is coupled with the presence of a strong producers' co-operative movement.

Let us now see what the regime's policy on co-operatives has been. The Greek co-operative movement has been growing steadily, although not without difficulties, since 1914, when a fundamental law (Law 602) 'on co-operation' was introduced by the government of Greece's famous liberal leader, Eleftherios Venizelos. The majority of the co-operatives formed were credit co-operatives, although producers' supply and marketing co-operatives were also formed at a later stage. All co-operatives were organized into co-operative unions by provinces and sub-provinces. These, in turn, had a central organization, the Pan-Hellenic Confederation of Agricultural Co-operative Unions (PASEGES).[13] In the early nineteen-sixties, agricultural co-operatives were growing in importance and their role would have expanded had the *coup* of 21 April not taken place.

The pattern of intervention observed in the case of labour unions was also applied here: mass arrests, replacement of the elected councils and officials of a very large number of co-operatives and especially those of the central organizations (see Decree 31/1967). The councils which suffered most were those of co-operatives connected with the marketing of agricultural produce. Thus, those co-operatives which proved successful in competing effectively with private enterprises had their councillors arbitrarily dismissed and replaced by figures docile to the regime. The export co-operatives of fruit producers in Naoussa, Skydra and Edessa in Northern Greece, the dairy co-operative 'Aspro' in Attica, a number of co-operatives connected with the collective harvesting, processing and marketing of tobacco, olive oil and olives, figs, cotton and cereals had been the victims of this attack by the military governors of their areas. These co-operatives and the Union of Co-operatives are just mentioned as examples because the number of co-operatives affected is much larger. An additional action taken by the regime was to strip the general assembly of the co-operatives (i.e. the highest decision-making body of the co-operative movement) of all its power. By decision of the Minister of Agriculture[14] the powers of this assembly are now vested with the regime-appointed councils.

Perhaps the most serious attack against the co-operatives is related to the hiving-off of a number of co-operative enterprises to private firms. The warehousing of grain, for example, which was handled by the co-operative movement, has been transferred to General Storehouses, a private firm.

Unfortunately, very little information is available about the functioning of the markets for agricultural products now that the new system of minimum intervention prices operates. There is no doubt that the exposure of the peasants to the market forces, under the conditions described above (i.e. weak and almost non-existent co-operatives and state-sponsored monopsonistic elements) works against the peasants' own interests. Those who profit are the wholesale merchants of agricultural products, especially those with exclusive buying rights, and the state which spends now substantially reduced sums in buying wheat and other products covered by the previous price-support policies. In 1966 the government spent £16·7 million on buying wheat; in 1969 just £143 thousand. Since the revenues of the budget are basically raised from the urban population, the reduction in the expenses for carrying the price-support policies for agricultural products benefits the taxpayers who are mainly urban dwellers.

No doubt the change in the system of agricultural income protection enabled the military regime to take the dramatic initiative of cancelling all debts to the agricultural bank. At the time the measure was taken (March 1968) the total debts amounted to £110 million. When this measure was however taken, most of the small producers had already paid back their debts. The Agricultural Bank as a rule never extended additional credit without prior payment of the existing debt. Only larger producers, with the necessary power to influence the Bank's decisions, and large co-operatives managed to have their debts frozen. It was precisely this group of credit recipients who basically profited from the cancellation of debts. The small producer has hardly felt the regime's benevolence. This act of cancelling farmers' debts has also enabled the regime to buy the political support of the big country producers and to create its own network of kulaks with whose support it hopes to keep the countryside under control. Most of the appointed local-government officials come from this group of people.

In other fields of agricultural policy, the regime has more or less continued the policies initiated in the late fifties for improvements in the productivity of the agricultural sector through irrigation, introduction of fertilizers, agricultural machinery, etc., and for a restructuring of agricultural production towards products with higher elasticity of demand. Perhaps one thing which would have happened had the *coup* not taken place was the progressive integration of Greek agricultural policies with the common agricultural policies of the Six. Because of the prevailing situation in the country, the EEC countries regard Greece's treaty of association with them as frozen and refuse to deal in this matter with the regime. Greek peasants and agricultural producers could have substantially profited from such an integration of Greece's agricultural policy with that of the Six.

What has been the overall income position of the Greek peasant relative to the income position of the urban household during this period? The income of the agricultural sector grew by 6% between 1966 and 1967, declined by 7% between 1967 and 1968 and grew again by 7% between 1968 and 1969.[15] Agricultural population was declining but not by more than one per cent annually, so that on a per capita basis the incomes in the agricultural sector were increasing by about three to four per cent at current prices (total 1966: 38,918 million drachma, total 1969: 41,280 million drachma). Even if the price level was growing at a slower pace in the countryside than in the towns, we cannot really say that the peasant's lot has been relatively better than the worker's. However, compared to the increases in the income from rents and profits, the peasant's income was growing much more slowly than that of the holder of property and capital.

The Greek peasant managed during this period to secure a small share from the growth of the national income and was offered a more extended social security system as well as a once-for-all cancellation of debts. Yet in the long run his prospects look rather bleak. His co-operatives are stripped of effective power, he has to face the market from a weak position with his position further weakened by the government's policy of strengthening rather than reducing the already substantial monopsonistic elements. As the Greek system of industrial relations has been turned into an employer's paradise, so the Greek countryside has been turned into a middleman's paradise. The peasant is left defenceless and in his despair he takes the long journey to Germany, to become a proletarian. At least, his children stand a better chance of being educated and of achieving their proper place in the meritocracy of the West. Staying in Greece, his children have less chance of this. He may not be in a position to pay additional expenses now that the regime has closed the village school and has abolished free school meals.[16]

A number of observers in the West have maintained that the regime has certain populist features. They have probably been impressed by such dramatic gestures as the cancellation of peasants' debts, and have rather uncritically forgotten to look at the statistical record and the other less spectacular but nevertheless rich anti-populist measures of the military regime. But even without looking at the record in detail one can still detect the basic attitudes of the regime towards the peasantry and the workers by perusing Papadopoulos' own proclamations. These attitudes

of the regime are aptly summarized in a passage from a speech he gave
on 15 December 1969. 'The Greek people,' proclaimed the leader of the
junta in one of his frequent moments of instant philosophizing 'must eat
less, work more and demand less.'

Reading, September 1971   *George Yannopoulos*

NOTES

1 Ministry of Co-ordination: *To Pentaetes Programma Oikonomikis Anaptyxeos*
   (The Five-Year Development Plan), 1968–72, Chapter 5, p. 40.

2 *Oikonomikos Tachydromos*, Athens, 27 May 1970. In 1971 (autumn) the
   regime authorized an annual increase of 6% in basic wage rates. This
   increase which is 2% below the previous increase in 1968 contrasts with
   the fact that the rate of growth of productivity was higher in 1971 than
   in 1968. For those groups of workers not covered by the National Collective Agreement the regime has frozen their wages by arbitrarily extending
   by government decree the duration of expired collective agreements.

3 Bank of Greece, Report of the Governor to the shareholders, 1971.

4 MARINOS, I. P., 'A Few Themes Worth Noticing'. *Eikonomikos Tachydromos*, 3 June 1971.

5 National Statistical Service of Greece, *National Accounts*, 1960–69, Athens
   1971, Table 2.

6 For a history of the Greek trade-union movement see: C. Jecchinis:
   Trade Unionism in Greece: a study in political paternalism, Franklin Roosevelt
   University Press, 1968.

7 For more details see: G. Katephores: 'Trades Unions and the new Constitution', *The Greek Observer*, No. 5, June 1969, pp. 22–23.

8 Ministry of Co-ordination: *The Five-Year Development Plan*, 1968–72,
   Chapter 5, p. 39.

9 See the magazine of the International Confederation of Free Trade Unions
   (ICFTU); *Free Labour World*, December 1970.

10 *Financial Times*, 12 May 1971.

11 Ministry of Co-ordination: *The Five-Year Development Plan*, Chapter 17,
   pp. 140–142.

12 KARAGIORGAS, DIONYSIOS, *Georgikai Epidotiseis* (Agricultural Subsidies),
   Centre for Planning and Economic Research (KEPE), Athens 1966.

13 For more details on the structure of the Greek co-operative movement
   see: Theodore Yannopoulos, 'The Greek Co-ops and the Junta Government', *The Greek Observer*, No. 6–7, August–October 1969, pp. 19–21.

14 *I Foni ton Synetairismon* (Voice of the Co-operatives), No. 2, 1968, p. 78.
15 National Statistical Service of Greece, *National Accounts*, 1960–69, Athens 1971, Table 2.
16 See the article 'Traditionalism and Reaction in Greek Education' in this volume (Chapter Seven).

CHAPTER SEVEN

Traditionalism and Reaction in Greek Education

Reviewing the development of education in Greece during the four full academic years which have elapsed since April 1967 would be relatively easy if we were still living in the times when success and progress in education were measured in absolute numbers. For numbers have risen. There are now more pupils in primary and secondary schools than there were in 1967, more students in the universities, the teaching staff at all levels has increased, and more money is being spent on education. It would have been very surprising if this were not so. Only strict legislation and an overt policy of restricting numbers can check the universal tendency for numbers in education to rise. But in Greece the Establishment has always found means of restricting the benefits of education without interfering with the trend of its statistics.

However, we have now learned that quantitative criteria in education have little significance. We have learned that in examining an educational ystem we must first consider *what* is taught at school, and only then *how many* are taught. The numerical factor becomes fully significant only after the establishment of its qualitative background. It is not difficult to see that rising figures in education in Nazi Germany, in socialist Sweden and in communist Russia cannot express the same general tendencies. This has now been established. What we have not yet found is a standardized and universally applicable method of 'measuring' and evaluating the non-numerical characteristics of education. A comparative review of statistical data within a particular educational system may produce some percentages more relevant than absolute figures (such an approach would considerably worsen the image created by the Greek increases mentioned above), but they would still give little indication of the aims and effects of the system.

Absolute numbers or percentages derive their significance from the principles which guide the educational system, from its philosophy.

Apart from the usual rhetorical clichés, there has been no explicit, comprehensive and authoritative statement on the philosophy behind the national educational system in Greece since April 1967. This is hardly surprising since educational philosophy is directly related to, and dependent upon, national philosophy, and observers have commented on the vagueness of national ideology in Greece today.[1] As a result one can only rely on official texts and statements regarding particular aspects of education, and on indirect indications, in an attempt to establish, if not the essence of the educational philosophy, then the aims of the system which has resulted from the educational measures taken since April 1967 in Greece.

The issue is particularly important in the case of Greece because by well-established tradition there is no alternative to the official national educational philosophy. The private sector, important as it may be in the actual functioning of the system, is deprived of any initiative either in the formation of policies or in their application. Talcott Parsons' assumption that there is constant interaction between the three levels – technical, managerial, and public interest – of any formal organization, does not seem to be true in the case of Greek education, though it has been established that it does apply to less rigid educational systems.[2] In Greece the flow of authority has always been unbroken, and it is even more so today, from the cabinet to each individual classroom throughout the country. Everything is regulated at the top. Curricula and syllabuses, appointments and promotions of teachers, methods of teaching and discipline, are all uniform for the whole country, for both state and private schools, and are prescribed by governmental laws and regulations. Even the subjects of essays which are to be written in secondary schools are laid down by the ministry. Education being a national issue, criticism on any of these matters is now discouraged, both officially and unofficially. It is within this framework that the texts which lay down the present policy must be examined. The most significant of these are the educational provisions of the 1968 Constitution.

Ever since 1823, Greek constitutions have included clauses on education. With the exception, perhaps, of the 1827 text, they have always established a tight governmental control over some level or another of education. But never before 1968 has there been a constitution which is more precise, and more thorough, in imposing the government's authority on all aspects of education.

These are the relevant articles. Passages in italics indicate significant additions to, and modifications of, the 1952 Constitution which was abrogated in 1967.

1   Education shall be under the highest supervision of the State, shall be offered at its expense, and shall aim at the ethical and intellectual training, as well as the development of the patriotic conscience of youth, based on the principles of Helleno-Christian civilization.

2   *The establishment of general directives of national policy on education is made as prescribed by law, after consultation with the National Council of Education.*

3   Elementary education shall be compulsory for all. The law determines the years of compulsory instruction which cannot be less than six.

4   The institutions of higher education are self-administered legal entities of public law and operate under the supervision and financial support of the State. Their teaching staff are civil servants. The administrative bodies of these institutions are elected by their regular professors. *The jurisdiction of the government commissioner appointed at each institution is defined by law.*

5   Subject to permission by the authorities, private citizens whose civil rights have not been revoked, as well as legal entities, may establish schools of elementary, middle and higher education, operating according to the Constitution and the laws of the State. *Those establishing private schools, and those teaching in them, are obliged to have the same moral and other qualifications as those required of public servants and prescribed by law.*

The significance of these constitutional provisions, their application and their effects will be discussed later in this paper. Their overall character is a sufficient indication of the essence of the new 'educational philosophy'.

A further aspect of this philosophy is the line followed since 1967 on the 'Language Question' which has always been directly related to education, to an apparently greater extent in Greece than in other countries. The issue is far too complex to be analysed here, and it is sufficient to note that modern Greek, though more or less uniform in its spoken form, has two distinctively different written forms, one 'purified', the *katharevousa*, and one common, the *dimotiki*. The latter incorporates the changes which have occurred in the language over many centuries, and presents lexical, morphological, structural and phonological differences from the ancient idioms from which it derives. But fundamentally its basis is the ancient linguistic pattern.

Katharevousa, on the other hand, aims to 'purify' the language of the non-Hellenic features which it has acquired over the centuries. It goes beyond the regulations of do's and don'ts common to all languages, for example Fowler and the rulings of the Académie Française, and beyond similar regulations to which Greek has been subjected for centuries through Atticism. *Katharevousa* represents an attempt to replace a naturally developed language by an artificial form of it, and to impose the latter as the national language. The issue, which has gained in importance since Greece acquired its independence in the early 19th century, has figured in Greece's constitutions. The 1968 Constitution lays it down that: 'The official language of the State *and the schools* is that in which the texts of the Constitution and Greek legislation are composed. Any intervention to alter the language is prohibited.'[3] 'And the schools' is an addition to the 1952 Constitution. The language 'in which the texts of the Constitution and Greek legislation are composed' is, of course, the *katharevousa*, which has almost invariably been identified with traditionalism and the Right, and which by 'its existence and the prestige which it enjoyed did much to hold back the intellectual and artistic development of the people'.[4]

Since the early decades of the 20th century, when the relationship between language and social stratification was brought home to the Greek public by such writers as Fotiadis and Skliros,[5] the 'Language Question' has remained in the forefront of educational controversy. So much so that the question of language sometimes appears to obscure the real socio-political aspects of any educational reform. This may be true, but then it would be very difficult to isolate the language problem from its socio-educational context, and proceed either to a progressive reform in education, or to a traditionalist counter-reform, ignoring the medium by which the intended change in spirit would be expressed. And it has been claimed by a foreign observer that the insistence on perpetuating the use of the *katharevousa* has 'kept an artificial barrier between the small educated minority and the mass of the people more vicious than any ever created in Britain by the public school'.[6]

Moreover, if, as Basil Bernstein seems to have proved, a change in language use 'involves the whole personality of the individual, the very character of his social relationships, his points of emotional and logical reference, and his conception of himself',[7] then it would not be too difficult to accept that similar effects would occur on a national scale when a change in language use is imposed on a national scale. For by insisting on the teaching and use of *katharevousa* at school, Greek traditionalist education disturbs, irreparably in most cases, the children's linguistic abilities. That is, if one accepts that a relationship between language and intellect does exist, it disturbs their intellectual abilities. Constant doubt over the use of words or grammatical forms, obsession with the correctness of the form of a word rather than concern over its proper meaning, have considerably reinforced some basic aspects of the Greek national character: vagueness, lack of precision, regard for appearance rather than essence. This may prove convenient to those in authority, of course, when it comes to concepts such as justice, democracy, authority and the like.

Since April 1967 *katharevousa* has in many ways regained its dominant place in Greek life in general, and in education in particular. As symptomatic of an entire philosophy, the insistence on *katharevousa* could be related to a number of measures taken at the same time: the ban on mini-skirts, beards, and long hair; compulsory church-going by pupils and teachers; the ceremony of saluting the flag every morning in all schools (a common feature in many of the United States); and more recently the compulsory carrying of satchels by schoolchildren (regardless of the fact that this adds to parents' expenses for their children's education, which is supposed to be free).

All these measures seem to be expressions of the same belief that a change in appearance, in external characteristics, will automatically change the essence, the inner characteristics. There seems to be no proof that the English who wrap their shopping in the Union Jack are less patriotic than the Americans who salute the Stars and Stripes every morning. Nor is there any indication that compulsory attendance at Mass (celebrated in an incomprehensible form of Greek) will automatically render the Greeks more devout. On the contrary, there are signs that it may well have the opposite effect. It is equally doubtful if the imposition of *katharevousa*, more akin to the language of their ancestors, will bring back their qualities to the modern Greeks.

In Greece today major issues – issues of essence – are pushed under the carpet. Problems such as drug-addiction among the young, sex education, handicapped children, changes in the composition of the population (mainly the result of emigration), lack of adequate medical facilities for the poor, the existence of slums, are declared to be non-existent in Greece and are not investigated. Their treatment is usually left to the initiative of private organizations, or to piecemeal legislation. It is characteristic that, following the campaign against smoking in Western Europe and the USA, an official Greek spokesman declared that 'the hysteria which is expressed in the English and American press on the matter is needless and harmful on account of the pathological anxiety which it creates'. (Tobacco accounts for 15% of Greek exports, and 11% of its revenue from indirect taxation.[8])

Within this constitutional and cultural framework one can seek other official expressions of the post-April 1967 Greek educational philosophy. Since the circumstances surrounding the creation of the National Council of Education provided for by the 1968 Constitution are somewhat obscure, and as nothing has yet been heard about the 'national policy on education' for which it is supposed to give 'general directives', one is forced to rely on the views put forward by official representatives of the government. Theofylaktos Papakonstantinou, for instance, one of the two ex-communist theoreticians of the 'Revolution' and a former Minister of Education under the military regime, has expressed his views on education in his book *Politiki Agogi* (Civics); an abridged version adapted for the teaching of civics in schools has also been published. According to Papakonstantinou the aims of the 'Revolution' in the field of education are:

'National orientation of education; purification and elevation of the teaching staff; meeting as far as possible immediate needs; offering to all youth the same opportunities of education; and the systematic creation of the preconditions for the expansion, modernization and development of education at all levels.'[9]

Before attempting to interpret such meaning as these lines may possess, one should first consider the last aim. *The systematic creation of the preconditions* seems to be an attempt both to justify the abolition of the 1964 reform (which will be discussed later) and to provide for an unlimited postponement of any measure which would *expand, modernize* and *develop* Greek education. It must be remembered that postponement is always the most common way of checking progress in education whenever it is feared that such progress would endanger the vested interests of the Establishment, political or otherwise.

As for the other parts of Papakonstantinou's statement, one can only observe that Greek education during the last four years seems slowly but steadily to have assumed a clear orientation towards an academic elitism. This is valueless in itself as it is based on an education of very doubtful quality. This tendency is apparent not so much through official statements as through certain measures taken or announced by the government. Not least among them is the reduction in the period of compulsory education from nine years (to which it had been raised by the 1964 reform) to six, and hence the reintroduction of an entrance examination into the academic schools, the only schools leading to any sort of respectable academic or social future. This happened twenty-three years after the 1944 Education (England and Wales) Act had established as a universal aim in education the provision of 'secondary education for all', an aim which has since been met by all Western European countries.

Lowering the school-leaving age must be seen in the context of the abolition, de-grading or merging of some 2,500 primary schools in September 1970. These were schools in small and often isolated villages, from which children will find it very difficult to travel (usually on foot) to the nearest village with an operative school in order to complete their 'compulsory' schooling. In view of the great differences in the social and economic composition of the population it can readily be understood that such measures, even if it is not their intention, will lead to the exclusion of a considerable section of Greeks from the benefits of education. It could, of course, be argued that, considering the quality of education offered today in Greece, the fewer who are subjected to it the better it will be for the country as a whole. But this type of argument should not be pushed too far, since any type of education offers some benefits which cannot be affected by any sort of indoctrination. Furthermore, it should be remembered that paper qualifications have become indispensable for any sort of financial survival in Greece – let alone progress – and these restrictions in education equal a condemnation to permanent financial and social misery.

This tendency towards elitism is also apparent in some of the regime's other measures. First came the regulation of a system of 'self-government' to be introduced into the schools. What is relevant here is not the fact that, as might be expected, student bodies will play only decorative roles, since they are deprived of any power to act or even to speak, but that their leaders will not be elected but nominated. The first three pupils, in order of academic achievement, will constitute the student officers of each form. This was followed by other, more important, measures, according special privileges to the academically most successful pupils. Thus those who get the equivalent of grade A (*arista*) at the end of their primary studies, and 85% or over at the entrance examination into secondary education, will be trained in the five model gymnasia in the country (almost the only state schools with full staff, laboratory facilities, etc.).

Further, there will be two special schools for 'the best' (*ton Aristouchon*): the Anavryta, near Athens, and the Anargyrios on the island of Spetses. These will cater for 'the best' to be selected through yet another academic examination among the pupils of all gymnasia in the country. For Anavryta, the school founded on the model of the English public schools to provide a suitably 'democratic' upbringing for the then Crown Prince Constantine, and for the Anargyrios, founded in 1927 on the initiative of Alexandros Delmouzos and other 'progressive' educationists under the auspices of Venizelos to become the 'Eton and Harrow of Greece', this is an interesting development. But the perspectives have changed since then, and one can now see these 'schools for the best' as part of a buying-off process which will render potential leaders of the lower classes acquiescent members of the Establishment. For the ruling classes have their own schools, the private, and very expensive, establishments which, though conforming to the regulations of the State, strengthen and perpetuate social segregation.

Figures relating to higher education since 1967 could also support the thesis of elitism. It is officially claimed that the number of students in the universities has been rising steadily; and so it has. There are, nevertheless, some interesting aspects to this claim, which might point in a different direction. During the reform year, beginning September 1964, 45·7% of all candidates were offered 'university' places. The proportion had drop-ped to 41·9% by the first examination to be held after April 1967, to 28·4% by September 1968, and reached a low of 25·8% during the last academic year under review, beginning September 1970. In absolute numbers this means that while 14,650 candidates found the doors to higher education closed in 1964, there were 39,840 who were left out in 1970.[10] There seems to have been no official anxiety over the academic and professional fate of these candidates, let alone over the psychological effects created by this failure. These effects are likely to have national implications in view of the great number of rejected candidates, but research into this problem is not likely to be encouraged by any official body. But it should be borne in mind that the wealthy can, and do, send their children to study in universities abroad (over one-quarter of the total Greek student population consists of those studying abroad). There is also a cramming-school industry, of unknown dimensions but extremely prosperous, which only survives because of the very narrow bottleneck at the entrance to higher education. It would be very difficult to establish the relationship between cause and effect in this situation.

But the point which might perhaps best clarify the educational philo-sophy of today's Greece is the reaction to the 'progressive' educational reform of the Centre Union government in 1964. This reaction is yet a further addition to the normal pattern of forward and backward steps which characterizes the history of Greek education, a further aspect of a vicious circle of reform and counter-reform. The 1967 counter-reform came with a violence and insistence reminiscent of previous similar situations when the Right, gaining power after a period in opposition, attacked all progressive and socialistic measures taken in the educational field by its predecessors. There is, however, a difference. The counter-reform this time has been extremely thorough, because the reform itself had been so complete and comprehensive. Still it should be noted that the abolition of the measures taken in 1964 was in 1967 an end in itself, regardless of the importance of the measures abolished or of the consequences of their abolition. The gradual return to the 1964 schemata which we witness now is sufficient proof of this. But in the meantime precious time has been wasted, and Greece is falling further behind any acceptable standard of education. Above all, this gradual and fragmented return to pre-1967 measures is now useless and perhaps, in some cases, harmful since it is not part of a thought-out whole, and especially since it is deprived of the coherent philosophy which had guided the original reform.

The following is a shortened list of the main points of the 1964 reform, with, respectively, subsequent developments:[11]

1   Free public education provided for all at all levels, including higher education. 1967: retained, although stamp tax on diplomas and other certificates partly introduced.

2   School leaving age raised from twelve to fifteen. 1967: reduced to twelve. 1970: government-backed conferences and teachers unions brought up the issue again, obviously preparing the ground for a new change.

3   Secondary studies divided into two cycles with three grades each. Compulsory education to include six years in primary school and three in secondary. 1967: abolished. 1970: Same moves as in 2.

4   Teaching of *dimotiki* established throughout the primary school and used as the medium of instruction. *Dimotiki* recognized as equal to *katharevousa* at all levels. 1967: abolished.

5   Curricula and syllabuses in primary and secondary schools reformed; more emphasis given to physical sciences and mathematics; new subjects introduced (economics, law, sociology and others). 1967: abolished: pre-1964 curricula and syllabuses re-introduced together with their old text-books. This means a return to a combination of 1913 and 1929 patterns and practices.

6   Methods of teaching ancient Greek changed. Translations replaced the original texts for the first secondary cycle. 1967: abolished.

7   Choice of subjects introduced into the curricula of the secondary cycle. 1967: abolished. 1971: re-introduced in certain schools.

8 Higher education entrance examinations reorganized on a more centralized scheme, giving active participation to secondary school teachers. 1967: abolished as such. A new scheme introduced combining old and new, decreasing the importance of secondary school teachers' participation, and abolishing the concept of 'general education' which guided the 1964 scheme. (A decree providing that at the September 1967 examinations 10% of the candidates would be admitted to higher education solely on the grounds of their 'high moral character and reproachless behaviour' was not applied, but all candidates are required to obtain a police certificate of 'good conduct' in order to be admitted.)

9 Teachers' training colleges (pedagogical academies) reorganized and the period of study extended from two to three years. 1967: abolished. 1971: a new three-year course introduced.

10 A new body, the Pedagogical Institute, was established to develop educational research and undertake the in-service training of teachers. 1967: abolished; the pre-1964 Board of Education was re-established according to 1914 regulations. It does not include educational research among its duties.

11 Half-year (semester) written examinations in secondary schools abolished. 1967: re-introduced. 1971: again abolished for most subjects.

12 Modern languages given a major status in secondary-school curricula (periods increased, higher coefficients, etc.). 1967: abolished. 1971: periods increased in certain schools.

13 Free meal service for primary-school children introduced. 1967: abolished.

In view of all this it is surprising, or perhaps significant, that the government has repeatedly included education as a sector where a fundamental reform will have to be completed before any return to democracy is considered. This was declared by an official spokesman to the two investigators of the Foreign Affairs Committee of the US Senate. Moreover, according to a statement by the Prime Minister on 21 April 1971, 'uplifting of the standard of education' was to be one of the three main targets of national policy during the fifth year in power of the government. This paper was written before the end of the fifth year, but there seems to be no indication that any sort of drastic measures will be taken in the matter in the foreseeable future.

In concluding this attempt to detect any philosophical background to educational developments in Greece since April 1967, it should be said that they bear all the characteristics of the existing policies of the Greek Right in the educational field, supplemented by a tighter control and an increased administrative incompetence. Education in Greece had little to be proud of in 1962, perhaps a lot to respect in 1964, but has certainly had nothing to pride herself on since 1967. It is not what has been done by the 'Revolutionary' government in education that counts, but what has been undone and what has not been done. History provides other examples of revolutions (genuine ones, such as the French) which felt it necessary to destroy the existing educational system in order to build a new one on different lines, but it would be difficult to associate any such precedents with the present Greek situation since what is lacking here was the dominant feature there: the philosophy.

A final word should be said about finance, before taking a closer look at some particular aspects of the situation. Since the end of World War II expenditure on education in the Greek national budget had been rising steadily, but it had been doing so much less steeply than had total expenditure. The picture changed during the period of the 1964 reform, when for the first time the expenditure of the Ministry of Education increased more rapidly than did the total national expenditure. In 1967 education accounted for 11·3% of the national budget. By 1970 the figure had dropped to 9·2%.

It is against this background, which leaves little doubt as to the regime's intentions, that one should see some particular aspects of the situation, such as measures taken in the field of higher or secondary education.

Higher education has been affected in three ways since 1967 (apart, of course, from the impact of the general lack of intellectual freedom) namely in the persecution of teaching staff, the control of the student movement, and the curtailment of the independence of educational institutions.

Of these the third is obvious from a study of the relevant clauses in the 1968 Constitution which have been discussed above. The Government Commissioners appointed to higher educational institutions in terms of this Constitution have not been merely decorative figures in the meetings of the governing bodies of their respective institutions of higher education. The rare information that reaches the outside world indicates that they not only participate actively in the running of these institutions (in both academic and administrative matters) but also see to it that their view is the one which prevails in the final instance. As a general rule, retired army officers are nominated to the posts.

A further indication of government interference is the decree issued in September 1970 according to which university deans will no longer be elected by the respective senates, but will be appointed by the Ministry from three candidates designated by the senates. The same arrangements apply to the rectors of the various faculties. Apparently these measures are not always sufficient to ensure the imposition of governmental policies or favouritism. In December 1970, for instance, the Senate of the University of Athens decided that facilities for additional examinations should not be provided for a certain category of students who had fallen below the required standards. Fifteen days later the same body reversed its decision, and according to press reports, it was 'one day after a letter had been received from the Ministry requiring the Senate to abide by the wishes expressed in the matter by the Ministry'.[12]

Wide publicity has been given to the dismissal at one stroke of some sixty university professors and lecturers, allegedly because of lack of loyalty to the national ideals or for professional incompetence. No objective observer had any doubt that the motives were purely political. Nor is it necessary to study the list of those dismissed who have since been offered chairs in European or American universities, a list that constantly grows longer, to realize the nature of their 'professional incompetence'. It should nevertheless be stressed that there seems to have been also a secondary aim behind this action, the lowering of the public image of the whole body of professors by including allegations of corruption (financial, sexual, etc.) among the purported reasons for the dismissals. The military's dislike of the intelligentsia is not a new factor, and the actions taken by the government to lower the image of those who were considered to be the intellectual leaders of the country's youth should come as no surprise.

One might even relate the dismissals to the attempts made during the first half of 1971 to ridicule and disgrace the Academy of Athens. This took the form first of a High Court ruling (the judiciary had undergone a similar purge) that the election of all the present academicians is null and void since it had been based on regulations which had not been properly legalized. Then came a more direct, and more personal, attack on two particular members who were publicly accused of having manoeuvred the election of a new member in exchange for favours to their friends. The fact that the attack was led by Theofylaktos Papakonstantinou, who had already been directly involved in the university purge and is, as mentioned above, one of the regime's few 'intellectuals', would suggest that we are here witnessing different stages of the same process.

But whatever the general framework within which the university dismissals have been carried out, they do not seem to have been comprehensive enough. Some of those who remained have apparently been reluctant to submit completely to the government's desires. For instance, in the University of Salonica, Professor D. Evrygenis was called before the university disciplinary committee, while Professor G. Savidis was forced to resign. Nor do academic standards appear to have improved to any considerable extent. For we find a professor blaming his colleagues rather than the students for the deplorable results of an examination. So despite all this, and the fact that new appointments have to be approved by the Ministry (and the police, through the certificate of 'good conduct'), the government has realized the weakness of the situation and turned to Greek scholars abroad. A register of these was compiled, and repeated appeals have been made to their 'patriotic feelings' in order to get them to come and teach in Greece. However, it seems that these academics place their patriotic priorities in a slightly different order, and the government will not find many who will repeat the exchange of an Oxford chair for one in Thessaloniki. But it should be noted that the idea of using eminent Greek professors in foreign institutions to contribute to the development of their homeland's higher education was one of the main targets of the 1964 reform, and a major feature in the planning of the new University of Patras. Thus we have yet again a return to previous policies without, however, the adoption of their underlying ideals.

Little can be said of the student movement, since here the post-1967 vacuum has replaced the very active movement of the years before the _coup_. Student unions have been banned, new regulations have been imposed, leaders have been arrested, and meetings are attended by 'secret' policemen who make their presence the more effective by disclosing their identity rather than by hiding it. Students' non-academic activities are restricted to planning and organizing travel, to participation in official ceremonies, and to issuing announcements about examinations. There have been endless prosecutions of students for participating in non-conformist groups or in more active 'resistance' movements, and two of the big political trials since 1967 were those of Rigas Feraios, a student anti-dictatorship organization. But activities of this kind have not been stopped, and to the 'good conduct' certificates and the trials in courts (military or civil) have been added measures taken, often against the same students, in disciplinary committees of the universities. These usually lead to long-term or even permanent expulsions from the universities, which in simple terms means the ruin of their lives, since there is little prospect of decent survival in Greece for non-graduates.

Higher education has also been affected in other ways by the general tendency to over-centralize. Among these, mention should be made of the abolition of five teacher-training colleges, the only higher education establishments functioning outside the big urban centres. They were, as might be expected, nuclei of an intellectual life and might have developed into 'dangerous' cradles of liberal ideas. By concentrating such institutions in larger urban areas, not only is their control easier, but also the rest of the country is deprived of any contact with means of popular instruction not under direct government control.

Then, under the pretext of cutting down expenses, the authorities have decreed that professors' books will be published by the government publishing office and sold at reduced prices. This, in fact, means that the pattern of the 'one book per subject for everybody' is extended from primary and secondary education to the universities. Generally a student in Greece is not given a list of books to study, but one or more of his professor's books to learn more or less by heart. There seems in this way to be no room for deviations which might endanger the proper indoctrination of the students. It also reinforces the principle of professorial infallibility which has always been so dear to Greek teachers at all levels.

Despite all this, during the four years under review, there have been few signs that liberalism has become alien to Greek students. The endless trials are an indication of their activities, and their massive expressions of admiration for the few professors who are known to be in opposition to the regime, such as Professor John Pesmazoglu for as long as he retained his chair, reveal their dedication to the ideals of freedom and democracy.

Similar indications can be seen in the attitude of secondary-school children on various occasions when they feel they can express their sentiments. This was the case in the school where, during an official ceremony, the students sang the national anthem in a deliberately very soft voice only to increase in volume at the words 'Hail, O hail, Liberty!' Or in another where the students clapped frantically at the end of a speech on the exclamation 'Hail, Greece!' but did not clap at all for 'Hail, 21 April!' In the same way the noise from the stadium which accompanied the Prime Minister's speech to the young people of Athens during an open-air ceremony may not have expressed a very definite spirit of 'resistance', but at least it showed a lack of respect which must have disappointed the educational experts in the government.[13]

But reassuring as these indications may be, they are no substitute for an efficient educational system, and the post-1967 situation in Greece appears to be far from efficient. Secondary education in particular has been directly affected by the attempt to Helleno-Christianize the nation which seems to underly all measures taken in education. There is a distinct impression that by over-emphasizing 'ancestral values', the authorities are once again trying to make the Greeks 'forget the present by focusing their attention on the past and its glories as a substitute for action today'.[14] But secondary education has suffered in other ways as well, and though no totalitarian regime has ever been really interested in improving general secondary education, Greece is now witnessing a degradation in its system which is without precedent in her history.

Purges in secondary education have been less publicized, and in percentage terms less sweeping, than those in higher eduction. Those dismissals which were made were based on ridiculous accusations such as listening to the national anthem with hands in pockets, playing records of Theodorakis to a class (before his music was banned) or praising the athletic achievements of Russia to a team of school athletes. But on the whole the bulk of the teachers were spared massive purging and, apart from having to sign the oath of loyalty, they did not at the beginning feel the impact of the change directly. They had to abandon their 1964 textbooks and use those they had been using for some decades before that. They had to return to their *katharevousa* grammars, forget modern mathematics and deliver the occasional speech in favour of the regime. But, all in all, this had no immediate impact on their status. Their prestige had been considerably raised following the 1964 reform and so had their salaries. But this did not last long. So much have things changed since 1967 that in 1971 the leadership of their union (which, if not appointed by, had been approved by the government) claimed that they did not know 'for how much longer they would be able to keep to themselves their bitterness and disappointment' about the way in which their financial status had been treated by the authorities.

It is easy to see how they arrived at this point. In June 1971 they had not been paid since 1969 for overtime (a service which, incidentally, was made compulsory in 1970), their promotions had been delayed for four years, and their scale of payment had fallen behind that of other civil servants of similar status who had received increments. For example, an agriculturalist appointed to government service in 1971 receives double the salary of his schoolmaster counterpart. It is not then surprising that the young are reluctant to accept teaching posts. From one group of appointments in March 1971, 20·9% of the appointees did not present themselves for service.

But these conditions are not likely to apply to the staff of the schools 'for the best' which have been mentioned above. They will obviously be treated in a special manner. It is the rest of the secondary schools which will suffer. So not only is a large section of the population deprived of secondary education, but those who do receive it have to make do with under-paid teachers who no longer have faith in their task – or 'mission' as they like to call it in Greece. So whatever little benefit one could expect for the future of the country from these indoctrination-oriented and malfunctioning schools, will be lost in an atmosphere of defeatism and fatalism. But this would not help to fulfil the aim of educating the nation and orientating it towards the 'new ideals' proclaimed by the regime. After four full academic years the government does not seem to have been very successful in imbuing secondary-school pupils with the 'spirit of Helleno-Christian civilization', this '19th-century creation' which, according to one observer, is 'an attempt to synthesize the essentially contradictory values of ancient Greece and Byzantium'.[15]

Greek education in 1972 is more classics-orientated, bookish and traditionalist than it has ever been. The short progressive period in the mid-1960s seems to have been an interlude, as were the earlier reforms of 1917 and 1929. But this time the return to the pre-reform patterns has been accompanied by chaos in all directions. Whether this is part of a deliberate attempt to keep the population in a semi-literate condition which would help condition it to accepting anything, or the result of gross incompetence, is of little concern as far as the future of the nation is concerned. But then all is not lost. There seem to be substitutes for intellectual achievement. Spain under similar conditions has been highly successful on several occasions in the Eurovision Song Contest. And in 1971 Greece reached the final of the European Cup football tournament. In both countries these achievements led to government-sponsored national celebrations. In the case of Greece these were particularly lavish, while the military regime did its best to humiliate the country's only Nobel prize-winner, the poet George Seferis.

Athens, August 1971   N.N.

NOTES

1   Beyond the occasional references to education in general works on post-1967 Greece, special mention should be made of the comprehensive study 'L'Enseignement Grec et son demantèlement par la Junte' by Dimos Anastasiou, in the special issue of *Les Temps Modernes* ('Aujourd'hui la Grèce'), 1969, no. 276 bis, p. 161 ff. On the question of ideology see, for instance, Chapter Three.

2 In A. W. Halpin (ed.) *Administrative Theory in Education*, Chicago 1958. For an analysis of Parsons' theory on a comparative basis see Brian Holmes, *Problems in Education*, London 1965.

3 It is interesting to note that on the initiative of the Faculty of Letters of the University of Athens (always a stronghold of conservatism and traditionalism in Greek education) it had been proposed to include in the article on language in the Constitutions of 1911 (when the question of language was first embodied in a constitution) and 1952, a clause which would have made *katharevousa* the language of the schools. The proposed amendments failed to get the approval of parliament. The English version of the text of the 1968 Constitution follows closely the translation published in the *Hellenic Review*, vol. I, no. 3 (London 1968).

4 BROWNING, Robert, *Medieval and Modern Greek*, London 1969, p. 107. This book provides a very accurate picture of the language question in Greece and of its implications. See also A. Mirambel, 'Les aspects psychologiques du purisme dans la Grèce moderne', *Journal de Psychologie moderne et pathologique*, No. 4 (Oct.–Dec.) 1964, p. 405 ff.

5 FOTIADIS, F., *To Glossikon Zitima kai i Ekpaideftiki mas Anagennisis* (The Language Question and our Educational Regeneration), Athens 1902. This is considered the first work to examine the social character and significance of the Language Question. G. Skliros (G. Konstantinidis) *To Koinonikon mas Zitima* (Our Social Question), Athens 1907. This is the first attempt at a marxist interpretation of the social evolution of Greece. The writer believes that 'the supporters of *dimotiki* have been summoned by History to play an important role in the regeneration of our society' (p. 53).

6 Quoted in Philip Williams, *Athens under the Spartans*, London 1967, Fabian Research Series, no. 264, 1967, p. 3.

7 'Social Class and Linguistic Development', in A. H. Halsey *et al.* (ed.), *Education, Economy and Society*, New York 1961, p. 291.

8 Thalis Andreadis, Honorary Director General of the (state) National Tobacco Organization in a speech of 17 March 1971.

9 Under the same title, adapted by D. V. Tountopoulos, Athens (O.E.D.V.), 1970, p. 245.

10 In the September 1971 examination (which falls outside the chronological limits adopted in this paper) there was a slight rise in the percentage of those accepted (30%) created by a substantial drop in the number of candidates and a small increase in places offered. But this still meant 33,608 refused candidates, and, more significantly, there was still no sign of official interest in the detection of the causes of this trend, or in the provision of alternatives.

11 Literature in English on Greek education in general is extremely scarce. Interesting discussion of aspects of Greek education can be found in the relevant chapters of *Tradition and Change in Education* by Andreas M.

Kazamias and Byron G. Massialas, Englewood Cliffs 1965, and Andreas M. Kazamias and Erwin H. Epstein (eds.) *Schools in Transition*, Boston 1968. For an analysis of the 1964 reform and a survey of later developments with comprehensive bibliography see Andreas M. Kazamias, 'Plans and Policies for Educational Reform in Greece' in *Comparative Education Review*, ii (1967) no. 3, p. 331 ff., and with a comprehensive picture of the reactions to the reform before April 1967, Karl Stolz, 'Das Schulsystem Griechenlands' in *Österreichische Schriften zur Entwicklungshilfe*, no. 5 (1965). The counter-reform is basically expressed in Law 129 (25 September 1967), for a short survey of which see 'Greek Regime's Intentions' in *The Times Educational Supplement*, 1 Dec. 1967. On some later developments in education see '*Battle for Young Minds*' by Campbell Page in *The Guardian*, 24 Feb. 1971.

12 Facts and information used in this paper are based on material which has appeared in the Greek press (a series in *To Vima* has been of particular value) and in the official journal of the Teacher's Union (*Deltion Omospondias Leitourgon Mesis Ekpaidefseos*).

13 Private communication.

14 SANDERS, Irwin T., *Rainbow in the Rock*, Cambridge, Mass., 1962, p. 249.

15 *The Times Educational Supplement*, loc. cit.

CHAPTER EIGHT

Culture and the Military

In a free society, cultural life follows a pattern of its own. Trends and fashions blossom and wither away in turn, tastes and styles compete with each other and undergo changes. But these developments usually occur over lengthy periods of time, and are mostly as remote from the daily drudgery of politics as are a healthy individual's intellectual and artistic experiences from his digestive functions. And this lofty independence applies both to the creation and to the enjoyment of culture – to the composer as much as to the concert-goer, to the poet as much as to his reader.

At the other end of the spectrum lies the totalitarian society, where all cultural life (as well as everything else) is controlled by the political rulers. It is for them to decide if the theory of relativity is acceptable, and if people should be allowed to read Kafka or listen to atonal music – the measure of all things being the Party's *Weltanschauung*, whether this be founded on a racial or a class ideology.

These two extremes, however, are not the whole picture. There is also the model of a society which is not free, but where the straitjacket forced upon it should be called authoritarian rather than totalitarian. The distinction is often blurred in liberal thinking, which tends to emphasize the resemblances between the two more than the differences. In the political field, this approach is largely justified: there is little to choose between two kinds of regime under which the right of citizens to elect and control their rulers is equally ignored, and respect for ordinary human rights is equally absent. Nevertheless, in other fields the differences are important, and should not be overlooked by those who wish to keep their terminology clear. This is particularly the case in cultural matters.

A totalitarian regime attempts to control all aspects of cultural life, which it regards as so many ways of promoting the realization of its ideal.

146

Its aim is to use cultural media, as well as all others, in order to spur the citizens on to dynamic action towards the Party's ultimate goal. Only such cultural manifestations as are deemed expedient for its purposes are tolerated, and these are practically forced down the public's throat. The general idea is that 'whoever is not with us is against us', and anything 'neutral' is suspect if not downright damnable.[1]

Things are different with an authoritarian regime whose chief aim is a static one, i.e. that the present rulers (or class of rulers) shall remain indefinitely in power. Its control over cultural life is normally limited to the suppression of anything that might imperil its self-preservation. In the words of a study recently published in Greece,[2] such regimes do not want to mobilize the masses but, on the contrary, to immobilize them. The catchword is here, 'as long as you are not against us, we don't mind'. 'Neutral' manifestations are tolerated, and even encouraged if sufficiently soporific.

These differences are crucial. On the one hand, there is comparatively greater cultural freedom in an authoritarian society than in a totalitarian one, and fewer or no attempts to enforce complete intellectual and artistic conformity; as long as the 'Man on Horseback' sits firmly in the saddle, he could not care less if the horse prefers abstract to representational art. On the other hand, those totalitarian rulers who are imbued with a sincere desire to improve humanity are more likely to care about the quality of some at least of the cultural food they serve to their flock – even if the choice of it is limited by a strict diet. They will be more inclined, say, to encourage good music, ballet, editions of the classics and free education than a selfish clique whose sole ambition is power for power's sake. The latter is more likely to encourage cheap culture-substitutes which tend to keep the masses in a condition of contented stupor – from football to pornography and from low-brow music to thrillers.

The line between totalitarianism and authoritarianism can seldom, of course, be drawn as strictly as that in actual practice. What begins as a revolution for the liberation of humanity by totalitarian means may well acquire, by degrees, some of the features of a conservative establishment concerned only with the maintenance of its own privileges. Conversely, an authoritarian power-group may find it expedient to disguise its *coup* as a revolution and to cloak its crude aims under a fictitious ideology, in the name of which it will go through the motions of 'mobilizing the people'; or its interests may be linked with, say, those of an established Church, in which case bigotry will be part of its cultural policy. In the first case, cultural freedom will probably be slightly increased; and it will probably suffer in the second.

It is useful to bear these distinctions in mind when trying to classify the present military dictatorship in Greece. This is not an easy task, because the regime itself is a curious blend. In essence, of course, it is an authoritarian dictatorship of the extreme Right, to which the Colonels' background and outlook lend a peasant, 'populist' flavour, while their wish to appear progressive sometimes supplies it with pseudo-radical overtones. On the other hand, their determination to establish their rule on as permanent a basis as possible often leads them to attempt to create an ideology, and to a type of propaganda, that smacks of totalitarianism. At the same time, however, international considerations force them to pay lip-service to democracy, which in turn makes it necessary for them every now and then to keep up a minimum of appearances. As a result of this unusual mixture, the general oppressiveness of the regime is at times sharpened to totalitarian extremes and at times tempered by conspicuous and much-advertised tolerance; it is never daunted by a fear of the ridiculous.

It is worth trying to show what part each one of these factors – which are to some extent contradictory – has played in shaping a cultural policy which often baffles by its apparent lack of pattern and sometimes total unpredictability.

THE AUTHORITARIAN SUBSTANCE:
NEGATION AND PROHIBITION

In the beginning, the regime was careful to emphasize its conservative nature. The *coup* that brought the military to power was described by the first post-*coup* premier, Kollias, as being 'not a revolution, but a counter-revolution . . . to prevent a communist revolution which was imminent'.

This frankly defensive policy was unmitigated, as far as cultural matters were concerned, by any radical or even pseudo-radical element. It was expressed by a marked preference for the 'purist' language – a traditional hallmark of Greek conservatism – and by the ruthless weeding-out of anything remotely reminiscent of communism. This included not only writings and songs of communist inspiration, but also anything written or composed by a communist, regardless of content. In the field of music, for instance, the typical example was the prohibition of public performances of all music by Mikis Theodorakis – even of his purely lyrical love-songs; at the same time, the sale of his records was forbidden, and later on existing stocks of such records were destroyed. The official programme of the Athens Festival had to be changed in a hurry, because it included Greek tragedies for which the incidental music had been composed by Theodorakis.

The chief weapon for the implementation of this policy in the fields of literature, learning, films and the theatre was pre-censorship. No book or magazine could be printed, no lecture delivered, without previous scrutiny and permission of the censors. Films and plays could be presented to the public only with their approval, and subject to cuts ordered by them. Existing books were taken care of by means of an 'Index' drawn up by the authorities and containing several hundred titles of books that could not be sold, bought, displayed, discussed or consulted in public libraries.

All this would have been bad enough if the witch-hunt had been confined to purely Marxist material. The regime's minions, however, preferred to err on the side of safety; quite often they vetoed not only communist revolutionary thinking, but everything connected with any revolution at all. Thus a revival of the film *Juarez*, dealing with the century-old Mexican Revolution, was stopped; a play about Robespierre was rejected with the explanation that Robespierre had been a communist; even films about the Greek War of Independence in 1821 were at first discouraged, since they would show a people rising against its oppressors; and a poet about to give a public reading of his works was told to change the word 'red' which occurred in a poem in connection with the beloved one's lips.

The Soviet Union and the Slavic countries of Eastern Europe being communist, everything that had to do with them came automatically under suspicion. On one occasion, a newspaper was not allowed to publish an essay on Tolstoy. The list of forbidden books included such items as a *Teach Yourself Russian* textbook, a Greek–Bulgarian dictionary and a biography of Peter the Great. China was also an obvious suspect. The censor forbade the editor of a world atlas to mention the predominant religions of China as being Confucianism, Taoism and so on (which the editor had thought of as a prudent anachronism) on the grounds that 'Taoism and all those philosophies lead to anarchy'.

Anything critical of the United States, at whatever period of its history, was thought to be the work of Moscow agents, even if originating in America itself. Thus, a translation of J. K. Galbraith's *The Triumph* was forbidden; and the film *Soldier Blue* was only allowed to pass after the sequences throwing a dubious light on the treatment of Red Indians by white Americans had been excised.

Authoritarian regimes with a conservative outlook tend to be pillars of religion and morality, at least outwardly. The Greek dictatorship has been no exception, and as censors are by nature cautious animals, here again they preferred to err on the side of safety. When a translation of Stendhal's *Cenci* was submitted to them, they took exception to some of its anti-clerical statements and ordered them to be expunged. A broadcast for the centenary of Claudel was forbidden because the officer in charge thought that the excerpts from the Catholic writer that were being presented were 'obscene'.

Some dead Greek writers were suspect because of their politics. But a few of them were too famous to be forbidden – like Kazantzakis and the poet Sikelianos – while others, like the novelist and essayist Theotokas, had been such obvious liberals that it was impossible to brand them communists. The censors struck a middle course: without actually forbidding the sale of their books, they allowed no reference to them to be published. In pursuance of this policy, a critic was given permission to publish a book of essays on Greek novelists only after he had deleted the chapter on Theotokas. It always remained possible, of course, to make oblique references to those writers without mentioning their names: the censors were not conversant enough with literature to detect the ruse. If one wanted to mention Sikelianos, say, one would refer to 'the poet of *Antidoron*' – a reference as clear, to the educated Greek, as one to 'the poet of *Paradise Lost*' would be to an Englishman.

Not unnaturally, it was writing – whether purely literary or, say, connected with the social sciences – that suffered the most, together with the theatre and the cinema. The more remote a field of cultural activity was from the spoken word, and the more remote the word was from social realities, the less did the impact of dictatorship make itself felt. The authorities did not, for instance, normally interfere with the visual arts, or with non-vocal music. Nor, for that matter, with handbooks on surgery or mathematics – for it is difficult to be subversive in such pursuits. On the other hand, the spirit of criticism and doubt was and is frowned upon as such, regardless of its object, and this tendency is particularly obvious in educational matters.

Education in present-day Greece is dealt with in another place in this volume (see Chapter Seven), but since it is intimately connected with cultural life – to the extent that education today will influence the culture of tomorrow – I may be allowed a short incursion into this neighbouring field.

University librarians have been ordered to purge their libraries of all 'leftist' literature, and academics are requested to keep down to a minimum the number of foreign books suggested in the reading lists given to students. One possible explanation of this ban may be inferred by an analogy from a famous speech of Colonel Ladas, a prominent member of the junta and now governor of Thessaly. Referring to philosophy, to which he has presumably devoted a thorough study, he declared on 6 December 1969 at the University of Jannina: 'no other people have any philosophers. The Greeks have exhausted the subject. . . . Foreigners can only imitate them. . . .'

Another explanation for this distrust of foreign textbooks could be that the police cannot understand everything those damned foreign intellectuals write, and some of it may well be subversive. (In fact, a man was sentenced to prison not long ago for having lent a Russian work on biology to a person not of age.) More generally, however, it is probably felt that students should not try to be too clever and learn too much. It is well known that students who wish to get good marks with the Security Police must avoid asking many questions at seminars, and generally thrusting themselves forward. The right kind of student – the 'safe' one from the police point of view – is the one who listens respectfully to his teachers, memorizes their words and repeats them faithfully at examinations. The other type, who has ideas of his own, is a fellow to be watched: he might take it into his head to start thinking for himself in politics, too.

The following incident will show that these are no idle exaggerations. Early in 1970, during the brief 'spring' that followed the lifting of pre-censorship in the press, the newspaper *Ethnos* conducted an inquiry among students on the subject of university reform. Several students replied, giving their names and expressing what were, by contemporary Western standards, remarkably mild views about the advisability, say, of increasing the number of teaching personnel and thereby facilitating individual contact between students and teachers. As a consequence, every one of them was summoned to the Security Police where they were insulted and threatened: 'Who do you think you are, having opinions about the university? Mind your own business. If you do it again, you may find yourself deported to an island with a couple of broken ribs.' (Four-letter words omitted.)

It is hardly necessary to stress the consequences that such a premium on servility and conformity, and such a penalization of intellectual independence and initiative, can have for the country's cultural life in the long run. The whole attitude of the regime towards scholarship was well illustrated by a speech pronounced by Premier Papadopoulos in the University of Thessaloniki on 5 January 1968. In a passage strongly marked by that bucolic flavour mentioned earlier in this study, he declared that students should henceforth dread, as a punishment far worse than any other, the sending of a letter of reprimand by the Rector to their village, which would be read aloud by the local priest in front of the entire congregation. . . .

There is no doubt that, in so far as it depends on the colonels, it is indeed the poor in spirit who will inherit their kingdom – and a large section of them (judging by the trend in radio and television broadcasts nowadays) will consist of football fans and of connoisseurs of the more insipid sentimental hits of the thirties.

THE TOTALITARIAN DREAM: IDEOLOGY AND REGIMENTATION

The conservative packaging in which the dictatorship first presented itself to the public did not prove entirely satisfactory. To begin with, very few Greeks were taken in by the excuse provided: even staunch conservatives regarded the alleged 'red peril' as an absurdity, and the more sophisticated among them were frankly appalled at what was going on in the name of their creed. It soon became apparent that the regime was sitting on bayonets alone, a position that has seldom proved comfortable after a time. Besides, mere 'anti-communism' was not a sufficiently inspiring ideal for men who looked upon themselves as called by Destiny to perform great deeds, and the fiction of a 'counter-revolution' could scarcely justify an indefinite tenure of power. The *coup* was therefore soon re-christened 'revolution' (to be more precise, 'national revolution', presumably in order not to be confused with 'non-national' or even 'anti-national' competitors) and the quest began for a positive ideology which might serve both as an excuse for remaining in office and as a bait for some popular support.

I shall not deal with the story of the quest, which has been described before in picturesque detail.[3] It is enough to mention that the concept finally adopted as the official motto of the regime was 'Greece of Christian Greeks'. Broadly speaking, it embraces a mixture of religious and moral bigotry on the one hand and rabid chauvinism on the other – together with a violent hatred of sexual permissiveness, communism, long hair, anarchy, decadent art and the Slavonic peoples.

Needless to say, there is nothing actually new in all this. It is little more than an attempt to perform a face-lift on the traditional conservative values, to turn them from static values into dynamic ones. Still, the adoption of this ideology could not remain entirely without consequences for the country's cultural life. The trouble is that it is not easy to deduce from it any coherent intellectual or aesthetic theory. True, an aesthetic theory has been put forward by Colonel Ladas. 'Good art,' he declared early in 1971 with his customary self-confidence, 'is that which is good for the Motherland. Bad art is that which is bad for the Motherland.' This admirable sentiment still does not take one very far. Nevertheless, the authorities have at times done their best to apply this simple yardstick.

On one occasion, a typical popular show of puppet shadow-theatre was to be broadcast on television. Now in all such shows – the tradition of which goes back to Ottoman domination – the cunning Greek hero (a kind of Till Eulenspiegel) gets a sound beating from the Turkish policeman for his tricks. Finding out at the last moment that such horrors were to be televised, the officer in charge of the supervision of broadcasts flew into a rage and ordered the plot to be changed in a hurry, so that the *Greek* puppet should beat up the *Turkish* puppet; national dishonour was thus averted.

On another occasion, a well-known critic delivered a lecture on modern Greek poetry – the first of a scheduled series. He had carefully steered clear of all controversial subjects, and was surprised when, a few days later, he was summoned to the Security Police and ordered to cancel the remaining lectures; the reason given was that, instead of discussing and praising 'good, patriotic poetry', he had dealt with 'decadent stuff'.

An ideological drive cannot confine itself to mere prohibitions. It has to foster the right kind of artistic production. An attempt in this direction was made in 1969: under the suggestive title 'The Popular Muse', the Government published a selection of verse written in its praise by supporters from all over the country. These amateur poets, who ranged from greengrocers to schoolchildren, certainly did their best to compensate for any literary deficiencies of their output with sheer enthusiasm; the net result, however, can hardly be said to justify the considerable amount of taxpayers' money involved in the process.

Some time before this, all newspapers were made to publish a reproduction of a picture presented to Premier Papadopoulos by a previously unknown painter. A symbolic representation of the 'national revolution', it showed an open book on the pages of which one could read '21 April 1967'. Hovering above it, with a twig in its beak, was a dove. Underneath, obviously crushed by the weight of the book, were some depressed-looking monsters, presumably standing for the forces of Evil. The entire composition was bathed in the rays of a jolly rising sun, and it was implied that this was the kind of art that patriotic painters ought to produce. (Rumours that the work had been inspired from a Soviet picture, with only the date altered, can be confidently dismissed as malicious gossip.)

In spite of such laudable efforts, though, it cannot be said that the 'Helleno-Christian' ideology has inspired many cultural manifestations. The Colonels probably feel that this is due, not to any inherent poverty of the ideology itself, but to the perverse mentality of artists and intellectuals brought up under the wrong political system – as indeed is the case with all Greeks having attained the age of consent. This is why the Premier has said, over and over again, that one of the tasks of the 'Revolution' is to re-educate the Greek people and to change their mental habits. Thus, somewhat paradoxically, the very reluctance of the Greeks to adopt Helleno-Christian attitudes, in cultural life or otherwise, is turned into an argument for the indefinite duration of the dictatorship.

In the meantime, it is only fair to say that totalitarian attempts at ideological regimentation, outside schools and youth organizations, have remained, up to now, sporadic and half-hearted. By and large, the prevailing line has been the normal authoritarian one: 'neutral' art and literature are tolerated. In some ways, even, the regime is doing its best to attract the good will of artists and intellectuals by promises of liberal prizes, stipends and pensions to those who merely behave, i.e. do not oppose it. This leniency may be due, among other things, to the fact that too much insistence on ideological conformity would become increasingly incompatible with the necessity to keep up a liberal façade.

THE LIBERAL FAÇADE: DECEIT AND COMPROMISE

From the very beginning, the Colonels were astonished and hurt to realize that they were unpopular in Western Europe, whose decadent peoples were still attached to such quaint notions as popular representation, human rights and the like. The Colonels' friends and well-wishers in the USA had not quite prepared them for so cold a reception, even by important sections of American opinion itself.

Unpleasant as the pill was, it had to be swallowed. Greece could not afford to be cut off from the Western World. Something had to be done to placate these spoil-sports; many of them are credulous enough, and you can get away with a lot of things provided you ostensibly accept their odd ideas. The cultural field seemed to offer opportunities for gestures of good will which posed no serious threat to the self-preservation of the regime.

The earliest of these gestures concerned the free sale of foreign books and newspapers, regardless of content. Quite soon after the *coup*, the Colonels and their advisers correctly estimated that the harm done to their image by censorship of foreign-language publications was far greater than the dangers involved in their free circulation: in fact these dangers were negligible, as only a tiny number of Greeks could both afford to buy such publications *and* understand foreign languages – and those were the educated ones who were in any case a write-off from the point of view of the Colonels. Hence it came about that even when the witch-hunt over Greek publications was at its height, one could find Marx, Lenin, Marcuse or the *Memoirs of Fanny Hill* displayed quite freely – in English or French. The same applied to *Le Monde* and the *Guardian*, even when they were carrying strong denunciations of the Greek dictatorship. Thus, while the bulk of the population was still protected from spiritual contamination, the tourists were allowed to read whatever they liked; many of them are still greatly impressed by the unexpected degree of freedom to be found in Greece.

It took the regime much longer to bring itself to relax its grip on Greek publications. Pre-censorship was lifted only in October 1969, and the book Index in the summer of 1970. At the same time, though, an extremely severe Press Law was passed, threatening with stiff sentences any writer or newspaperman who might offend the Colonels in any foreseeable way. The idea evidently was that the dictatorship would thus both have its cultural cake and eat it: it would be able to blazon forth that there was full freedom of expression in Greece, while writers would be too frightened to dare try any mischief – the more so since offences under the new law remained under the jurisdiction of Courts Martial, which everybody knew were not to be trifled with.

The Colonels went even further: in the spring of 1970 they released Theodorakis and allowed him to go abroad (even though his music was still forbidden) and in the following autumn they released the poet Ritsos. Moreover, they have hitherto shown comparative indulgence towards the intellectuals who have been impertinent enough not to take the hint, and actually to make use of the semi-freedom granted to them. That is to say, only one of these intellectuals has been arrested up to now,[4] though others have lost their jobs or been deprived of their passports.[5]

For a regime like the Greek one, this is exceptionally lenient treatment, and it stands in marked contrast to the severity shown to newspapermen; it is probably due, again, to a deference to the unaccountable foible Western societies appear to have for egg-heads.

But what have the egg-heads actually been up to?

THE INTELLECTUALS' DILEMMA: TO SPEAK OR NOT TO SPEAK

From the very first day of the dictatorship, nearly all Greek writers went on a spontaneous, silent strike: that is to say, they decided not to publish a word under censorship. This was both a protest against the dictatorship and a measure for the preservation of their own integrity; to write only innocuous things that might be passed by the censors would be tantamount to condoning the whole system.

There were, of course, exceptions, but they were to be found mostly among elderly members of the Academy. The greater number of writers – and, incidentally, the best ones – went on strike as one man; among them, most conspicuous of all, the greatest poet of modern Greece, Nobel prize-winner George Seferis, who actually withdrew a book from the printers. At the same time, the two most important literary reviews closed down: the liberal *Epoches* of its own accord, the left-wing *Epitheorisi Technis* because most of its staff were arrested.

Painters and sculptors joined in – a gesture the more meritorious since they did not have the same reasons as writers for objecting to censorship, which did not apply to them. For a long time no self-respecting artist agreed to exhibit his work in public; later on they began to exhibit in private galleries but still refused to participate in State-sponsored exhibitions at home or abroad – a refusal involving considerable financial sacrifice.

The theatre and the cinema dragged along; but many of Greece's best actors and directors chose to leave the country,[6] and our best tragic actress, Anna Synodinou, refused to perform on the stage.

Overnight, there descended upon Greece a kind of medieval obscurity. Its foremost intellectuals were either in prison, or in self-imposed exile abroad, or silent.[7] The only notable books to be published in the first three years of the regime, apart from translations, were works of scientific or scholarly interest which the censors would not even trouble to read. Even the literary columns of daily newspapers – a traditional ground for lively intellectual argument and dispute – went dead. (Again, of course, with a few exceptions such as those that provided the examples, quoted earlier, of the workings of pre-censorship.)

The first to break that ominous silence was Seferis. In March 1969 he handed out a memorable statement of protest against the dictatorship, which was heard over foreign broadcasts and circulated in typewritten copies. (Needless to say, the newspapers were not allowed to print it, though they had to print a vicious personal attack on Seferis produced by the official propaganda service.)

'A regime has been imposed on us,' he said, 'which is entirely opposed to the ideals for which our world fought during the last war. Our spiritual values . . . have been submerged in the muddy and stagnant waters of a swamp. . . . Tragedy lies in wait inevitably at the end . . . the longer this abnormal situation lasts, the worse it becomes. . . .'[8]

After Seferis had taken the first step, things began to move in literary circles. In April 1969 eighteen other writers, mostly belonging to a younger generation,[9] handed out a collective protest against both censorship and the high-handed decision of the junta to force all newspapers to publish short stories by Greek writers without the latter's consent. The protest stated among other things: 'There can be no intellectual freedom . . . as long as there is censorship; as long as books are banned; as long as intellectuals are being persecuted for their convictions alone. . . . Freedom is indivisible; and the relevance of intellectual freedom to the dignity of man has been reaffirmed recently by the Czechoslovak people's heroic struggle to attain it. . . .'

At approximately the same time, Anna Synodinou made public a passionate plea of her own: 'Our country is subjected to a cruel and unworthy destiny. A heavy silence has spread over the land. . . . It is the silence that accompanies the abolition of freedom. . . .'

The Security people began to worry. What on earth was going on? Each of the eighteen writers was summoned to Security Police Headquarters and subjected to what was partly an interrogation, partly an attempt at appeasement and partly a threat of prosecution. Here are, verbatim, excerpts from one of those conversations:

POLICE OFFICER: What have you got against censorship? Has any of your works been rejected by it?

WRITER: I would never submit anything to censorship. I object to it on grounds of principle.

OFFICER: But why? It is there only to prevent the publishing of things contrary to religion and to the national interest.

WRITER: We had laws before, that took care of blasphemous and treasonable publications.

OFFICER: Ah, but those could be applied only after the harm had been done. With censorship it is prevented altogether.

WRITER: I know the argument, it is being used in the Soviet Union. I still prefer the Western system.

OFFICER: What are your political beliefs?

WRITER: I believe in democracy.

OFFICER: But so do all of us! The greatest democrat of all is the Premier. And he is especially fond of intellectuals, he wants you on his side.

OFFICER: You don't seem to realize the communist danger.

WRITER: There was no such danger. The communists had polled less than twelve per cent at the last election.

OFFICER: Oh, but a well-organized minority can seize power. Look at the way these people did it now.

WRITER: There is a difference. The communists had no tanks.

OFFICER: No, but they had insidious propaganda, subversion. . . . Anyway, do you realize that what you and your colleagues have done is unlawful, and may get you into trouble?

WRITER: I know, as with Daniel and Sinyavsky in Russia.

When pre-censorship was abolished with regard to writing (though not with regard to films and plays) in autumn 1969, intellectuals were faced with a dilemma: should they begin to publish again, or not?

The argument for going on with the silent strike was that there had been no real change. The new Press Law being as it was (and still is), writers would still be unable to express themselves freely, while putting an end to their strike would be used by the regime's propaganda to prove that there *was* freedom of expression. Besides, it would not be honourable to start publishing as long as a number of our colleagues were still prevented from doing so – either because they had been deprived of their personal liberty or because their works were banned.[10] The argument for resuming publication was that the semi-freedom granted could and should be used for fighting the dictatorship on the intellectual level, and that this fight would be waged on behalf of our gagged colleagues as well. Besides, it was added, too prolonged an intellectual strike would harm the nation's cultural level more than the Colonels' regime; it would allow the latter's voice to be heard alone. We owed it to our own people, and more particularly to the young, to do our best to keep free thought alive.

After many months of passionate discussion, a group of writers finally decided to take the plunge, to find out how wide, in effect, was the margin of freedom granted. Needless to say, the experiment was to be carried out by means of writings *with* political implications – more or less thinly disguised; these were no times for *ars gratia artis*, and besides it was known that non-political stuff was allowed in any case. The legal and editorial responsibility was to be assumed, collectively, by seven writers.[11] Thus, if the regime decided to prosecute, it would have to prosecute no fewer than seven. (There is a certain strength in numbers.)

The result was the publication, in July 1970, of a book called *Eighteen Texts*, consisting of contributions by as many authors – poems, short stories or essays.[12] Few of them, if any, were devoid of political intent, though none named the Greek dictatorship by name: everything was done by innuendo, transposition and the use of metaphors which the reader could easily understand, but for which it would be difficult for the authorities to prosecute. For example, four of the contributors published short stories dealing with a fictitious Latin American country with a military dictatorship, sometimes christened 'Boliguay'. No reader could possibly miss the point, though the authorities would look rather silly if the Public Prosecutor tried to prove in court that so appalling a country bore a close resemblance to contemporary Greece.

The success of the book exceeded its editors' wildest hopes. It immediately became a best-seller by Greek standards, by running into four editions of three thousand copies each within less than six months. Messages of congratulation and encouragement poured in from abroad, from prisons, from detention camps. All this emboldened the editors to publish a book of similar nature. It came out in February 1971 and was called *New Texts*; going a step farther than the first, it included straight political studies in an undisguised liberal vein. It too became a best-seller.

This time, the junta lashed out – but in words alone. Its spokesmen denounced both books, their authors and those who had been fooled by them: yet there was still no attempt at prosecution. The colonels obviously feared that police action, and a trial involving several prominent intellectuals because of their opinions alone, would ruin the international image they were trying so hard to build up. To the editors and contributors of the books, the regime's verbal attacks spelt success; they had got under the dictatorship's skin. They have decided to go ahead: further volumes can be expected, each representing a step in an escalation to sharpen the regime's dilemma: should it allow this subversion to go unchecked or should it prosecute? The future will tell what the decision will finally be.

In the meantime, intellectual life is, at the time of writing (summer 1971) very different both from what it used to be before 1967 and from what it was between 1967 and 1970. It differs from pre-*coup* life in that it has become more politically minded. Intellectuals who had shunned that kind of commitment all their lives, to whom *littérature engagée* was at best in poor taste and at worst a nightmare, now find themselves incapable of writing any other kind. One can call this the 'toothache effect'. George Orwell once remarked that when your tooth is aching you cannot enjoy *King Lear*, or anything else for that matter. Life under a dictatorship is a permanent Great Toothache – you can hardly think of anything else: your writing turns round and round the sore spot like a probing tongue; and the time comes when, to quote one of our writers, 'you take up your pen like a sword' to fight the Toothache.

Another great difference is that intellectuals whose politics used to diverge sharply have now been brought close together by a common indignation and the sense of a common duty. Former conservatives and former communists who hardly spoke to each other in the old days now work hand in hand; their disappointment and disgust with American and Soviet policies respectively have contributed a great deal to throw bridges across the previously existing gulf.

The difference between 1968 and 1971 is hardly less considerable. Mournful silence has been replaced by the noise and excitement of battle. Controversial books have begun to appear in increasing numbers, newspapers are coming cautiously to life once more. Plays have been performed in which the censors had seen no harm, but where sly hints were greeted with loud applause by audiences – and by the time such a play is forbidden, some effect has been produced. Around the editorial group of *Eighteen Texts* and *New Texts* a larger group of intellectuals and artists has crystallized; their names are to be found under a series of liberal protests and manifestos that have come out since 1970. They have gradually acquired a sense of solidarity and unity of purpose, as well as the feeling of being once again in touch with the wider public. The latter's response has been characteristically enthusiastic, and shows a remarkable sensitivity to even the subtlest anti-dictatorial innuendo; this is particularly noticeable among the young, and can be regarded as a most hopeful sign.

The list of contributors to the two books which started the ball rolling makes an interesting study. It cuts across not only former political barriers, but also age groups, professions and personal circumstances. It included Seferis, the venerated Grand Old Man of Greek letters, as well as beginners in their twenties; lawyers as well as poets, economists as well as novelists. Four of the contributors are in prison,[13] and others have tasted prison or deportation. They all share a common faith in their struggle for freedom, and a readiness to take the consequences of their action.

The struggle may have to go on for months or years. There may be further victims. Our cultural life may still have to suffer both from the restraints imposed on it by the dictatorship and from the excessive pre-occupation with politics made necessary by the struggle itself. But it has by now been proved that the spirit of freedom is hard to exorcise; when kicked out of the door it has a way of coming back through the window – even through a narrow window almost inadvertently half-opened by contemptuous jackbooted authoritarians.

Two years ago the painter Kaniaris delighted the Athenian public by what was at the time a very daring manifestation. He exhibited a series of compositions in which the main materials were plaster (an allusion to the favourite metaphor of Premier Papadopoulos, according to which Greece is a recalcitrant patient who has to be immobilized in plaster for her own good) and barbed wire – a reminder of prisons and detention camps. Yet there was a message of hope in his work, for out of the plaster and through the barbed wire hands were extended, and they were holding red carnations – a symbol of resurrection and of freedom.

Athens, August 1971   *Rodis Roufos*

NOTES

1 Wishful thinkers who believe that, as far as Europe is concerned, such extreme views have been buried with Stalin would do well to ponder a recent statement by the Romanian President Ceauşescu, which is reminiscent of the famous Zhdanov doctrine in the middle forties.

2 A. Peponis, 'Mass Media and Political Message' in *Nea Keimena* (New Texts) Athens 1971.

3 *Vérité sur la Grèce*, Lausanne 1970. To this book and to its anonymous author, I am indebted for a lot of material I have used in this study. This book is to be published as 'Athenian', *Inside the Colonels' Greece*, Chatto and Windus, London, and Norton, New York, 1972. (Editors' note.) See also Chapter Three on the regime's ideology.

4   Dimitrios Maronitis, a distinguished former professor of classics at the University of Thessaloniki.

5   Nikos Kasdaglis, a novelist, was sacked by the Bank of Agriculture, of which he had been an employee for nearly twenty years, for having signed two liberal manifestos. Among those deprived of their passports I may cite Kay Cicellis, an English-language novelist; the measure was extended to her husband, a business consultant who had nothing to do with politics.

6   Such as the film directors Cacoyannis and Coundouros, and the actress Aspassia Papathanassiou.

7   Some writers had circulated their work in roneotype, clandestinely, after the example of the Soviet *samizdat*. This practice, however, was made difficult by a provision of Martial Law compelling all those possessing duplicating machines to register them and holding them responsible for the way they are used. The police can refuse permission to possess them, or even a photocopier.

8   The full text of this, and subsequent protests, is to be found in *Free Greek Voices* edited by Helen Vlachos, London, 1971.

9   See *Free Greek Voices*, p. 138.

10 Such was the case of, among many others, the poet Varnalis and the novelist Vassilikos.

11 Anagnostakis, Arghyriou, Frangopoulos, Kasdaglis, Kotzias, Koufopoulos, Roufos. Later N. Kasdaglis was replaced by A. Peponis.

12 The book is being published in translation by Harvard University Press.

13 D. Maronitis, mentioned earlier; G. Mangakis, former Professor of Criminal Law in the University of Athens; Sp. Plaskovitis, novelist and former member of the Council of the State; P. Zannas, the translator of Proust into Greek.

CHAPTER NINE

The State of the Opposition Forces*
since the Military Coup

Greek political life had been undergoing profound changes in the course of the 1960s – at least up to the time of the *coup*. The liberal–socialist forces of the country, jointly operating under the umbrella of a coalition party (the Centre Union), were challenging the political supremacy of the right-wing forces and their self-acquired right to monopolize the government of the country – a supremacy that had been established as a result of the civil war of 1946–49. Their 'unrelenting struggle' brought them eventually to the government of the country after the elections of November 1963 and February 1964. The events of July 1965[1] had subsequently shown that the centrists might have succeeded in becoming the government of the country but had not succeeded in getting hold of the reins of power. A second 'unrelenting struggle' had to be launched. The forces that had rallied behind the first 'unrelenting struggle' rallied in an even more determined way behind the second: the workers of the working-class suburbs of Athens and other urban centres, the students who belonged to a new generation that had no personal memories of the civil war, the peasants and the agricultural workers in the countryside. A growing economy had made all of them conscious that the liberalization of the country's political life, an end to the primitive anti-communism of the right, the establishment of the principle of popular sovereignty – would have enabled them to enjoy their fair share of the growing

* In writing this paper I have greatly profited from an unpublished article sent from Greece by a courageous man who, however, in view of the nature of the article prefers to remain anonymous. Although parts of this chapter are based on his article, final responsibility for what is presented here is entirely mine.

national income. The concept of popular sovereignty had for them not just a metaphysical meaning but rather a concrete relationship with the improvement of their poverty-stricken lives. It was precisely because these social groups felt this way that the Centre Union's simple pro-gramme of political reform had appealed to them and brought about an alliance that was bound to achieve power in the elections scheduled for 28 May 1967. These elections were forestalled by the *coup*.

The *coup* of 21 April meant the dissolution of political parties, the prohibi-tion of all forms of political activity, the silencing of the press and of the communications media. Political life cannot function under conditions of martial law and with a complete absence of the rule of law. Thus, the political evolution that was taking its own course before the *coup*, despite the setback of the events of July 1965, came to an apparent halt. This does not imply that the Greeks suddenly lost any interest in politics or that the regime, which came to power in a conspiratorial manner, has acquired a broad popular base in the course of the few years following its takeover. Far from it. The regime so well realises its lack of any significant popular base that it publicly declares that it needs the 'shadow of fear', the maintenance of martial law, to keep the popula-tion under control.[2] This lack of popular support forces the regime to hesitate (to the embarrassment of its major ally, the United States govern-ment) in implementing its own constitution, which it put to a rigged referendum in 1968. For the same reason the regime has not allowed, up to now, and it is unlikely that it will do so, any kind of free elections within labour organizations, co-operatives, local government or even student unions.

The dissolution and effective dismantling of the party political machines was not a difficult task. The organization of the political parties was based on a system of political clientelism. In pre-Franco Spain and in Southern Italy the existence of such a system originated in the feudal character of the economy. In Greece, the power of the local political bosses was derived from their links with the highly centralized state machinery of the country. Under such conditions of party political organization, the arrest of the key political leaders automatically brings about the collapse of the party machinery. It is true that to some extent the left-communist alliance of the United Democratic Left (EDA) had tried to create an efficient and modern organizational structure, and that the left wing of the Centre Union had attempted just a few weeks before the *coup* to overcome the organizational deficiencies of the Centre Union party by forming the 'Democratic Leagues'.³ But the political parties were badly organized to face the eventuality of an army *coup*. In their overwhelming majority, politicians of the centre and the left believed that the threat of a dictatorship by the army generals was used as a kind of bluff by the King to force them to make concessions. They had thus decided to steer a firm course and to induce the King to show his hand. They were, however, somewhat mistaken. In the end it was the American military and intelligence mission in Athens which showed its hand.

On the morning of 21 April 1967 the Greek masses, who had been constantly mobilized over the preceding two-year period and were led to believe by the rhetoric of the parties that dictatorship would be met by 'popular revolution', were left at the mercy of a gang of ruthless conspirators composed of unknown, crude, colonels. The failure of the leaderships of the left and the centre to grasp the realities of the Greek situation in those days, and their incompetence in forestalling the trend towards dictatorship, has led to an apparent feeling of mistrust toward the old political leaderships and parties by the party cadres, the political activists and especially the young. It is not enough to arm the crowd only with enthusiasm when you know the opponent is ready to resort to the brutal force of modern weapons. This distrust of the old political formations, this feeling that the old leaderships had proved to be incompetent, led eventually to the development of a national ideological crisis of enormous dimensions – a crisis in which everything previously considered worthwhile (the political parties, their leaders, their programmes and ideology) crumbled.⁴ This state of affairs into which Greece was plunged has paralysed resistance and created a fertile ground from which the Colonels have been desperately trying to reap rich harvests through their incessant, hypocritical, propaganda about the weaknesses and failures of the pre-*coup* system. That such harvests were not reaped by the Colonels is a reflection of the fact that the average Greek realizes that it is not so much the state of affairs that existed on 20 April 1967 that matters, but rather the fact that the period before the *coup* sustained a genuine movement toward political emancipation and progress, whereas the post-*coup* situation is characterized by a forced backward movement to the pre-war type of paternalistic society of a predominantly peasant country.⁵ As an observer has put it, the result of the *coup* is regression, both economic and, what is in the long run more damaging, political.⁶

Three years after the *coup* the leadership of the Athens group of the communist resistance organization 'Patriotic Front' has explicitly recognized the existence of a national ideological crisis (by which the left has been affected more than any other group) when it wrote in its underground paper: 'The arrest, imprisonment and detention in the dictatorship's concentration camps of a very large number of the cadres of the left was undoubtedly a very serious blow. The problem, however, is that a large number of the cadres who remained free, people who spent much of their lives in the struggle for democracy and social progress, have no inclination to participate in the *organized* anti-dictatorship struggle. The damage from this stand is not just limited to the loss to the struggle of expert cadres. The loss is basically in the paralysing influence that this stand exerts on a broader circle of the masses and especially on the youth. . . . The *coup* of 21 April 1967, especially in the manner it imposed itself, caused a real crisis in the consciousness of the people, brought the people suddenly to a very painful reality. . . . The *coup* made the masses at large feel the bitter taste of crisis that had been maturing for some time in the left movement. It has destroyed values, broken idols . . . has brought to an unbelievably low level the prestige of the leading figures of the movement – sometimes in a very indiscriminate way. . . . The movement's condition, as revealed in the above matters, has created an image of chaos and brought bitter disappointment to all honest fighters.'[7]

This picture of disappointment, bitterness, lack of confidence in established leaderships, is not confined to the left alone. It is also, to a considerable extent, the experience of the centre and the right. Thus the most significant political development in present-day Greece is the continuous political reorientation of the population – a reorientation that began almost immediately after the *coup*. The Greeks are now taking stock of what existed before and trying to discover what was particularly unhealthy in the country's political life which enabled a tiny group of military conspirators, together with their foreign instigators, to take over the country so quickly and easily and to neutralize the masses so easily. In this search for something sounder and stronger which will not allow the reappearance of dictatorships, Greeks are looking for political movements which can express more closely their new orientations. In this respect, the old political formations – the rightist National Radical Union (ERE), the liberal-socialist Centre Union, and the communist United Democratic Left – are unlikely to reappear as forces representing the same strata and alliances of social groups that they represented before the *coup*. There is no doubt that with this reorientation the whole Greek political spectrum has significantly shifted to the left.

The impact of this process of political reorientation has brought the

development of new movements within and between the political formations of the past. The communists, i.e. the traditional Greek left, are now
grouping themselves around three movements. The pro-Moscow Greek
Communist Party (KKE, known also as the Koliyannis group from the
name of its Secretary General) is based in Eastern Europe and supported
financially and morally by the Soviet party. The second group, which is
called the Greek Communist Party of the Interior, was formed by old
KKE leaders who disagreed with the Koliyannis policy and who wanted
to pursue a more independent line. This group is based in Rome and its
General Secretary is B. Drakopoulos, although the best-known figure
associated with the KKE of the Interior is Mikis Theodorakis, the composer. It is very difficult to pinpoint exactly the causes of the split between
the leading cadres of the Greek Communist party. Formally this split
was finalized in the 12th plenary session of the KKE which took place in
February 1968. The disagreement developed, strangely enough, in the
second part of the meeting devoted to 'internal party affairs', whereas no
disagreement had manifested itself in the first part when ideological and
policy planning questions were being examined. But during the discussion on internal party affairs it became apparent that Koliyannis – like
every general after a defeat – was looking for scapegoats who could then
be held responsible for the ineffectiveness of the party mechanism inside
Greeec. Three members of the party Politburo, who realized that they
were to be singled out as victims, seized the party's radio station and
declared that the Koliyannis group was using unorthodox methods in
running the party's internal affairs.[8] One day later the remaining members
of the Politburo dismissed the three 'rebels' from the party. These three
members, with the collaboration of party cadres from inside Greece –
who had not in fact been invited to the 12th plenary session, thus making
its legitimacy questionable for many KKE followers – subsequently formed
the second group referred to above – the KKE of the Interior.

The third group that developed in the area of the traditional Greek
left, unlike the previous two, does not possess any formal party structure
and is thus nebulous both in form and ideology; it is in fact a movement
in flux. This movement is usually known by the name 'Chaos', and one
of the former leading KKE figures who can be described as belonging to
it is Manolis Glezos – a hero of the anti-Nazi resistance. But the movement
of 'Chaos' began to develop inside Greece in the Partheni camp in Leros
among communist cadres there. They considered that both factions into
which the Politburo was split after February 1968 were responsible for
the fate of the left in Greece. Those who follow this movement believe

that the traditional forms of political organization in the communist movement are obsolete, and, moreover, that because of the disintegration of the class struggle at the international level into power-bloc politics the only way to further working-class interests in Greece is the formation of a broadly based progressive movement. For the same reason they question the advisability of resistance against the Colonels ('it would mean a confrontation with the United States ultimately') and advocate any solution which would bring an end to the present system of the military-police state.[9] It is very difficult to estimate the relative strength of each of these groups. If we accept, however, that there is a process of political re-orientation taking place, then the political bases of both the pro-Moscow KKE and the KKE of the Interior ought to be shrinking, for both are closely linked with the party's past policies. It is also worth noting that today the Greek communists do not find it expedient to use the cover name of EDA to hide the activities of their party. The reasons that forced them to do so – and I do not mean the legal prohibition of the party – no longer exist.

The Centre Union used to house together two basic groups: liberals and socialists.[10] In Greece, because of the civil war and the fervent anti-communist propaganda pursued by the right-wing governments of the past, the word socialism was purposely interpreted by the police and the right-wing press as equalling communism. As a result of this, the Greek socialists found it expedient in the 1960s to call themselves centre-left, and the Greek word for it, *kentroaristera*, came to be synonymous with the Greek socialist movement. The ideological division between centre-right and centre-left which existed in the old Centre Union party, and manifested itself so openly during the events of July 1965, remains today. But the most significant development within the Centre Union party is the enormous strengthening of the centre-left since the *coup*. Because of the continuous weakening of the centre-right, the major spokesmen of this group (George Mavros, John Zighdis and others) are now paving the way for an alliance with the progressive wing of the ERE party which groups around its pre-*coup* leader, Panayotis Kanellopoulos. It is even conceivable that these two groups may join forces in the foreseeable future. This rapprochement between these two wings of ERE and the Centre Union has also been influenced by pressure on both sides from European conservative and social democratic statesmen, who insist that without a 'viable' alternative acceptable to the United States, any effort on their part to work for a change in American policy towards the regime would be doomed to failure. The movement towards the development of a common platform between the centre-right and the progressive wing of the conservatives started with a common statement issued two years after the *coup* (July 1969) and signed by Panayotis Kanellopoulos and the leading figure of the centre-right, George Mavros. Perhaps because the statement was too general, and because the signature of Mavros was not sufficient for all groups within the centre-right, the whole affair had little impact either inside or outside Greece. It is fair to say that Kanellopoulos tried, before taking any initiative to collaborate with the centre, to bring in the centre-left as well. He sent the former ERE deputy E. Kefaloyannis to England to meet Andreas Papandreou, who at that time was attending the Socialist International Conference at Eastbourne (in June 1969). Papandreou, although not putting any obstacles in the way of this rapprochement, felt that in view of the nature of the agreement he could not, as head of a resistance organization, be part of it.

A more serious attempt by these two groups to present a common platform was made in March 1971, on the eve of the initiatives that were about to be taken by the US Congress on the question of military aid to Greece. A much stronger statement was signed by the two persons mentioned above, but also by another leading figure of the centre party, John Zighdis (who was serving a four-and-a-half year prison sentence because of a declaration on Cyprus he had made a year earlier), and by Dimitrios Papaspyrou, the former Speaker of the Greek Parliament and the leading personality in the group of centre dissidents. A further clarification of the intentions of this four-man leadership was made in a later statement that they issued on 10 July 1971 on the occasion of the first Congress decision on discontinuing military aid to the regime. The main point of this was the strong reiteration of the adherence of the four men 'to the democratic principles that inspired the decision of Greece to enter the defence organization of NATO and share the responsibility with the other members of the alliance for the maintenance of peace'. It thus became obvious that the aim of this initiative was to show the existence of a 'viable' alternative. In a hasty manoeuvre Papadopoulos attempted to show the lack of any appreciable strength in this alliance by starting his 'dialogue' with former deputies of both parties who defied the party line. The small number of deputies who accepted the invitations made Papadopoulos' effort look ridiculous. Much more important, however, is the fact that, despite the creation of the much-demanded 'viable' alternative, no evidence has been produced of a willingness for change in policy by the US administration. On the contrary, the dispatch to Athens of

Vice-President Spiro Agnew was calculated to thwart any further efforts to intensify the opposition to the junta in conservative circles. Apart, however, from the moves by former parliamentarians to present a unified group of the former centre-right and of the progressive wing of the ERE party, outside the circle of former politicians movements are taking place among professionals and intellectuals which are indicative of the future trends in this area of the Greek political spectrum. The formation of the 'Society for the Study of Greek Problems' by professional people and intellectuals belonging to this part of the spectrum is a movement in the direction mentioned above. But among broad strata of the population it is the centre-left which is probably gaining most in strength. Its pre-*coup* attitudes – giving emphasis to the danger of a dictatorship and warning the party to take measures to meet the eventuality of a dictatorship – now permit its leaders easily to shift the burden of the defeat away from their own shoulders. The disillusion that has developed also in the communist camp, the inevitable splits, the bitterness arising from revelations about the mistakes of the past, and the present policy of the Eastern bloc toward the Colonels, all these make the centre-left a pole of attraction for many of the dissatisfied followers of the communist movement. To what extent this will continue in the future depends very much on the ability of the centre-left to develop a robust and effective liberation movement. The charismatic leadership of Andreas Papandreou is, of course, an asset for the centre-left; but his leadership has not gone without challenge from within the ranks of the movement, and especially from the leading figures of the resistance organization 'Democratic Defence'. But, despite these challenges, Papandreou has managed – mainly as a result of his uncompromising stand – to maintain his leading position within the movement.

On the right, the following movements have now developed. The first movement is very eloquently expressed by the leader of ERE before the *coup*, Kanellopoulos, and represents a position of total refusal to recognize the regime or to compromise with it. The second tendency within the Greek right started almost as a one-man campaign by the former Foreign Affairs Minister in the Karamanlis government, Evanghelos Averoff, but has by now acquired more importance. According to the views of this group, former politicians should recognize the necessity of the 'Revolution of 21 April', should accept the legitimacy of the regime by endorsing the 1968 Constitution and recognize George Papadopoulos as a well-intentioned leader and co-operate with him. They believe that Papadopoulos will lift martial law and lead the country to some kind of elections on the basis of the junta's constitution in which the former ERE deputies will be welcome to participate. Finally, the third tendency within the anti-junta right has developed since 1969 mainly through the leading articles that have appeared in a right-wing newspaper *Vradyni*, whose editor is closely associated with the founder of the ERE party, Karamanlis. The aim of this group – put in a crude form – is to split the junta by supporting the opponents of Papadopoulos inside the revolutionary council. This group, like the second, recognizes the legitimacy of the so-called Revolution and accepts the 1968 Constitution.

It should be noted that the policy advocated by the second of these groups is also accepted by a handful of former Centre Union MPs. During the summer of 1971, a number of the MPs of the ERE party (joined by four Centre Union deputies) started what they termed a 'dialogue' with the dictator by holding individual meetings with Papadopoulos. The whole basis of this group's approach was badly shaken, however, when the junta leader refused to include any of these MPs in the government following the reshuffle that took place in August 1971.

The above three tendencies refer of course to what may be described in very broad (although to some extent misleading) terms as the anti-junta right. But many ERE members supported the Colonels. George Papadopoulos himself, it should be remembered, was a known ERE supporter. He was vigorously defended in 1964 by the pro-ERE press when George Papandreou tried unsuccessfully to dismiss him from the army, because of the report that he masterminded alleged sabotage in an army tank division that he commanded. There is no way to estimate how the loyalties of the right wing were split at the time of the *coup* and to show how many right-wingers backed the Colonels (either as 'saviours' as they saw themselves, or as a 'necessary evil') during the first few months after the *coup*, and how many remained loyal to their leader, Kanellopoulos, who was the Prime Minister actually deposed by the junta. The proportion at that time was most likely significant. The King publicly had appeared to accept the Colonels, and what was good enough for the King was good enough for most conservatives. It was also believed that the *coup* had been supported by the entire Armed Forces – a cow sacred enough for any right-winger. In addition, many believed that the *coup* was necessary to forestall the electoral victory of the Centre Union party which – according to what ERE supporters were led to believe by their party propagandists – was in some kind of secret agreement with the communists.

Less than a year later many of these assumptions, upon which a number of right-wingers were prepared to accept the regime, were proved to be erroneous. There had been no proof produced of the greatly advertised 'red peril': not a shred of evidence was produced to substantiate the view that the communists had been engaged in unlawful, let alone dangerous, activities. The Armed Forces had been progressively purged even before the King's counter-*coup* in December 1967. After the counter-*coup* many more officers who sided with the King were dismissed. More than 1,500 officers were summarily retired. It also became slowly established that the Navy – as well as the Air Force – were not siding with the Papado-poulos junta. As early as August 1967 reports appeared in the foreign press[11] that a purge of more than sixty high-ranking naval officers was ordered because of the Navy's growing opposition to the military regime. Later, in 1968, a group of naval NCOs was accused of plotting sabotage in the Navy. Finally, it became increasingly clear that the military dictators regarded themselves as anything but temporary: the Colonels had wanted power and they had no intention of letting it go. The realization of all this caused many of the ERE supporters, who had been prepared initially to side with the regime, to look at it with growing hostility; those who were left to support the Colonels were those who did not care a straw for human rights, or even common decency, provided that there was a 'strong government' to prohibit strikes, etc. Given this analysis of the political reorientation of the former supporters of the right-wing party, and given the electoral results of 1964, and also making allowance for the fact that one can find in all parties people with no convictions at all, who can be bought off by a favour or an appointment, it is unlikely that the total number of junta supporters from all parties has ever been more than a very small percentage, which would in fact be counted on the fingers of both hands.

The developments described above are taking place inside Greece. Apart from these movements and tendencies which have evolved inside the country, the climate of political reorientation that developed after the *coup* also led to the formation of various groups of a political nature among Greeks living abroad. These groups remain small and without true counterparts inside the country. For this reason they seem to be more a byproduct of the psychological strains and the loss of orientation developing in exile than genuine expressions of the search for new ideas and programmes. A few of these groups are: 'Anexartiti Aristera' (Independent Left – based in Italy), 'Revolutionary Socialist Groups' (based in Paris and London), 'Revolutionary Greek Communist Party' (based in Germany), 'International Greek Workers Movement' (Trotskyite – based in London and Germany). These are just a few of the groups that sprang up in the climate of exile. It must also be noted that of all the movements with a real existence inside Greece, only the centre-left and the two organized groups of the traditional left have set up organizations abroad after the *coup*. The major branches of these organizations are naturally to be found in West Germany, where more than 300,000 Greek workers now live.

It has been demonstrated above that popular support for the regime is, for practical purposes, almost non-existent. Many Greeks are resentful of the regime's suppression of freedom and violation of basic human rights. Others, who tolerated the regime at the beginning, are now critical of the regime's inability to cope with the country's basic problems. The lack of any political programme and the low quality of the junta's collaborators are evidence enough that the regime cannot claim to lead the country towards modernization.

Support from the regime emanates not from the public at large, but from other quarters. There are three major sources of its support.

The first is the Army, which forms the regime's only safe 'constituency'.[12] The main support here comes from the younger officers, the colonels, the majors and the captains. In contrast to the generals, who always aspired to become members of the various palace cliques, these younger officers are very critical of the Monarchy's involvement in the running of the affairs of the armed forces. This critical stand towards the Monarchy stems from a number of reasons. Having tasted for themselves the fruits of power, the officers of the 'Revolution of 21 April' naturally do not want the palace cliques to come back again and interfere with the procedure of promotions in the Army. There is also a fear that the politicians of the old right-wing establishment would inevitably come back with the King and would challenge the junta's claim to represent the 'nationalist Greeks'. The anti-monarchism of the junta would disappear if the King would give assurances to dispel these fears.

The economic and financial oligarchy of the country constitutes the second basis of support for the regime. This group has been tremendously revitalized by the establishment in Greece of a number of monopolistic concerns, following the measures initiated long before the regime came to power (but highly accelerated after April 1967) to attract foreign capital. Papas and Pechiney are symbols of this revitalization of the country's economic oligarchy. Tom Papas was the first to praise the regime publicly in the United States. The Greek shipowners have provided much of the financial backing needed by the Colonels in exchange for lucrative concessions ranging from tax exemptions to outright violations of the International Maritime Convention.[13]

The third and most important power basis of the regime, however, is the government of the United States, which supplies moral, military and economic support to the regime. The reasons for this support have been convincingly given by many experts in Greek affairs and were very aptly summarized by the present (1971) Deputy Assistant Secretary of State for Near Eastern Affairs Rodger Davies in testimony before a committee of the Congress in the summer of 1969. 'I think,' said Mr Davies, 'the fact that our ships can put into Greek ports is extremely important. At the present time, we have no other area in the Eastern Mediterranean where our Sixth Fleet ships freely could put into port.' The present-day policy-makers in the United States look on Greece essentially as a part of American military real estate in Europe.[14] This military real estate is managed by the national security managers in the United States – a military caste whose aims – as those of any modern military caste – are essentially expansionist. For them, management of national security in the world of modern military technology requires control over foreign policy. And with the conflict of the two super-powers for world domination this essentially means the consolidation of their system of influence. For the military caste running the US Defense Department, assertion of national independence by small nations and their demand for an equal voice within the alliance systems, is considered subversive arrogance which has to be eliminated. The Colonels have proved completely docile: they never raised any problem concerning the use of bases and they even agreed, in the course of Secretary Laird's visit to Athens in October 1970, to the establishment of a nuclear submarine base in the Western Peloponnese.[15]

Yet, despite the lack of popular support for the regime, there has not been active popular opposition to it. In a state of affairs where normal parliamentary opposition is not allowed to function, disapproval of the government can manifest either as (a) silent discontent, (b) passive resistance (go-slows by civil servants and the like), (c) active non-violent resistance such as writing slogans on walls, distribution of leaflets, etc., or (d) active violent resistance (bomb-throwing, political assassinations and guerrilla warfare). Sometimes the lack of widespread active violent resistance is mistaken for apathy by foreign observers. 'Apathy even more resoundingly than order reigns in Athens,' wrote Sam White in the London *Evening Standard* after a visit to Greece in the summer of 1971. 'To someone like myself,' he continued, 'who has not been in Greece since the Colonels took over more than four years ago, this apparent docility – or possibly more accurately resignation – comes as something of a shock. One recalls the general strikes in Athens and Salonica and the massive demonstrations just before the Colonels' *coup*, and by contrast the Greece of today resembles a nation of sleepwalkers.'[16] However, it would be a mistake to describe the state of affairs prevailing in Greece today as apathetic. When a country is under martial law and the government knows no limits to its power; when citizen's rights are not guaranteed because the government itself is not prepared to respect its own Constitution; when the judiciary has been purged of all 'unsound' judges and magistrates; when all local government bodies, trade unions and a host of professional organizations and farmers' co-operatives are run by government appointees; when any man can be deprived of his personal freedom, his job or his passport by means of an administrative decision – then it would be surprising not to encounter this silence and apparent resignation. No shopkeeper can refuse to adorn his premises with the portrait of Big Brother when strongly advised to do so by the police, and no one can afford, in a small town or a village where everyone knows everyone else, not to join the 'cheering crowds' assembled to welcome a member of the government or the junta. The larger the town, the less inclined are the Colonels to hold big meetings. There have been hardly any in Athens itself, and for good reason. When occasion has permitted, and the tiny loopholes of the martial law have been open to exploitation, the people of Greece have shown their true feelings in an unmistakable way. Thus any book, film, play or public lecture which has – or is thought to have – some anti-dictatorial content is assured of immediate success. This can be demonstrated in a more convincing manner in the case of the press. Ever since preventive censorship was lifted and the anti-regime newspapers managed to convey – in the usual cautious way – their opposition to the junta, their sales have soared enormously. A comparative study of the sales of daily newspapers during the brief 'thaw' between the lifting of the preventive censorship and the closing down of the newspaper *Ethnos* shows that the sales of the pro-junta dailies hardly ever exceeded 10% of the total, despite the fact that in the countryside, where police control is tightest, many people dare not buy anti-regime newspapers (see Chapter Four). Another sign of the population's feelings has been the unprecedented audience for foreign broadcasts from London, Paris, Cologne and Moscow – particularly during the period of the preventive censorship.

But all these manifestations of popular opposition to the dictatorship fade away before the events of 3 November 1968. On that day, at the funeral of the Centre Union leader George Papandreou, there was a spontaneous mass demonstration for democracy such as the Greek capital has rarely seen. In defiance of martial law a crowd of between 300,000 to 500,000 people occupied the centre of the city for hours, crying 'Long live freedom', 'We want elections', 'The Army to the barracks' and 'To-day we vote'. This last remark referred to the junta's referendum which had taken place five weeks earlier and had produced a 92% vote in favour of the Colonels' Constitution. This opportunity of expressing popular feeling turned out to cost the temporary loss of freedom for about forty men and women who were arrested at random for participation in the demonstration, court-martialled and imprisoned. A similar manifestation – although of smaller size – took place in September 1971 during the funeral of Greece's famous poet and Nobel prize winner George Seferis. The reduced size of the crowd (about 100,000 strong) should not be interpreted as a sign of increasing apathy, for George Seferis had never been a political activist and thus was relatively unknown to the common people of his country.

Nor is it true, although hostility and opposition manifest themselves in many ways in the large urban areas, that apathy and resignation (or even approval) are prevalent in the countryside among the peasants. Apart from the well known difficulties of political organization of the peasantry, one has to understand the attitudes of the Greek peasants as they have been shaped by many years of oppression from the capital, from Athens. Especially during the period following the civil war, the Greek peasants lived under constant police and army control, with the possible exception of the eighteen-month period of the Papandreou government. An American anthropologist, studying Greek peasant communities several years ago, accurately captured the mood of the Greek peasantry when he wrote that a basic fact in the Greek countryside is 'the peasant's chronic tendency to assume that he is not getting a square deal, or everything that is due to him because throughout his memory or that of his forebears he has been used to what he considers exploitation by a government or those from the city who would take advantage of him. No aid programme can ever create a contented peasantry.'[17] It is useful to bear this anthro-pologist's description of Greek peasant attitudes in mind before we derive any conclusion concerning their stand toward the Colonels' regime.

So much then for the lack of passive resistance or the apparent apathy. But the significance of active resistance, even in its violent form, should not be underestimated either. Resistance has not yet reached the stage of guerilla warfare, but bomb-throwing has now become so widespread that hardly a week passes by without a bomb explosion somewhere in Athens. This, for example, was the situation in Greece during the first fortnight of July 1971, according to news agency dispatches from Athens:

'3 July: bus belonging to a US communication centre is bombed and destroyed in Crete. 6 July: a bomb exploded and seriously damaged the entrance of the Ministry of Public Order, Athens. 9 July: a bomb goes off on the tracks of the Athens–Piraeus subway (owned by the staunch supporter of the junta, Andreadis). On the same day three oil trucks belonging to the Esso–Papas Co. are hit and destroyed outside the company garage.' What happened during this fortnight is fairly typical of the frequency of bomb blasts as well as of the targets selected. The reason that not much is said about this sign of instability in the Colonels' regime is obviously due to the fact that the resistance has tried so carefully to avoid human casualties.

There exists, however, a problem whose importance must not be underestimated. Although there have been many attempts to organize resistance on a broad basis, the resistance organizations have not yet managed to persuade the masses to join their ranks. The resistance has not yet been successful in attracting people to its support. This problem will be discussed later after a brief sketch of the history of the resistance movement in Greece since 1967.

It is obvious that a fight against a dictatorship requires a different form of organizational apparatus than the kind required to contest elections in a parliamentary democracy. Realizing this, the Greeks have set up, very often spontaneously, their resistance organizations, hundreds of whose members now languish in the Colonels' prisons. It is very difficult to estimate the precise number of these prisoners – all genuinely political prisoners. The estimates given are often based on the cases that have appeared before the Athens or Thessaloniki military courts. Statistics now available in the *Greek Statistical Yearbook* (1969) show that the number of those in prison for political 'crimes' may exceed 3,000. The number of those condemned for violation of the martial law legislation is, according to the same source,[18] as follows: 1967, 4,567; 1968, 3,286.

The efforts to organize resistance to the regime started almost immediately after the *coup*. Despite the inability of the organized pre-*coup* parties to stage a campaign of non-co-operation in the crucial stages of the first few days after the putsch, a number of people associated with the youth movements of the centre and the left (EDIN and 'Lambrakis Youth' respectively), as well as with groups of intellectuals of radical or left tendencies, started exchanging views under the most difficult of circumstances (meetings of more than five people being prohibited by martial law) about the prospects of organizing resistance against the military junta.

As early as the beginning of July 1967, foreign press reporters in Athens were dispatching news about the wide circulation of underground leaflets and newspapers.[19] Towards the end of July 1967, the first major trial of a resistance group calling itself the Greek Democratic Movement of Resistance (EDKA), led by the centre-left deputy Katsikopoulos, the former head of the political office of Andreas G. Papandreou, A. Livanis, and the former head of the Greek Radio, A. Peponis, took place in the special military court of Athens. This organization – composed mainly of followers of the centre-left – had distributed leaflets in the Athens area repeatedly since April 1967 and had set up a small printing network. All the defendants were given heavy sentences. In the summer of 1967 two other trials took place in the island of Crete. In the first trial, a group of democrats from Iraklion were imprisoned for long periods because they attempted to stage a demonstration on the day of the *coup*. This was in fact the only reported instance of an immediate, spontaneous response to the *coup*. In the second trial, a group of left-wingers from Canea were accused and subsequently sentenced for illegally printing and distributing anti-regime leaflets.

A certain fragmentation of the resistance effort became apparent from the first days of the movement. The mistrust of the old structures of organized political activity led various groups of people to experiment with what they considered more appropriate forms of organization. Sometimes the hope that the regime was going to fall soon, through international isolation, led people on the one hand to believe that co-operation with communists or communist sympathizers would jeopardize the chances for a successful Western boycott of the regime, and on the other hand to maintain their identity in small groups whose contribution to the resistance effort could become more easily traceable. Whatever the true reasons were, the fact remains that the centre-left was already split in the first months after the *coup* into two major groups: the group of former party activists and youth leaders, and the group of radical intellectuals and professional people. Most of the active leaders of the EDIN youth movement, as well as the cadres of the Centre Union party loyal to the leadership of Andreas Papandreou, grouped initially under EDKA (see above) and later, after the arrest of a number of them and the dissolution of the organization, into the Democratic Greek Resistance Movement (DEKA). This group was also disbanded very quickly when, in October 1967, a cache of arms and radio equipment was discovered in the house of the brother of Papandreou's lawyer in the Aspida affair, the retired gendarmerie officer Koutsoyiorghas. However, the amnesty that the regime was forced to grant under international pressure in December 1967 led to the release of most of these people from prison. Many of them seemed to have participated later as leading cadres in the Panhellenic Liberation Movement (PAK) which was set up by Andreas Papandreou, after his release from prison and his exile abroad in 1968, or in other groups closely working with PAK, such as the Hellenic Resistance, which with the help of Alexander Panagoulis organized the unsuccessful assassination attempt against Papadopoulos in August 1968; the Democratic Union (later renamed Greek Democratic Resistance) which accepted responsibility for a series of explosions that took place in Athens late in the summer of 1969; and the Liberation Commandos, who made a late but spectacular start by placing a bomb inside the American Embassy in Athens at the time of the arrival of the new ambassador in early 1970, and by exploding a bomb near the Prime Minister's office at the time of his discussions with US Defense Secretary Melvin Laird in October 1970. By the beginning of 1971, most of these people had been re-arrested, together with a group of prominent Greeks such as the former examining magistrate in the Lambrakis affair, Christos Sartzetakis, Dimitrios Maronitis, Professor of Classical literature in the University of Thessaloniki, and others following a big wave of arrests by the Military Police between November 1970 and March 1971. The explosion at the time of Laird's visit and the arrest of lawyer Koronaios, linked with another explosion that damaged the Truman statue in Athens, led to an almost unprecedented wave of arrests by the security authorities, which is all the more unusual since none of those held had yet been brought to trial (October 1971). Two centre-left MPs, J. Alevras and T. Kefallinos, were also implicated in this affair by the police.

The nucleus of the group of intellectuals of the centre-left who opted for the establishment of a separate resistance organization under a leadership other than that of Andreas Papandreou, came basically from the Alexandros Papanastassiou Club – a kind of Fabian Society, essentially an elitist movement, which was established slightly more than a year before the *coup*, with the aim of contributing constructively to the debate and of participating actively in the effort to accelerate Greece's political, social and economic development. Their group was finally named

Democratic Defence, and Vassilis Filias, the chairman of the Papanastassiou Club, was subsequently described as the leader of the organization.
Democratic Defence circulated its first manifesto in August 1967, and in
October of the same year it circulated inside Greece its first eight-page
newspaper, which was printed in London and smuggled in bulk quantities
for distribution within Greece.[20] The newspaper and various leaflets were
continuously distributed in Athens and Thessaloniki despite the fact that
by the autumn of 1967 several alleged leading figures of the organization
had been arrested in Athens and Thessaloniki (Notaras, Zannas, Protopapas, Pyrzas, Nestor and others), and Filias had gone underground, until
his arrest in the middle of 1968. But the big blow to the resistance network
of the Democratic Defence came in July 1969 when a bomb accidentally
exploded in the hands of Professor Karayiorgas in his home outside
Athens. The discovery of a cache of bombs, allegedly brought into Greece
from Sweden, was immediately linked to the series of explosions that
were rocking Athens in the spring and early summer of 1969, and led to
the arrest of a large number of people. A few escaped abroad. But the
rest were tortured in a brutal, medieval manner, and 34 were finally
brought to trial in April 1970 (a 35th died during the trial). The great
display of courage by the defendants, and especially by Professor
Karayiorgas, Professor Mangakis and Kharalambos Protopapas, created
an atmosphere of tension in Greece throughout the spring of 1970.

Intellectuals and former youth leaders associated with EDA started,
almost from the day of the *coup*, their efforts to form the broadly based
Patriotic Front (PAM) to organize resistance against the regime. The moving force behind the attempt to organize PAM was Greece's famous
composer, Mikis Theodorakis, who escaped arrest and went underground
until his capture in September 1967. Apart from leaflets and slogan
painting, the group often used concealed loudspeakers to boom out
anti-regime slogans, and they have regularly printed and circulated inside
Greece since May 1967 their underground newspaper *Nea Ellada*. The
first trial of Patriotic Front members took place in November 1967, and
showed that at that time the Front was in fact broadly based. Prominent
among the defendants were two leading personalities of the centre-left,
Mr Loulis, the MP from Volos, and Sylva Akrita, the wife of the Minister
of Education in the Papandreou government and herself a parliamentary
candidate in the elections scheduled for May 1967.

Many trials, involving hundreds of members of the Patriotic Front,
took place in subsequent years in Athens, Thessaloniki, Patras, Larissa and
other towns, but the broad political image that the trial of November

1967 conveyed does not seem to have been maintained. The development of active resistance organizations of the centre-left and the splits in the communist camp led to a narrowing of the base of the Patriotic Front. In fact, after the split in the Greek Communist Party, a second Patriotic Front under a Central Committee (the first Patriotic Front is run by a National Council) was set up by the pro-Moscow Koliyannis group. Trials of members of this second group of PAM also took place in July 1970 and July 1971. The most important ones involved members of the Eastern Europe based Central Committee of the KKE, including Nikolaos Kaloudis and Zenon Zorzovilis, who were sent illegally into Greece to organize resistance cells. Despite the narrowing of its base, the Patriotic Front associated with the anti-Koliyannis group of the KKE intensified its resistance effort, with the formation of a sabotage group (Group Aris) which tried unsuccessfully to damage the American Embassy in Athens in September 1970 with a powerful bomb. The bomb went off before it was placed in the building and two young people lost their lives in the attempt. A further 31 alleged members of PAM were arrested in November 1971 including two members of the KKE (Interior).

The National Council of the Patriotic Front set up, towards the end of 1967, a youth branch – active mainly among University students – named after the hero of the struggle for Greek Independence, Rigas Ferraios. The group prints a mimeographed paper, *Thourios*. The student divisions of the Athens police and the Thessaloniki gendarmerie have tried desperately to stop the spread of this organization among university students. More than a hundred students, most of them former members of the Lambrakis youth movement, have been arrested, severely tortured and heavily sentenced. Their University Senates were pressured into expelling them so that they are left without any prospect of obtaining their degrees. Long after the outcry that followed the publication of the report of the Human Rights Commission of the Council of Europe, students – members of the Rigas Ferraios group – while being tried by a special military court in Athens in August 1971 revealed the inhuman treatment they had received under interrogation by the security police. They gave evidence once more that the use of torture is systematic government policy.

The attempt to maintain Rigas Ferraios as a broadly based student movement, coupled with the disillusionment prevalent among young people as a result of the splits in the left, led eventually to the increasing autonomy of this organization *vis-à-vis* the National Council of PAM. Indeed, when towards the end of 1970, the National Council of PAM decided to form an alliance with certain underground groups of royalist-conservative tendencies, Rigas Ferraios strongly criticized them for the concessions they made in their effort to arrive at a minimum programme. Apart from its strong links with the student resistance organization Rigas Ferraios, PAM also maintains an underground Trade Union group, the Anti-dictatorship Workers' Front (AEM). PAM also tried – without much visible success – to create a peasants' resistance organization, the Anti-dictatorship Peasants' Front of the Countryside (AAMY). A group of people were tried for alleged participation in this organization in July 1970.

Outside Athens and Thessaloniki the most important resistance organization is the Democratic Resistance of Crete. It operates as an autonomous group *vis-à-vis* the others and has shown its presence almost constantly throughout the years of the dictatorship. It groups together many movements of the centre and a few sections of the left. A large cell of this organization operating under the alleged leadership of the former EDIN youth leader, Foivos Ioannidis, was broken up in November 1967, and a considerable quantity of explosives and weapons was confiscated. Leaflets are circulated from time to time, as for example on the occasion of the visit of Spiro Agnew to the island (October 1971), and bombs have also been planted on a number of occasions, as, for instance, in cars belonging to the American base at Iraklion (July 1971).

The right wing in Greece tried to organize some form of resistance a few months after the collapse of the King's counter-*coup* in December 1967. Up to that time all leading figures of the right (excluding of course those like Pipinelis who collaborated outright with the junta) were preoccupied with the organization of the royal counter-*coup* rather than with resistance. A royal counter-*coup* would have made the King and his close collaborators on the right absolute masters of the situation, without having to accommodate themselves with the radicals of the right or of the left. Realizing what was in preparation, the Colonels became very hostile to a number of the leading ERE politicians, and in fact they tried in July 1967 to imprison first Evanghelos Averoff and then George Rallis for alleged violations of the existing martial law. In a letter to the King, the leader of ERE, Kanellopoulos, encouraged him to move against Papadopoulos and his junta. The old leader of the Centre Union, Papandreou, and a number of the leading MPs of his party were also persuaded to approve of the King's planned action and addressed similar letters to him. After the King had failed (being outmanoeuvred by Papadopoulos[21]) a number of cashiered officers formed a rightist resistance group, the Free Greeks. The Free Greeks started publishing their mimeographed newspaper at the end of 1968 and collaborated with Democratic Defence in manufacturing and planting bombs in Athens in the spring of 1969. Late in May 1969 almost the whole network of this organization of about 50 retired officers (including by then a few civilians and a few former officers known for their centrist sympathies) was broken up by the military police, and its alleged members were banished to remote islands or mountain villages. All of them were freed when martial law was partially lifted in December 1971. An offshoot of this organization (which was started abroad under the alleged leadership of the former colonel and former classmate of Papadopuolos in the Army Cadet College, D. Opropoulos) is called 'Defenders of Freedom'. A trial in the summer of 1970 revealed the existence of another small rightist underground group calling itself 'Defenders of the King and the Nation'. A leading defendant in the trial was N. Doulger who, as he himself revealed, had been an agent of the political police since the years of the Karamanlis government. The King's counter-*coup* certainly created many splits in the main body of traditional right-wing supporters.

Apart from the traditional political formations one can find other organized resistance groups. Indeed, after the severe losses inflicted on the resistance movement through several waves of mass arrests of members of broadly based organizations, a tendency has developed for the formation of small, flexible groups using their own particular names. Such groups possess certain advantages in security and flexibility, and can easily confuse the police. It is very difficult in such cases to identify the political orientation of the group, if the group itself does not reveal it through a statement or a declaration. One group of this type is EMA (Greek Fighting Resistance). Other groups, however, have made their identity public, and most of them are groups of the radical left. Prominent among these groups is the 'Movement of 20 October', which was founded towards the end of 1969. The movement has accepted responsibility for many bomb explosions in Athens, and circulates an underground paper, *Synergasia*, in Greece. In the past there has been collaboration between the 'Movement of 20 October' and PAK. The 'Movement of 20 October' has managed to acquire the support of prominent European intellectuals of the left, and especially of Jean-Paul Sartre, who in a public declaration in the summer of 1971 personally endorsed the movement. Other groups of the radical left include the 'People's Revolutionary Resistance' which made its appearance in 1971, the 'Struggle of the People' which used to be active in Thessaloniki and had nine of its alleged members, seven of whom were students, brought to trial in Thessaloniki in January 1970; the group of the Greek Marxist–Leninists (pro-Chinese), which publishes the newspaper *Proletarian Flag*, and had five of its alleged Thessaloniki branch members brought to trial in the summer of 1971; the group known from its initials as AAA and the National Anti-Dictatorship Army, three members of which were given long prison sentences in 1970.

The fact that so many resistance organizations exist does not necessarily mean that the resistance movement is terribly fragmented. Co-ordination is achieved by various methods, and often via the cells of the organizations abroad. Many times, in order to confuse the police, a number of organizations purposely use different names on different occasions. Many cases can be cited to corroborate this view, but the recent trial (January 1972) of eight people accused of planting bombs in the centre of Athens between 1969 and 1971 provides evidence for this. Their group, The Commandos of Democracy, under the alleged leadership of Josef Valyrakis, certainly did not operate in isolation, This trial, too, confirmed reports of some of the most brutal aspects of the regime when defendants accused police officers of having tortured them.

Attempts to co-ordinate the efforts of the resistance organizations date from February 1968 when an agreement to exchange information and co-operation in the technical field was signed between PAM and Democratic Defence. In August 1968, after a meeting between the leader of PAK and the then representative of PAM abroad, A. Brillakis, in Rome, the two organizations agreed on many issues relating to the strategy and tactics of the anti-dictatorship struggle and agreed regularly to exchange views and co-operate on resistance matters. This agreement, far-reaching as it then was, created many problems for the leader of PAK, who had to face a considerable protest from the anti-communist group of his supporters. However, events have moved so rapidly that three years later it was these conservative elements of the Centre who advocated closer ties with PAM in the framework of a National Resistance Council. The two separate agreements were followed by an agreement between the three organizations, which envisaged the creation of a number of common organs of action. At the same time inside Greece, as has been stated earlier, co-operation had developed between Democratic Defence and the Free Greeks. The effort to unify the resistance took a new turn with the arrival of Mikis Theodorakis abroad in April 1970. During his first press conference in Paris, the Chairman of the National Council of PAM proposed the creation of a National Council of Resistance on the basis of a minimum programme which he himself outlined in nine points.[22]

The essence of the programme was that only points of agreement in the programmes of the organizations should form the basis of a minimum programme, whereas any points of disagreement should be buried for the moment. This essentially meant that questions like the future of the Monarchy or the future of the country's system of alliances should not be raised by the members of the National Resistance Council. Otherwise there was no possibility of persuading the resistance groups of the right, the Free Greeks, and its offspring, Defenders of Freedom, to join the Council. Theodorakis and his PAM people felt that the participation of these groups was important since this would have brought the group of retired royalist officers closer to the resistance, and they would then provide the expert knowledge that the resistance movement so badly needed. Moreover, the whole idea was in accordance with the traditional policy of the communist movement in Greece who had always advocated, but more emphatically so since the *coup*, the broadest possible alliance of the progressive forces. The objective of the strategy of PAM, as was declared in repeated statements, was not revolution but national unity against the junta and its foreign supporters. This strategy also fits in well with the long-term policy of the KKE which has, since the Civil War, advocated legality in preference to revolution.[23]

Eventually, a National Resistance Council (EAS) was formed (in February 1971) comprising four organizations: the Free Greeks and the Defenders of Freedom on the right, Democratic Defence in the centre, and PAM on the left. PAK would not agree to participate on the basis of a minimum programme which did not provide for the freedom of the Greek people to vote on the question of the Monarchy after the fall of the junta. 'Liberation struggles,' wrote Papandreou to the representatives of the organizations participating in EAS, 'are not waged on the basis of programmes that do not provide a vision about the future to those who are called to fight. Such a vision cannot be found in a minimum programme based on compromises.' The question of the Monarchy has thus become, yet again, a divisive factor in Greek politics. The pre-*coup* polarity between communism and nationalism has now turned into a new polarity between republicanism and monarchy. It is also interesting to note that most of the other organizations which stayed outside EAS, such as Rigas Ferraios, the 'Movement of the 20 October', etc., are basically in agreement with the position taken by PAK although they do not agree in other matters. It is extremely doubtful, however, if this question of the nature of elections to be held after the fall of the junta was in fact the fundamental question that created obstacles to that broad unity of the resistance forces that would have made a significant impact in the whole campaign for Greece's freedom.

At the root of all these difficulties in creating unity there is one basic obstacle: the deep ideological crisis which prevails in all parts of the Greek political spectrum. The entire Greek political process is in a state of flux. Old alignments and coalitions are breaking down and old party loyalties are rapidly disintegrating. No doubt, out of these shattered fragments of the Greek political process a new national consensus will one day be formed. This new national consensus will then be lasting if it is grounded not so much on political manoeuvring as on ideology.

The formation of EAS indicated clearly that there are two streams of thought prevailing among the opposition and resistance forces in Greece. Those in the EAS or close to it believe that it is ultimately possible to remove the junta by forcing a change in the policy of the United States toward the regime. This could be achieved through pressure and persuasion and by offering guarantees that there will be no chaos in Greece after the junta goes. A unity among the Greeks and their resistance organisations would offer that guarantee. This policy, if successful, could also undermine the other source of power of the regime, namely the Armed Forces. The NATO orientation of the Greek Armed Forces means that when the signal is given in Washington, a profound change of attitudes towards the ruling junta could be expected in the Army. The second stream of thought, although it does not challenge the logic of this approach, does not subscribe to its underlying assumptions. According to this second view, the United States has never been interested in the question of the unity of the Greeks. It is interested only in the privileges that it can enjoy for its military and industrial establishment. This the US can do by having a tame and easily manipulated regime. Such a regime, according to this view, is one based on the Armed Forces or supervised by them, since the Greek Army is totally infiltrated by the American military mission in Greece. Thus the maximum that the US will be prepared to concede to the 'united' Greeks will be the promise to press for the implementation of the Constitution of 1968. This Constitution is, according to those adhering to this point of view and to all democratic Greeks, a legal camouflage for the legitimization of the regime. Thus the only way to change the present situation is through a change in the power relationship between the Greek people and their resistance organizations and the United States. Those who emphasize this point finally conclude that the only way the power relationship can change is through the development of a robust liberation movement which has to be modelled along the lines of the liberation movements of the third world. Therefore its ideological orientation will have to be anti-imperialist and anti-NATO. Thus, although the resistance movement began as basically an anti-junta, anti-dictatorship movement, a section of it now adopts a new position by emphasizing the need for a liberation movement, because experience has revealed the true nature of the US policy toward the junta. The organizations that now subscribe to this view (essentially PAK and the various groups of the radical left) further point out that a great liberation struggle calls for vision, and that visions are seldom incorporated in minimum programmes.

These two streams of thought will continue to dominate the thinking of the opposition and the resistance until theorizing is finally replaced by concrete action on a large scale, until, in other words, a substantial qualitative change in the resistance effort takes place. This can happen only when the ranks of the resistance are joined by the masses at large. There are, however, important obstacles which at this stage make this task extremely difficult. The paralysing influence of the deep ideological crisis which has affected all political tendencies has repeatedly been emphasized. This does not mean that it is the only one by any means.

The development of technology gives a modern totalitarian regime a monopoly of effective weapons and of swift communications. It can control all mass media; computers and up-to-date electronic gadgets enable it to keep tabs on the entire population. State interference in economic affairs permit it to exercise an effective economic warfare against its opponents. The development of modern methods of psychological warfare and of 'scientific techniques of interrogation' permit an authoritarian regime to penalize its opponents not simply by putting them in prison but by invoking the threat of torture. The Greek regime has perfected the methods and techniques of torture to an unbelievable extent.[24] And it does not hesitate to let these methods become publicly known despite the international outcry they cause because it wants to make all potential members of the resistance fully aware of what awaits them in the dungeons of the security police. That risk becomes a serious handicap since ordinary men and women consider such a fate out of all proportion to the results that can be hoped for in a struggle against a regime backed by the United States with the tacit connivance of the Eastern bloc.

The Greeks passed through a cruel civil war twenty years ago and, although the younger generation are not so much affected by memories that they never themselves experienced, nevertheless the left especially has been deprived of people with the kind of knowledge useful for a resistance organization. The modern safety valve of the Greek state, namely emigration of the unemployed and underemployed to Western Europe, results in a loss of the young workers and peasants and reduces any economic difficulties with which the regime might have been faced. Finally, this regime consists of members of the intelligence services of the Greek Army and their knowledge has been put to use in perfecting the mechanisms of oppression by improving the methods through which the population can be kept under constant surveillance in a manner similar to that used by Big Brother in Orwell's *1984*.

There is no doubt that under these circumstances it requires immense courage, almost heroic qualities, actively to oppose the regime. And it should be mentioned that resistance activity is not necessarily confined to the framework of the organizations mentioned above. Resistance is often carried out by tiny, secret, closely-knit groups whose activities range from collecting and relaying information about torture to helping opponents escape from the country. The arrest and trial of Lady Fleming, in September 1971, reminded us once more of the existence of these innumerable resistance cells. Assisting the families of prisoners and deportees, who often find themselves in very difficult financial circumstances, is also a clandestine activity involving risks – for the junta's laws forbid it.

Yet despite the torture, despite the control and surveillance of all forms of organized social life, despite the setbacks of the past and the present, despite the climate of demoralizing expectations that the sirens of compromise and bridge-building with the oppressors create, the resistance has constantly shown its presence with the leaflet, with the concealed loudspeaker, with the open defiance of the writer or the poet, or with the bomb. The presence of this resistance, in all of these forms, has kept the Greek problem constantly alive on the international scene and blocked the way to final subjugation of a people who, since their first war for independence in 1821, have constantly struggled for freedom, democracy and social justice. It is indeed amazing that under conditions of such a highly perfected repression so few men have appeared to counsel compromise and submission. Perhaps because the Greek is what Kazantzakis called in the prologue of his *Freedom or Death*, 'a real man'. 'The real man is not discouraged; he knows that in this changeable, dishonest world there exist several basic principles . . . which he had moulded with blood, sweat and tears. And although they dwell in but few hearts, they are immortal. Most of these were born in Greece and two are the noblest: the Freedom and Dignity of Man.'

Reading, October 1971   *George Yannopoulos*

NOTES

1 See Chapter One. For further information the reader should consult Margaret Papandreou, *Nightmare in Athens*, Englewood Cliffs, New Jersey 1970, Chapters 10–14.

2 See the interview given to Sir Hugh Greene by Papadopoulos, *Sunday Telegraph*, 2 August 1970.

3 PAPANDREOU, A. G., *Democracy at Gunpoint: The Greek Front*, London 1971, pp. 15–18.

4 National Union of Greek Students (EFEE), *Greece 1963–1970*, London 1970.

5 See Chapter Three on the regime's ideology.

6 FORREST, W. G., 'Greece: Tyranny without a Future', *The New York Review of Books*, 24 September 1970.

7 *Eleftheri Athina*, the newspaper of the Athens organization of PAM, No. 5, August 1970.

8 For further detail about the events that led to this split see 'To chroniko mias diaspasis' (The chronicle of a split), *Aghonas*, February 1971, No. 2, pp. 126–135.

9 An analysis of the views of 'Chaos' can be found in A. Kranis, 'Merikes apopseis tou Chaous' (Some views of Chaos), *Aghonas*, February 1971, No. 2, pp. 27–40.

10 In social democratic circles in Europe the name of the Social Democratic Union of Greece is often heard. Such a group did exist in Greece, but has never managed to gain representation in parliament. When it contested the election of 1963 its candidates received a few hundred votes only. After April 1967, more than half of the members of this group joined the junta. One of these, G. Voyatzis, became Minister of Labour and subsequently President of the so-called Mini-Parliament. Another, Vyron Stamatopoulos, became press spokesman of the regime in 1968 and in 1971 Under-Secretary for Press and Information. Stamatopoulos used to publish a journal reflecting the views of this group entitled *Diethnis Zoi* (International Life). This journal was well-known for its 'anticommunist' stand.

11 *Guardian*, 14 August 1967.

12 'Thucydides', 'Greek Politics: Myth and Reality', *Political Quarterly*, October–December 1970, pp. 455–466.

13 *Greek Observer*, July 1969, pp. 19–21 and February–March 1970, p. 12.

14 MACRIDIS, R. C., 'On the eve of civil war', *The Nation*, 1 January 1968.

15 *Financial Times*, 5 October 1970.

16 *Evening Standard*, 3 September 1971.

17 SANDERS, I. T., *Rainbow in the Rock: The people of rural Greece*, Cambridge, Mass. 1962, p. 239.

18   National Statistical Service of Greece, *Statistical Yearbook*, 1969, p. 63.
19   *Observer*, 23 July 1967.
20   The publication of this newspaper was made possible through a financial contribution from the Maltese Labour Party.
21   PAPANDREOU, A. G., op. cit., p. 224.
22   *Greek Observer*, April–May 1970, Nos. 13–14.
23   STAVRIANOS, L. S., 'Greece's other history', *The New York Review of Books*, 17 June 1971.
24   See, for instance the four-volume report of the European Commission of Human Rights of the Council of Europe, Strasbourg 1969, and James Becket, *Barbarism in Greece*, New York 1970.

CHAPTER TEN

The Military Regime's Foreign Policy[1]

Until April 1967, Greece had been playing her normal part as one of the smaller states in the Western European–Atlantic orbit. Her economy was developing at a rapid pace, and her political structures were gradually readjusting to the conditions of modern parliamentary democracy prevailing in Western Europe. This readjustment, which covered the years 1950 to 1963, was not without stresses, due to the havoc that war, enemy occupation and civil war had wrought, from 1940 to 1949, on the political, social and economic fabric of the country. However weakened and distorted it may have been by these stresses, some of which originated in 1936 with the Metaxas dictatorship, the democratic parliamentary framework on the whole withstood them. It did not break down even at the most 'militarized' moments of the civil war. From 1963, with the end of the eight-year Karamanlis administration, the country showed signs of setting itself a new course of modernizing and renewing its political structures. By their stand from 1963 onwards, the Greek people showed that, given the leadership they deserved, they could attain political maturity as fast as any other European people. They were ready to claim a new articulation of their political and social structures, which could thus give a healthier long-term frame to the rapidly developing economy.

In these conditions, there was no reason for Greek external policy to diverge from the course generally followed by the Western bloc of opposing communism by a policy of military vigilance and economic improvement. Internal policy conformed in a general way to the principles set out in the preamble of the NATO alliance, as well as in more specific European documents such as the charters of the Council of Europe and of the European Economic Community.

The authenticity and strength of Greece's democratic institutions were generally taken for granted, despite doubts voiced by some earlier members of NATO, who had succeeded in keeping the Spanish dictatorship outside the fold, although Portugal had been admitted – apparently more on the strength of its military assets than of its only relatively anti-totalitarian war record.

Greece's policy inside the NATO alliance (Greece became a member in 1951) and in the international organizations with specific European targets, such as the OECD, of which Greece had been a member since 1948, or the Council of Europe, of which Greece had been a member since 1950, was therefore not very different from the policies of more important members of these organizations, such as France or Britain, and it was conditioned in inverse ratio to its size and economic strength by a military and economic strategy increasingly worked out in Washington.

Beyond defence against communism, economic development, and eventual political integration of Europe, it was possible for Greece to direct special attention to issues which her geographic and historic position in the Mediterranean made more specifically Greek, as distinct from European (and Western). In fact, they became European and Western issues chiefly through Greece's concern with them, and it was in meeting the problems they posed that Greece could offer a positive contribution to the making of Europe.

These specifically Greek issues were: (1) Cyprus. (2) Greece's part in the Middle East conflict, from the perspective of the Arab–Israeli dispute rather than from that of oil supplies. (3) Balkan coexistence.

(1) On Cyprus, the critical nature of the problem, to which a solution of sorts had been given in 1959–1960, had been blunted by the patient course chosen by President-Archbishop Makarios. Navigating cautiously between the siren's call of *Enosis* and the Scylla and Charybdis of partition, he managed to maintain, despite periodic outbreaks of crisis, the island's independence and integrity, as guaranteed chiefly by its membership of the United Nations, and secondarily by specific if double-edged provi-tions of the treaties signed between Greece and Turkey. The call of *Enosis*, heard in recent years more strongly from Athens than from Nicosia, was muted by 1967. The growing pains of political and economic development in Greece, and Cyprus' membership of the Commonwealth, contributed to make the advantages of independence evident to increasing numbers of Cypriots (leaving aside a fringe of fanatics for instant union with Greece and/or Turkey clamouring in the wings), and to relegate union with the mother country to the realm of sentimental national

aspirations whose fulfilment is not always assured, however strongly it may be prayed for.

In Athens, lacking a statesman of the calibre of Makarios, *Enosis* was not a slogan that the politicians could afford to reject unscathed. No one had the political courage of the Cretan Venizelos who early in the century had opposed the unionist moves of his countrymen because he considered them untimely. The Cyprus issue tended, in fact, to become a Helladic more than a Hellenic problem, and one whose perpetuation or solution was not always pursued with the interests of the Cypriots themselves as the main consideration. It also became the main issue in Greek–Turkish relations.

These had gone through a moment of tension in 1963–64 over Cyprus, but had settled to an uneasy calm. The Turks, pressed by the United States to keep the peace, did so reluctantly but grasped the opportunity to extract other insular thorns from their side – Imbros and Tenedos were gradually emptied of their Greek majority population by colonizing the islands with convicts from the mainland jails; the last remnants of the Greek minority in Istanbul, including the Oecumenical Patriarchate, were submitted to ever-growing pressures. Turkey may not have obtained a portion of Cyprus to date, but it has got its pound of flesh inside its own boundaries, while Greece, entangled in the ties of its alliances, was hoping (*a*) that NATO, in the form of the United States, would come to her rescue, and (*b*) that her NATO ally, Turkey, would respect the alliance as Greece was trying to do, and that it would prefer to press its communist neighbours against whom NATO was directed more than its neighbour with whom it was linked by the alliance.

(2) In the Middle East, Greece, without being opposed to Israel (with whom, in fact, its main differences were of a financial or commercial nature), had long followed a course which kept her close to the Arabs. The Greeks had been bound to them not only by the long common experience of subjection to the Turk, but also by the existence for two centuries at least of large and prosperous Greek communities in most of the Arab countries, and by a common religion, Greek Orthodoxy, shared with many Arabs. These communities had, generally speaking, remained in the Arab countries long after the colonial powers and their nationals had been driven out. Greece, with Spain, was the only Mediterranean country which did not recognize Israel *de jure*, and this added to her prestige with the Arabs.

Greece, with her sister state, Cyprus (and with the non-colonialist connections of both with Western Europe) was in a position to play a role in the Arab–Israeli conflict which no other Mediterranean country could play.

(3) In the Balkans, Greece had strengthened her ties with Yugoslavia, and had paved the way for a settlement of all differences outstanding since World War II with Rumania and Bulgaria. The only difference that remained unsolved was with Albania. Northern Epirus, as the Greeks call Southern Albania, was, along with Cyprus, the last vestige of the great irredentist problem whose solution had been the object of Greece's external efforts since she became independent.

The problem of Northern Epirus, dormant before the war when the numerous Greek minority was guaranteed educational and religious autonomy, had become a major issue since 1940, when the Greek army occupied it during the war against Italy. After the war, the resentment at its remaining within Albanian borders[2] was compounded by the fact that Albania had become a communist state. The redemption of Northern Epirus became thus a doubly hallowed mission which no Greek post-war government – made up from the country's conservative forces – dared solve in the only way possible short of war, that of some compromise with Albania that would have ensured the survival of the Greek minority. Consequently, in 1967, Greece remained technically still at war with Albania and their borders were hermetically sealed.

Greece drew much benefit from its close ties with Yugoslavia. At a time when Yugoslav independence was threatened from Moscow, and when Yugoslav relations with Italy and Austria were not friendly, Greece represented a unique and most valuable contact. The services Greece thus rendered were appreciated both by the Yugoslavs and by the West. They came after the Yugoslavs had closed their borders to the Greek communist forces fighting in Northern Greece (1949) and had broken with the Cominform, and helped to re-establish on a firm ground the old Greek–Yugoslav friendship which had withstood many tests through the nineteenth and twentieth centuries.

After the military *coup d'état* of 21 April 1967, the permanent and 'general' issues of external policy (anti-communist alliance with the West, economic and political integration with Europe) naturally remained to be dealt with as part of the routine of Greek diplomacy. The specifically 'Greek' issues remained too (Cyprus and relations with Turkey, relations with the Arabs, Balkan co-existence). Each of them, however, took on a new complexity owing to the nature of the regime forcibly ruling the country.

There were also new problems stemming directly and exclusively from the nature of this regime. There was a general revulsion in the West, and especially in Western Europe, against the establishment of the first totalitarian regime in this area since the war. This revulsion was strong enough to force the governments of Western Europe into demonstrations of immediate disapproval which were expressed in diplomatic démarches or public statements. The regime, which at the outset proclaimed itself a temporary 'parenthesis' in the country's life, was put by Western European countries into a sort of quarantine or, at best, on probation. In this quarantine the Eastern European countries took no part. They recognized and did business with the regime from the first.

The dictatorship soon became generally known as the 'junta', an appropriate term since it denotes an origin in a 'clique or cabal of men who have combined for a common purpose' (*OED*), in fact a group of mutinous officers, deprived of any articulate ideology other than the most simplistic and nationalist slogans. This revulsion began to be expressed in a more manifest way, as the junta's undemocratic and un-European activities, and its objective of permanence became clearer (with martial law maintained, political prisoners and deportees numbering many thousands, accusations of torture, rigorous press censorship, suppression of articles of the Constitution guaranteeing basic human rights such as inviolability of the home, of correspondence, association and meeting, etc.). Certain collective practical steps were taken, particularly in the main European organizations. Greece was indicted before the Council of Europe and, on 12 December 1969, was expelled (the more decorous expression of 'withdrawal' was used by the regime) from the Council after protracted discussion had produced ample evidence of the junta's unsavoury practices.

Meanwhile, the European Economic Community executive had decided to withhold the balance of the development loan due to Greece, and to reduce dealings with the junta to current relations, thus in fact freezing all progress towards full membership which is to be attained by 1984.

In NATO, more than half the member countries (Iceland, Norway, Denmark, Holland, Belgium, Luxembourg, Germany, Italy and Canada) repeatedly and in various sessions of the Council and other organs raised the problem of Greece's participation in the alliance, only to be countered by such pressure by the United States, inside and outside the conference room, that their strongly expressed doubts were watered down to general expressions of concern in the final communiqués. However vague these may have been, they betray a strong malaise inside the Alliance, which is far from having abated. Of the four remaining members of the alliance, it was natural that Portugal and Turkey should stick closely to the United States line; Britain and France, pressed by public opinion, were by no means vocal supporters of the junta. In fact, a clear majority in the alliance was so unfavourably disposed towards it that they agreed at least to discuss certain concrete manifestations of disapproval (refusal to participate in manoeuvres with Greek forces, or to use Greek NATO installations) which were finally not decided upon collectively but applied by some countries individually.

With this increasing alienation from Western Europe, with the organic difficulty for the regime of leaning even more on Eastern Europe, the junta's reliance on the United States became ever more patent and exclusive. Whatever the original involvement, it was a fact that of all the Western Governments, the United States administration from the outset was the least unfavourable to the junta. There was considerable evidence pointing to *post factum* approval and support of the *coup* by American services such as the Pentagon and the CIA working hand in hand.

United States collusion with the dictatorship after its installation appeared a natural and indisputable fact, both to the Greek people as a whole, conditioned in the troubled two years preceding the *coup* by random American interventions in Greek politics by businessmen and covert agents, and to the greater part of foreign public opinion, opposed as it was to United States policy in the Far East. If there were some doubt as to American non-involvement in the actual execution of the *coup*, the attitude of the American services after it had prevailed did nothing to turn this doubt to certainty. The junta, on the other hand, did all it could to stress and underline the close ties it maintained, if not with the United States administration as a whole, at least with these services. The frequent visits of American admirals and generals to Athens, with their lavishly favourable statements, or of some congressmen sponsored by Greek–American organizations whose pro-junta attitude was blatant, cancelled out every time the feeble expressions of disapproval occasionally uttered by the State Department. As for the suspension of supplies of heavy military equipment, announced soon after the *coup* (May 1967) as a healthy reflex of distaste expressed by Washington and greeted then with approval both inside and outside Greece, it was frustrated in practice, first covertly by various administrative manipulations, then overtly during the Czech crisis of August–September 1968, so that in fact, the value of yearly deliveries has now been found to exceed that supplied in

1966. Now the continuation or suspension of these supplies has lost all but symbolic significance as a political step. But all the manipulations surrounding it have damaged American prestige in Greece even more, whether in the small circle of the junta, or with the Greek people in general.

To sum up, there has developed a very large body of public opinion in Western Europe, and a growing one in the United States, morally and politically opposed to the regime ruling Greece. And this opposition is taking on new forms of private and public demonstrations of hostility. However great may be the number of tourists who visit Greece, however unabated the commercial exchanges, it is a fact that Greece is morally and politically isolated from her natural friends and allies in Western Europe. Even with the United States, what was before 1967 a relationship based more on a traditional long-term friendship between the peoples than on the common short-term interest of Dullesian anti-communism, has now become complicity in low-level military and security deals and opportunist calculations aimed at American targets whose fulfilment requires the collaboration of a subservient regime on a short-term material basis, virtually on a 'real-estate' basis. In such a relationship, the Greek people's feelings, confidence and interests are more of a nuisance than an asset, and it is all in the interest of short-term tranquillity that any concern they may show is immediately discounted, and violently put down if it is manifested more actively.

How has the junta coped with this new external problem, which is also an internal one since Greek public opinion, in its vast majority opposed to the junta, was encouraged by foreign manifestations of hostility towards it?

(1) It spent two-and-a-half years (April 1967 to December 1969) fighting the hostility of Western Europe in Western European organizations, aided by the expertise of diplomats of the 'old regime' well known in Greece for their reactionary and authoritarian convictions (Foreign Ministers P. Ekonomou-Gouras and P. Pipinelis, and Foreign Under-Secretary G. Christopoulos). Its efforts came to naught, both in the Council of Europe (whence Pipinelis was forced to a hasty withdrawal on 12 December 1969) and in the European Economic Community whence, besides the freezing of relations to the level of routine current exchanges, there were issued a number of statements directly critical of the undemocratic state of affairs in Greece. Moreover, the Council of Association with the EEC which met twenty-four times in the five years 1962–April 1967 (of which ten meetings were at ministerial level) has

only met seven times between 1967 and 1971, of which none have been at ministerial level. Internally, the junta tried to make light of the expulsion from the Council of Europe and in a crude fashion tried to make nationalist capital out of it.[3]

There was very little conventional diplomacy during all this period. Actual diplomatic exchanges between Greece and Western European chanceries had been much restricted, with coolness shown on both sides. Even social contacts with Greek diplomats were avoided in Western European countries. In Germany, Italy, Sweden and Denmark, where the embassies and consulates became involved in Greek secret-police operations against Greek workers and students, there occurred demonstrations and even bomb attacks against them. The career ambassadors in Paris and London (nominees of the regime) were replaced by retired generals, perhaps because they had not succeeded in convincing the governments to which they were accredited of the virtues of dictatorship. Bonn has retained its career Greek envoy by signifying that it would not accept a military ambassador. The ambassador in Brussels had to be recalled after repeated representations from the Belgian government to the effect that he was responsible for violent demonstrations in the Brussels streets between junta supporters and Belgian and Greek opponents of the regime.[4] The Greek envoys in Oslo, Copenhagen and Stockholm have been withdrawn for over three years; there are only chargés d'affaires of Norway, Denmark and Sweden in Athens where previously there had been full ambassadors.

Except for a brief visit by Colonel Makarezos, as Minister of Coordination, to Paris in 1969, and two or three working visits of other ministers to London or to Washington, up to September 1971 no junta minister has visited a Western European country officially. Of course, the twice-yearly meetings of the NATO Council were regularly attended by the junta's Finance and Foreign Ministers (while the latter post was filled by Pipinelis), but neither the Defence Minister (Colonel Papadopoulos himself) nor the Foreign Minister (after Pipinelis' death also Colonel Papadopoulos) have attended a NATO Council session, and Greece has missed two turns as President of the Council. Not one Western European minister, except the Spanish Foreign Minister (in August 1971) has come to Greece officially.

In such circumstances it is impossible to speak of a tightening of relations and very difficult to speak of the resumption of fully normal diplomatic relations between Greece and its natural partners in Western Europe. Such *froideur* could in the long run become detrimental to Greece despite the continuing commercial and tourist exchanges. Official cultural exchanges, normally organized through diplomatic channels, are practically non-existent.[5]

In the fifth year of the dictatorship, the junta has become accustomed to the lowering of diplomatic relations to such a formal minimum, and shrugs off the evil effects such an isolation of Greece can have by publicly abusing the Western European countries in its press, and by administering diplomatic snubs to 'satisfy the Greek people's pride'.[6]

(2) With Eastern Europe, no such *froideur* has been officially displayed. While the Eastern bloc press and radio have not refrained from violent attacks on the junta, the regime has drawn much comfort from the recent visits to Athens of the Foreign Ministers of Bulgaria and Yugoslavia and of the Rumanian Prime Minister. Much play has been made of the first invitation extended to Colonel Papadopoulos to visit officially a foreign country, Rumania, although no date has been fixed as yet. The Foreign Under-Secretary (C. Xanthopoulos-Palamas) has recently officially visited Sofia and Belgrade. In June 1971 the Minister of Commerce, Spyridon Zappas, paid an official visit to Bucharest.

The acceptance by the regime and its press of such cordial exchanges with countries ruled by the hated communists has two explanations. Firstly, they come as a psychological compensation to a regime badly in need of domestic and international approval. Since it cannot get it in Greece or in Western Europe, it might as well take it from Eastern Europe. Besides currently maintaining commercial exchanges at the satisfactory level they had reached before the *coup*, and obtaining imporsant investments from the USSR and the German Democratic Republic, they give the regime a vaguely 'Nasserist' image of damning the communists within and liberally consorting with them abroad.

It is also aimed at the American administration, whose naivety the junta overestimates, as a hint of blackmail that the junta could move away from NATO and closer to political co-operation with the USSR. The junta could not carry out such a volte-face. Nasser could not do it in more difficult circumstances even with the strength he drew from the support of his people; the junta cannot do it for lack of such support. The United States may not realize, however, that Moscow and the Moscow-oriented Greek communists seem satisfied to wait until the junta's continued rule has so weakened the fabric of Greek society that in a number of years the conditions will be objectively created for a takeover by their specific brand of conservative communism.[7]

(3) In its quest for international approval, the junta has left few stones

unturned. It has in the last year inaugurated an African policy (with, it is said, American blessing) which has significantly developed not into an opening to the North African or Arab countries, but one of increasing relations with the black African countries, carefully south of the countries bordering on the Mediterranean that would have been natural partners in any really serious diplomatic venture. Thus Brigadier Pattakos, the First Deputy Prime Minister, visited, to the accompaniment of great flourishes in the Greek press, Egypt and Ethiopia (February 1971), Libya (March 1971), Congo-Kinshasa and the Central African Republic (May 1971) and Athens received (April 1971) Colonel Bokassa, President of the Central African Republic, one of the only two Heads of State (the other being the Greek-born President of Panama) to visit Greece officially since 1967. Pattakos visited Libya and Egypt more or less self-invited, and the lack of rapturous headlines in the junta press would appear to confirm that these visits were not taken over-seriously by the Libyan and Egyptian governments.[8]

If one abstracts the courtesies exchanged at official receptions, the practical result of these visits can be detected mainly in the commercial field. Greek exports have secured some additional outlets in these countries which can take Greek industrial products not acceptable in Western or Eastern Europe. No improvement has been secured in any field with the Arab countries bordering the Mediterranean from Tangier to Lattakieh. These somewhat improvised ventures toward Africa, like the regime's unexpected dependence on Eastern Europe, underline the growing sense of isolation which the junta feels.

(4) To this political and psychological problem, the easiest outlet was, of course, the United States. Dependence of the regime on the continued backing of the Pentagon is doubled by dependence on the State Department to counter repeated Western European moves against the junta, and by dependence on United States financiers and businessmen to ensure a continuous flow of easy, although costly, dollars to keep the economy going. It would be interesting for an economist to compare the number and quality of American firms which have set foot in Greece in the last four years with those operating in Greece before the *coup*. But the long-term cost, not only to the country's economy, but also to the country's political independence, of their establishment in Greece with practically extraterritorial privileges, is a political matter, made all the more acute by the use that the United States administration makes of private capitalism as a means of political control and vice versa, by the use of administration services by private capitalism.[9] The number of former

State Department officials who have served in Greece and who are now working with big private firms with interests in Greece is a pointer to this interlocking of public administrative and private enterprise to further a palatable, streamlined patron–client relationship which comes very close to colonialism. Greek foreign policy is thus presently bound not only by the requirements of Western defence and economic integration under obligations the Greek people have legitimately and voluntarily under-written through governments having their consent, it is also hamstrung by an ever-thickening web of draconian obligations to protect foreign investment, service its rapidly increasing foreign debt, protect the ever more numerous foreign nationals allowed to work in Greece and so on. And such obligations are undertaken by a regime subject to none of the checks or controls normal to democracies. The country was never so open to foreign pressures, and these not principally through diplomatic channels, as it is now. The greatest pressures naturally come from the major and strongest foreign partner, the United States, which is on the way to becoming Greece's sole partner in foreign policy. The vehement assertions that 'Greece will go it alone' or 'hands off Greece' sometimes heard in the highest quarters, and the frequent statements that no foreign intervention will be brooked, appear to come only at moments when the junta fears that such 'intervention' or 'pressures' go against its own interests.

What the consequences of such developments can be, is made clear by examining the present position of issues that I have termed specifically 'Greek'.

(1) *Cyprus* The Greek-Turkish conference at Keşan and Alexandrou-polis (September 1967) on the Thracian border, proposed by the Turks and incautiously accepted by the regime (without even informing the Cyprus desk in the Greek Foreign Ministry), ended in a diplomatic disaster for Prime Minister Kollias, Foreign Minister Ekonomou-Gouras and Minister to the Prime Minister, Colonel George Papadopoulos, who were the chief Greek delegates. The demand for *Enosis*, which was openly sought by the Greek delegates, was equally openly rejected by the Turks who, being more consistent diplomats, took advantage to improve their position on other points of the Greek-Turkish nexus, i.e. the Turkish minority in Western Thrace, the Greek community and the Patriarchate in Istanbul. The fate of the Tenedos and Imbros Greeks was sealed then. Nothing more has been heard of them since, except when one reads of a boat coming in from one of those islands carrying a few desperate

refugees. In November 1967, after bloody collisions in Cyprus which brought threats of Turkish intervention, Cyrus Vance was rushed to Athens, Nicosia and Ankara. He was successful in forestalling a Greek-Turkish military confrontation and the main outcome of his efforts was an agreement to withdraw from the island all Greek and Turkish forces other than those allowed by the Zurich and London agreements. This meant, in fact, that the Greek forces introduced on the island in 1964 by the Papandreou government to defend it against Turkish threats of intervention. It was easier for the Turks to camouflage the two or three thousand Turkish soldiers who had been introduced as Turkish Cypriots, than it was for the Athens regime to disguise units twelve to fourteen thousand strong as peaceable Greek Cypriots. Since there was no mechanism fixed for the control of the withdrawal, it ensured that while the greater number of Greeks were withdrawn, most of the Turks remained and are still there to this day.

Since then, the Athens regime has lost even the relative freedom it had to conduct its own policy in Cyprus. It has been wide open to pressures from Ankara or Washington. The Turkish pressures would have been greater had Turkey's internal situation not been so precarious. The American line was for settling Cyprus at any price, which could mean, in fact, at the price of dividing the island between Greeks and Turks. This 'solution' would have the added advantage, in Washington's eyes, of bringing Cyprus into NATO. The British, satisfied with their two exclusive bases on the island, became Makarios' best supporters in his efforts to keep the island in one piece, even at the cost of promoting its independence instead of *Enosis*. The dictatorship in Greece had to conform with American plans and especially now that Cyprus – with the Arabs whipped into an anti-American frenzy after the six-day war, with Turkey developing an ever more virulent anti-Americanism – had become the only tranquil country east of Greece. The United States would have welcomed the possibility of using its ports for the Sixth Fleet. The USSR, whose fleet also did not put into Cyprus ports, became more and more concerned to keep the island a neutral area; naturally they did not wish to see the island changed into a NATO outpost. This happened also to be the view of President Makarios, who had learnt only too well that if he was to keep his island independent and intact, he would have to be very wary of any attempt to press him toward one or the other bloc.

Makarios, who had the support of the vast majority of his countrymen, thus became the main obstacle to the plan for dividing the island, the only plan which appeared, even before 1967, to muster support in important sections of the Turkish and United States governments, and even in some Greek quarters. For them it held up the temptation of a nationalistic triumph, even if won at a discount. A large portion of Cyprus would do for the junta's prestige, any portion would be welcomed by Turkey, and the Americans could at last use territory that had been denied them since Cyprus was not a member of NATO. These converging lines became fatally entangled and, with the Cypriot intercommunal negotiations deadlocked, the crisis culminated with the abortive attempt to assassinate Makarios (in March 1970), and the successful liquidation of his Minister of the Interior, Georgadzis (in April 1970). It is considered in Cyprus that the latter was eliminated because he knew too much about the part taken by certain secret services in the plot against the Archbishop. However that may be, Georgadzis' bloody elimination showed the lengths to which those anxious to intervene in the island were prepared to go.

With the statements of Colonel Papadopoulos to the Turkish newspaper *Milliyet* (30 May 1971) that he believed in a Greco-Turkish federation, and that the two countries 'should convince our communities (in Cyprus) that we are not disposed to spoil the relations between us and quarrel for their sake; consequently they should settle their differences, indeed in a manner acceptable to us also. . . . If we tell them this . . . then they will recover their senses. . . .' Makarios' hold over the Cypriots was in fact strengthened. Many of the *Enosis* supporters went over to him as it appeared that the Athens regime was preparing to sell them down the river for the sake of friendship with Turkey. This attitude on the part of Athens may not have been imposed from Washington, but it was formulated in Athens with the aim of falling in line with American efforts to 'tidy up' the whole Eastern Mediterranean sector in view of the Soviet threat and the continuing Arab–Israeli conflict. Makarios' visit to Moscow, in the spring of 1971, Soviet statements that the USSR was concerned in the maintenance of an independent and unpartitioned Cyprus, could be construed, with malice, to prove that Makarios is pro-communist and that there is, therefore, all the more need to cast him aside. A recent attempt apparently to impose a Greek-Turkish solution of the Cyprus issue, initiated by Foreign Minister Olçay and Undersecretary Palamas, came to naught during Makarios' latest visit to Athens (3–5 September 1971) when he refused to consider any further concession to the Turkish Cypriot community beyond those already made by the Greek Cypriots during three years of protracted negotiations. The junta thus finds itself in the invidious position not only of having to curb its own 'enosist' aspirations, but also of going back on what is generally believed to have been agreed between Palamas and Olçay, that the two would have met at the United Nations General Assembly in September in order to hammer out the final details of their 'solution' which would have suited everyone except the Greek Cypriots, and indeed of incurring American dissatisfaction for not having reached such a solution.[10]

In fact, the dictatorship has managed, after four-and-a-half years, to weaken Greece's position over Cyprus. Cyprus is forced to look elsewhere for support and in the future calls for *Enosis*, especially when they originate in Athens, will meet with even more doubts and hesitations. The junta, since the Keşan–Alexandroupolis conference, has become indifferent to the wishes of the Cypriots because it would prefer a Cyprus (or part of it) united and docile to Greece – which would give it the credit of fulfilling the last irredentist aspiration of Greece – to a Cyprus functioning as an independent sister country of Greece in the Eastern Mediterranean, whose interests, not only its ties of blood, would keep it closer to Greece than to any other country in the area. This has come about because of the junta's incautiously nationalistic approach, and because of its concern to serve American interests in the belief that it thus furthers its own cause. Thus one healthy divergence between Greek and American foreign policy has been smoothed away. The policies have been aligned and the junta appears to support an 'at all costs' solution of the issue which would end with the partition of the island and the disappearance of a valuable little country from the Eastern Mediterranean.

(2) *The Middle East*   Greece's role in the Middle East conflict has been reduced since 1967 to that of an onlooker, torn between her traditional affinities with the Arabs and the junta's desire not to hinder United States' support of Israel. This conflict of interests became patent when, in September 1970, the United States asked the junta to grant facilities for passage and refuelling not only for planes flown to the Middle East to evacuate American nationals from Jordan, but also for military reconnaissance planes that would naturally have flown mainly over Arab countries.[11] This ambivalent attitude has cost Greece much of the credit of goodwill it had accumulated with the Arabs up to 1967.

The Greek Colonels could not but admire the military power of the Israelis and, as the short-term advantages of being, like the Israelis, exclusive clients of the United States became more obvious to them, they adjusted their policy even closer to that of the United States in the area.[12] They have appointed for the first time a full Ambassador as 'diplomatic agent' in Jerusalem, where they still maintain a Consul-General who, in the past, in accordance with the United Nations arrangements, also acted as 'representative' to Israel. So that a *de facto* recognition of Israel has gone a long way to becoming a *de jure* one. Perhaps a restraining factor for the junta is not so much Arab misgivings as the latent anti-semitism of Greek reactionary circles supporting the junta, such as the newspaper *Estia* and the overtly fascist magazine *Fourth of August* whose pages are full of virulent anti-semitic material (see Chapter Three).

(3) *The Balkans* In the field of Balkan co-existence, some progress has been apparent. Differences arising from the war have finally been settled with Bulgaria and commercial exchanges have been expanded. Since Bulgaria is Moscow's most faithful ally in the Balkans, and NATO's first-line adversary there, her willingness to improve relations with Greece (to the extent of foregoing any mention of the small group of Slav-speaking Greeks in Greek Macedonia which she considers Bulgarians), must be seen in the context of the striving toward a global détente between the USSR and the USA during the period 1968–1970, with green lights given by Moscow and Washington to Sofia and Athens to institute a local détente.

With Albania, an agreement has been reached establishing diplomatic relations and opening the way for commercial exchanges. This agreement, however, makes no mention of the Greek minority in southern Albania (Northern Epirus to the Greeks) or to war damage caused by the Albanians when they were allied with fascist Italy. The nonchalance with which the junta appears to have given up this Greek population has caused some shock in the Greek nationalist circles from which the regime draws the greatest part of its limited support. Neither can it have escaped the notice of the Cypriot people. Of course, relations with Albania had to be re-established, but it would have been an opportunity for the Greek regime to obtain firm assurances, if not guarantees, for a large population that was protected, before the war, by international agreements.

Greece's relations with her third northern neighbour, Yugoslavia, have remained stagnant in the sense that neither side has made any move further to improve them or even to reassert their previous excellence. The expeditiousness and cordiality with which Greco-Bulgarian relations were improved could not but cause some questioning in Belgrade, whose relations with Sofia were not of the best in precisely the same period, mainly because of the question of Yugoslav Macedonia, considered by the Bulgarians to be inhabited by their kin. The traditional friendship between Greece and Yugoslavia is still there, but the privileged relationship that was an old feature, from which both countries drew strength, appears to be a thing of the past. Greek–Yugoslav relations are now on the same functional, practical level as Greek–Bulgarian or Greek–

Albanian relations. This should be debited to the junta as an offering on the altar of USA–USSR détente. The future will show whether it will bring Greece any advantage.

With Turkey, Greece's eastern Balkan neighbour, relations have been least good; bad, in fact, since both are linked by NATO ties. The main reason, of course, is the Cyprus issue whose vicissitudes have already been examined. However, there are other problems too, all of which have remained unsolved, when they have not been solved unilaterally. With Cyprus as a pretext, the Turks have refused any arrangement either with regard to the Greek community in Istanbul or to the Oecumenical Patriarchate. Indeed, in August 1971, the Patriarchate's theological college on the island of Halki, an old foundation and still the principal training school for the clergy of the Greek Orthodox world outside Greece itself, was closed down by the authorities following a law against all private institutions of higher learning. In answer to Colonel Papadopoulos' statement to *Milliyet* (see above), Prime Minister Erim showed such diplomatic restraint that Papadopoulos, speaking in Thessaloniki (2 August 1971) of the Turkish attitude, expressed his 'bitterness because Turkey did not offer her hand with the same faith in the necessity of friendship and co-fraternal co-operation as we did'.

The consistent use by the Turks of the Cyprus issue to put pressure on the Greeks and to make all other problems dependent on its solution, has put the junta in an awkward position no democratic parliamentary government need have faced. If the Greeks came out in full and unhesitant support of an independent and unitary Cyprus, it would be impossible for the Turks to claim anything more than a fair treatment according to international norms for the 18% of Cypriot Turks on the island.

At the time of writing, the results in the diplomatic field of four-and-a-half years of dictatorship can be summed up as follows.

Cyprus Loss of the Greek military foothold, widening of rift between Athens and Nicosia: Makarios has spoken openly and repeatedly of the necessity of maintaining a common line between the two capitals, implying that there were certain divergencies or 'disruptions' as he called them before his visit to Athens (*Cyprus Bulletin*, 5 September 1971). Greece turned into a power just as indifferent to the people of Cyprus as Turkey, the United Kingdom, the United States or the USSR (i.e. pursuing her own interests and calculations regardless of whether they are acceptable to the Cypriots).

Western Europe Merely correct diplomatic relations with none of the cordiality and will to improve them of the past. Narrow commercial and financial interests foremost. Expulsion of Greece from the Council of Europe, freezing of relations with the EEC, absence of Greece from moves of European countries on vital pan-European issues such as entry of new countries to the EEC, political integration, European Security Conference.

United States Relations on a love-hate basis between the Greek officers composing the junta and their colleagues in the United States Military Mission, complicated by a more general patron-client relationship.[13] Having successfully exploited the Pentagon's preponderant voice in Greek affairs, the junta is being unpleasantly surprised to find this voice being questioned in the United States more generally and, particularly regarding Greece, in Congress. Growth of anti-American feelings both among the large majority of Greek people opposed to the junta, and also among certain of the junta's most jingoistic younger officers. Loss for any Greek–American relationship in the future of the cornerstone of trust and confidence between the peoples that existed in the past.

Eastern Europe Dependence on the Soviet bloc for tacit moral approval derived from official 'non-intervention in internal affairs'. Reliance for bolstering economy on Eastern European commercial outlets and even on investments. This could prove dangerous if support were suddenly withdrawn for political reasons.

Eastern Mediterranean Lessening of Arab confidence and respect because of junta's devotion to the United States, albeit no improvement in relations with Israel.

International Organizations In the United Nations family of organizations, Greece has been much less active than in the past and in some has been the subject of investigation or censure (viz. ILO, GATT). Greece's situation in the European organizations has already been described.

For small countries diplomatic activity and active participation in international exchanges in all their complexity is an essential condition of guarding the maximum independence that can be a small country's lot in the world of today. Only by taking part in and understanding this kind of continuous interplay can it hope to avoid becoming a simple pawn or client of one of the great powers. It is characteristic of the military mentality to ignore or denigrate the subtleties and flexibility required to carry out constructively this aspect of national life, as it ignores the general complexities and variety that make up the social and cultural fabric of a country. The past years of military dictatorship have brought about a lowering of the international status of Greece and a gradually more serious isolation from precisely those countries who should be, and were in varying measure until 1967, her most natural partners in this constructive international interplay, the Western European, the Balkan and the Eastern Mediterranean countries.

Athens, September 1971 *A. G. Xydis*

NOTES

1 The author, living in Greece, has used the Greek and foreign press as his main sources for this article.

2 Its return to Greece had been ruled out by Eden's statement on the integrity of Albania in December 1942.

3 For instance, the government-appointed Municipal Council of Athens ordered that the day should be marked by flags flying for three days to 'celebrate' the fourth Greek '*ochi*' (no) to the 'powers of darkness', the first being that of Leonidas at Thermopylae, the second that of Metaxas in 1940 to the Italians, the third that of the victory over the Communists in 1949. The organs of the controlled Greek press closest to the regime suddenly burgeoned with stories of the degeneracy and depravity of the Scandinavians and the savagery of the British, the Germans and the Italians in their colonial wars. The most crudely nationalistic chords were struck to show that Greece was well rid of such a Europe. Typical is the leader in *Nea Politeia* of 14 December 1969, 'Greece fought fascism alone in 1940. Greece fought nazism alone in 1941. She blocked alone the communist tide in the European area. Now she is fighting to save Europe. And she is not alone. Not the governments but all the free men of Europe, the USA, Asia and Africa and Australia are at her side. Soon all will have to speak of Greece as they did in 1940.' In the same issue there is an announcement 'From the day after tomorrow sensational facts on British atrocities' and an article by the Director of the National Theatre, V. Frangos, entitled 'European vitiation of Greek freedom'.

4 He was subsequently promoted, awarded the highest decoration for his services to the regime, and rewarded with the embassy in Madrid.

5 Most important European artists, musicians, singers, dancers, have refused to take part in the regime-organized Athens Festival, sometimes even in privately sponsored events in Greece.

6 Such as forbidding junta ministers to attend National Day receptions at foreign embassies in Athens or by statements by Papadopoulos and others to the effect that Greece will 'go it alone'.

7 The whole course taken by the 'orthodox' Greek Communist Party

appears to be, in the short term, despite much verbal opposition, favourable to the junta.

8 The Egyptian Foreign Minister Mahmoud Riad passed through Athens (April 1971) on a forty-eight hour visit in the course of a round-the-world tour to canvas support for his country's line in the Arab–Israeli conflict.

9 A visit to Mr Tom Papas, the well-known businessman and financier, is put by the US Embassy on the programme of most American officials visiting Athens, from Defense Secretary Laird downwards.

10 The Turks' irritation was obvious in Olçay's statement (UPI 21 September 1971) that 'the Greeks are changing their position on Cyprus. . . . From our side there is not the least change. It is the Greeks' turn to give us explanations on the situation in the island.' On the same day, Makarios declared to UPI, 'We will fire at [Turkish] planes if they overfly the island illegally, and we will fight if the [Turks] invade'.

11 In another instance after the six-days war, the junta, anxious to achieve the strictest neutrality, was careful to see that the Greek Red Cross shipped relief supplies to Jordan, Syria and Israel, despite the disproportion of casualties and needs.

12 Professor D. G. Kousoulas (an adviser of Colonel Papadopoulos) declared that: 'Greece . . . contributes indirectly . . . but to a very great measure to the protection and survival possibilities of Israel.' (Hearings of House Sub-Committee on Foreign Affairs, Washington, June 1971, as published in *Vima*, 7 October 1971).

13 Which leads, for instance, to the Governor of the Greek Investment Bank, Totomis, alone among the Europeans, to commend Washington's 10% tax on imports as a constructive measure, not an obstacle to economic development (*Nea Politeia*, 7 October 1971).

CHAPTER ELEVEN

Europe and the Greek Dictatorship

For the past five years the Greek case has clearly demonstrated a clash between two schools of European thought in foreign policy. On the one hand, there is the pragmatic school which has dominated the thinking of the so-called free world since the end of World War II. According to this school, Greece ought to be supported, regardless of its regime, and as good and friendly relations as possible established with the Colonels. Even if we dislike and distrust the present Greek regime, there is no reason why we should change our policy.

On the other hand, we find those who favour a more idealistic course toward what they consider to be a disgrace to Europe. They are not willing to accept 'hard realities' as put forward by the pragmatists, but rather see this policy as determined by short-term considerations. There may be some short-term military advantages in keeping the regime content. But these short-term considerations will in the long run have a disastrous effect, and in fact produce results quite the opposite of those intended.[1]

When considering the Greek situation, it is interesting to note that this idealistic attitude has been much stronger than is normal in matters of foreign policy. As one explanation for this one can point to the very active public-relations work done by the regime's opponents.

This emphasis on moral arguments has in most European countries created a climate of public opinion consciously aware of what has been going on inside Greece. Those Western countries that are members of the same international organizations and alliances as Greece have felt this pressure especially strongly.[2] Under the pressure of a strong domestic public opinion there has been no choice for many of them other than to take a strongly critical and actively hostile attitude towards the Greek regime. This, too, is remarkable. There are few cases where public opinion could be said to have played such an important part in forming the policy line of governments as in the Greek case. This is clearly the case with regard to many of the Western European countries, but it also has some relevance to the Eastern bloc countries which have been confronted with active Greek minority groups who have been able to exercise a certain pressure.

These introductory remarks have made it clear that when talking about 'a European attitude towards the Greek regime' both Eastern and Western Europe are included. For obvious reasons, as the present author is a Norwegian, a prominent place is given to Scandinavian reactions to and relations with Greece. This has certain drawbacks but also some advantages, for the Scandinavian countries have been extraordinarily active in the Greek case. The Scandinavian countries, as a result of their distance from Greece, felt freer to act in accordance with their own ideals. But this fact should not obscure the positive, indeed unique, importance of the Strasbourg case, in which Scandinavia played such an important role. As Professor Drouan puts it: 'The decision taken by the Council of Europe constitutes an extremely important example for the future of Europe. This time it is not material interests which are at stake. It is human rights – and respect for these human rights.'[3]

Some historians will regard the Strasbourg case as an expression of idealism in foreign policy relations, indeed some have already done so. To defend human rights and freedoms is seen as something outdated and unrealistic – as a kind of anachronism. If nothing else, this indicates the tremendous influence which the pragmatic school of foreign policy thinking has had on our views concerning international relations.

It was with high hopes that some Western European states on 4 November 1950 signed the European Convention on Human Rights. At the time the Convention was something extraordinary, and so it is still. Its basis lies in the supposition that there exists in Western Europe a common heritage of political traditions, ideals, freedoms and belief in human rights. Such a Convention can only exist and be effective if this common heritage is shared by all member countries. In the Greek case, these same member countries found themselves confronted with a fundamental lack of respect for this common heritage. For the Greek Colonels human rights were something outdated. In their eagerness to create 'super-Greeks of Helleno-Christian traditions' the Colonels forgot that such a common heritage existed. The Director of Legal Affairs at the Norwegian Ministry of Foreign Affairs, Jens Evensen, who presented the Scandinavian case, put it like this:

'It is with deep regret and with anxiety for the future of Western Europe that we today must confess that the basis for this common heritage no longer exists. Barely twenty years after the signing of the European Convention on Human Rights one of the member countries has so far departed from this common heritage that it is not only infringing ordinary human rights, but it is even applying extensive use of torture and maltreatment to dissenting citizens. And it is worth mentioning that this Convention on Human Rights is concerned only with the basic minimum of fundamental individual human rights and freedoms in a civilized society.'[4]

In this case concern for human rights and freedoms defeated pragmatism and prompted the Scandinavian countries to act. Thus they forced the representatives of the Greek regime to defend itself. This proved that Greece, despite the support it was receiving from across the Atlantic, at least had to go to a European capital to defend its actions.

The question has arisen and will do so again: why should the Scandinavians of all people feel obliged to become crusaders for Greek democracy? The factor of distance has already been mentioned. Scandinavia is far removed from the central decisions in Europe – and in the world. We belong to the periphery of Europe. This, together with limited experience in foreign-policy matters – perhaps with the exception of Sweden – makes for a sort of aloofness. Generally speaking, we are newcomers on the world political scene.

Another factor may be added: although we have intrigued against and exploited each other, we have never been subjected to colonial rule from outside Scandinavia. Norway and Denmark were under German occupation for five years during World War II, but with that exception we have always had our independence and national sovereignty. This has made Scandinavia a quiet corner of the world in foreign affairs. Internally, also, we have so far been able to solve the conflicts within society through peaceful means by established parliamentary institutions. This has given the Scandinavian countries a certain reputation for democratic procedure and institutions which, together with a Lutheran pietistic heritage, sometimes makes for what foreigners would call a sense of self-righteousness.

There is a further point which has probably some relevance to Scandinavian behaviour in the Greek case. Norway especially – and to some extent Sweden and Denmark also – is characterized by a strong anti-communism which has dominated its political thinking in the 1950s and early 1960s. The labour movement is strong in all three countries and has always been dominated by the Social Democrats. The communists have had limited influence, except for a short period after World War II, and have never been able to present themselves to the working class as a real alternative to the Social Democratic parties. The urge for a more radical policy in the aftermath of the war and the growing influence of the communist parties prompted the Social Democratic parties to launch an anti-communist campaign in order to neutralize the communists and safeguard their own monopoly position in the labour movement.

This campaign ran parallel to the entry of Norway and Denmark into the North Atlantic Treaty Organization in 1949. The anti-communist campaign was more or less linked to the question of joining NATO. To be against entry was to be against the safeguarding of democracy and free institutions, and was considered to be communist-inspired. In Denmark and Norway both the Social Democratic parties then in power and the bourgeois parties agreed on the need for NATO. Thus foreign policy questions were taken out of the political sphere and left to the so-called specialists, the Minister of Foreign Affairs and his officials. Debate on foreign policy was, therefore, very limited and did not affect the public to any significant degree until the question of the Vietnam war arose.

The debate about Vietnam helped to stimulate interest in the Greek question. The moral aspects were stressed: how could Nazi and medieval methods be tolerated in an alliance which was intended to preserve democracy and freedom? Should we take no notice of the establishment of a military dictatorship in a country with more than eight million people, a country deeply integrated into an international alliance? And what if this had happened in another European country with, let us say, a population of fifteen million – would it still have been a question for the military and the military alone?

We see, therefore, in the Greek case the peculiar fact that public opinion did play a dominant part in forming government policies. It is no exaggeration to say that the Danish and Norwegian initiatives in the Council of Europe and in NATO were first and foremost a product of an active and concerned public opinion.

The question of raising the Greek case with the European Commission of Human Rights was proposed for the first time in a seven-column front-page article in the influential Danish newspaper *Politiken* on 30 April 1967.[5] The paper quoted a statement by Professor Max Sørensen, the legal adviser to the Danish Ministry of Foreign Affairs, saying that a complaint to the Commission about the Greek military regime's suppression of human rights and freedoms was a possibility, and had been tried once before in international law when Greece in 1956 complained about British behaviour in Cyprus. The paper continued by suggesting the

possibility of a joint Nordic action, and referred to the Norwegian
Premier, Per Borten, who recently had regretted that 'we have allies in
NATO who are not willing to observe the fundamental rules of human
rights'. The article concluded that 'there is reason to believe that the
Committee on Foreign Relations would pay attention to this possibility
and note the opportunity for making a step forward in the question of
the Greek regime on the basis of international law'.

The many alarming reports from Greece during the summer of 1967
and the broad coverage which these received in the Scandinavian press,
together with the report of a parliamentary delegation to Athens in
mid-August of the same year, strengthened the need for rapid government
action.[6] On 21 September 1967 the three Scandinavian countries presented
their complaint to the European Commission of Human Rights. One
week later this complaint was supported, on a more limited scale, by the
Netherlands. On 25 March 1968 the Scandinavian countries included
extensive use of torture in their complaint against the Greek military
regime. In making this complaint the Scandinavian countries took upon
themselves an historic mission. For the first time in history a case of this
nature and scale was raised before an international court against a friendly
country with the sole object of protecting fundamental human rights and
freedoms.

The procedure that followed was long and tiresome. In addition to four
major sessions, running from January 1968 to June 1969, exhaustive verbal
evidence and thousands of pages of written evidence and documentation
were presented. To quote *Politiken*[7] again: 'There is no reason to hope
for a quick decision. In the first instance the Greek government will, of
course, claim that the Council of Europe is not competent to accept the
complaint, and there is, furthermore, no reason to expect that the Greek
regime will contribute any kind of assistance during the investigation by
the Human Rights Sub-Commission. Sooner or later, however, the
Greek regime will be sentenced.'

The United States of America was most certainly upset at the idea of
expelling Greece from the Council of Europe, for such an expulsion would
have made it more difficult for the Americans to support the Greek
regime openly. Throughout 1969 there were consistent rumours that the
US would finally resume deliveries of heavy arms to Greece.[8] Such a
resumption would have been politically impossible for their European
allies to defend. A condemnation in the Council could, from the American
viewpoint, cause trouble within the NATO alliance. Both the Danish and
the Norwegian governments had quite clearly stressed that they would

await the outcome of the Strasbourg case before they were ready to take further action in other international organizations. By this they could have meant only NATO as a possible next step.

On 14 July 1969 the official Danish news agency, *Ritzaus Bureau*, claimed that Washington was actively working against the Scandinavian efforts to get Greece expelled from the Council. The despatch stated that 'the Scandinavian countries fear that the United States will try to interfere in the internal procedures of the Council of Europe to avoid the expulsion of Greece. Even if this is a purely European business, Denmark, along with Norway and Sweden, does not think that the United States would be prepared to see Greece sentenced for violations of the Human Rights Convention. Such a sentence would automatically lead to Greece's expulsion from the Council.'

This statement was published while the Scandinavian lawyers were completing their complaint. *Ritzaus Bureau* quoted high Scandinavian officials as the source of the information, and concluded by saying that the United States would not suffer the loss of prestige of seeing an ally which it strongly supported being condemned by its European allies. There were indications that the United States, if they chose, had many means of direct pressure of an economic and political nature. Norwegian officials confronted with the telegram from *Ritzaus Bureau* said that it contained some exaggerations. 'It is, however, no secret that Washington openly opposes the expulsion of Greece from the Council of Europe. In the American view such an expulsion would be a threat to Greece's membership of NATO as well.'[9]

There is no reason to believe that such a careful and sober news agency as the official Danish *Ritzaus Bureau* would have presented such a telegram if they were not relying on very good sources. The publication of what appears to have been a deliberate leak could be seen as a strong indication of a tough confrontation between the US officials and the Scandinavians involved. The *Ritzaus Bureau* leak was probably intended as a warning to Big Brother: so far but no further.

It is difficult to tell whether there has been pressure by the Americans, in other forms and at other levels, to coerce the Scandinavians by means of economic sanctions, as happened when the Swedish government recognized North Vietnam somewhat earlier. What is certain is that the United States was very much opposed to Greece's expulsion from the Council of Europe and that the Americans very actively tried to convince the Western European governments of the serious effects of such an expulsion, and in this way tried to influence the decision-making processes in these countries.[10] It is also perhaps fair to say that had not the Scandinavian lawyers been men of mettle, it would have been easy for them to give in to the blandishments offered.

The Greek withdrawal from the Council of Europe in December 1969, after a final threat of expulsion, gave the Greek question a new dimension. The main object of the Scandinavian complaint was to ensure that elementary human rights were respected. The Council of Europe could, however, do little to change the Greek regime. In that respect NATO was in a qualitatively different position. After the final decision in Strasbourg it was only natural to try to follow up the Greek case in NATO.

As early as August 1967 the leader of the Nordic parliamentary delegation to Greece, the Norwegian Labour MP, Aase Lionaes, stated: 'There is no place for a dictatorship within the framework of Western co-operation.[11] The preamble to the North Atlantic Treaty is quite clear on this point. Not only does it affirm the determination of the parties "to safeguard the freedom, common heritage, and civilization of their peoples founded on the principles of democracy, individual liberty and the rule of law", but Article 2 enjoins upon the parties the obligation of "strengthening their free institutions".'

Words and declarations have not, however, been followed by deeds in this case. On the contrary, the NATO alliance and its member countries have not shown great restraint in their relations with the dictatorial regime in Greece. This has bred disillusionment among people who honestly believed what the ministers and military brass had said about the protection of freedom and individual liberties. The Greek case has openly demonstrated the true character of NATO as a pure military alliance with no interest in civil liberties within the alliance. This is even more serious when one considers the responsibility which NATO must share for the *coup d'état* and for keeping the Colonels in power. It has been admitted that the April *coup* was carried out on the basis of the NATO emergency plan for Greece, called 'Prometheus'.[12] Even though it has been strongly denied by NATO, and by officials of the member governments, there is good reason to believe that such plans do exist for all NATO countries.[13] The now famous McConnell plan of 1962, with its league table in which the NATO countries are ranked according to the strategic significance of their geographical location, is a part of the same pattern.[14]

The sensitivity of the Greek question for NATO is clearly demonstrated by the unwillingness of the NATO countries to place it on the agenda. When the then Danish Premier and Minister of Foreign Affairs Jens Otto Krag tried to raise the Greek question in a NATO ministerial meeting in

Paris in May 1967 his move was bluntly rejected by the Secretary-General Manlio Brosio as an unacceptable interference in the internal affairs of a member country.[15] It was claimed that the Greek *coup d'état* was a purely Greek matter and in no way affected the alliance as such. When the then Minister of Foreign Affairs in West Germany, Willy Brandt, raised the Greek question in the Council of NATO a couple of days after King Constantine's failed counter-*coup*, his effort met a similar fate.

The case before the Council of Europe and the controversy over expulsion deflected interest away from NATO for a time. The Greek question remained, however, a potentially explosive issue. When the procedure in Strasbourg was over, the battleground slowly shifted to NATO. The strong influence of public opinion in the Scandinavian countries on the Greek question has already been mentioned. It was the main factor in influencing the Norwegian Parliament on 10 December 1969 to pass a unanimous resolution condemning delivery of weapons to Greece on behalf of the NATO alliance, and urged a full halt to such deliveries as they helped to support the regime. New factors such as the 'Trial of the Thirty-Four' resistance activists in Athens in the early spring of 1970, and fresh reports of continuing use of torture once again created a public demand for action. This was strengthened when a parliamentary delegation was denied entry to Greece to attend as observers at the trial. A former Norwegian Minister of Justice, the Labour MP Jens Haugland, who waited a whole night at Athens airport, said on returning that this was the first time a NATO country had denied admittance to Members of Parliament of another NATO country. 'Greece is a dead body in the NATO organism,' he said.

This created the first real opportunity to confront the US at NATO level. A debate in the Norwegian Parliament on 21 May showed growing support for the demand that Greece should be suspended as a member of NATO. Two proposals in this direction were put forward. The Labour Party (74 out of 150 seats, and the Government from spring 1971) proposed what was later called a 'three-stage policy' for NATO action. The resolution reads as follows:

'The Norwegian Labour Party resolves that Norway must actively work in the Ministerial Council in Rome on 26–27 May to get democratic rule re-established in Greece within the framework of NATO:

1 The Norwegian government must during this meeting in Rome follow up the resolution taken by the Norwegian Parliament on 10 December 1969 about discontinuation of all deliveries of weapons to Greece.

2   Action must be taken to secure a boycott of Greece by using the right of veto in all matters regarding economic and material support to the junta.

3   In this first meeting Norway must make contact with other member countries of NATO to prepare for the suspension of Greece from NATO, if the means mentioned under points 1 and 2 do not lead to the re-establishment of democratic institutions in Greece.'
A less far-reaching proposal was made by the bourgeois parties.

None of these proposals was put to the vote but following the debate the Cabinet instructed the Minister of Foreign Affairs to demand at the NATO ministerial meeting an end to US arms deliveries to Greece. A similar debate took place in Denmark before the Rome meeting. Immediately before this meeting took place in the spring of 1970 there was heavy pressure on some governments to discourage them from raising the question. The Secretary for the Air Force of the US Defence Department, Mr Seaman, was visiting Oslo and Copenhagen during the second week of May and sought to use his influence. Some days later photographs showing him with leading members of the Greek regime appeared in the Athens newspapers.[16]

During the Rome meeting, Secretary-General Manlio Brosio took a series of initiatives to persuade the Scandinavians not to raise the problem of the Greek dictatorship at ministerial level. In his efforts to block the discussion he was assisted by the US Secretary of State, William Rogers, and even by his British colleague, Michael Stewart. Brosio arranged a meeting for the Scandinavian representatives to meet with the junta's Minister of Foreign Affairs, Panayiotis Pipinelis, in the presence of the Foreign Ministers of the US, Great Britain, West Germany and Italy. There should be no doubt that critical remarks directed at Greece were not welcomed by any of the major NATO partners.

In the event, the Scandinavians were distinctly muted. Some lofty remarks were uttered on conditions within the alliance which did not in certain cases correspond with the ideals expressed in the NATO treaty. The Danish Foreign Minister, Hartling, along with the Norwegian Stray and Dutch Luns, expressed in different ways their concern for high principles but none of them was prepared to make remarks that might lead to anything in the least resembling an open confrontation with the US.

A similar performance was given in Lisbon in June 1971. On this occasion the newly appointed Norwegian Minister of Foreign Affairs, Andreas Cappelen, was alone in speaking about principles. In the end he was half-heartedly supported by his Danish colleague. But on this occasion too there was no indication that Norway, for instance, was willing to draw the appropriate conclusions from its rhetoric. There were no concrete threats such as Norway refusing to take part in NATO military maneouvres for as long as the US remained unwilling to put pressure on Greece. Nor were there any indications that the unanimity rule might be invoked to block all multilateral aid to Greece, or threats on the part of any of the allied countries that either they or Greece must withdraw from NATO as long as the situation in the country remained the same. The raising of the Greek question in NATO has therefore more or less taken the form of a farce, where words have been given one value, deeds quite another. This criticism applies equally to the Scandinavian countries which have more or less taken it upon themselves to act as the conscience of the alliance.

NATO is well aware of the strategic importance of its south-east flank. Therefore, the argument runs, NATO is well served with the Colonels who maintain calm and order in an otherwise unstable area. The likelihood of any change in this attitude is not very strong. It seems that belief in the unity of the alliance – in NATO as an established and permanent force for good – is too deeply rooted in the established parties and in their leaders. The experience of the last four years has shown that beyond a certain point the Western Europeans are unwilling to draw the necessary conclusions. The prospect of a real confrontation with the US at NATO level is therefore very slight. To bring about a major change in the attitudes of European statesmen, a drastic change in the internal Greek situation must manifest itself, in the form of a much more active and broadly based resistance than has so far emerged. It is also possible that the European-Atlantic Action Committee, under the chairmanship of Sir Hugh Greene, may be able to bring home to the statesmen of NATO the implications of their fine-sounding rhetoric.

When one looks more generally at relations between Greece and the countries of Western Europe the contrast between rhetoric and action is again marked. On a few occasions Western European governments have directly intervened, as in the case of the death sentence on Alexander Panagoulis, where they probably saved his life. This was again demonstrated in the case of Lady Fleming.[17] This type of reaction serves to keep the Greek regime morally isolated in the Western family of nations. Also, the suspension of the treaty of association between Greece and the EEC has had a harmful economic impact on the regime, besides its moral impact upon international public opinion. These examples help to give the impression that the Western countries are pursuing an active line in making life as difficult as possible for the Colonels.

The figures, however, give a somewhat different picture. Trade and investment are important in this connection. While it is somewhat difficult to get a clear idea as to the inflow of investment, the trade figures are interesting. In 1966 the EEC countries exported goods worth 485 million dollars to Greece. By 1969 this had increased to 610 million dollars, comprising 43% of Greece's total imports. The other Western European countries increased their exports to Greece at a rate of 49% during the same three-year period. The United States follows as the third greatest exporter to Greece, supplying 14% of total imports, a share which has substantially increased since the military take over. In comparison, the exports of the Eastern European countries, including the Soviet Union, to Greece were 7% of the total in 1969. Their rate of increase during 1970 and 1971 seems to have been about the same.[18]

Another illuminating example is to be found in European attitudes to weapon deliveries to Greece. In Norway the delivery of three NASTY motor torpedo boats in May 1967 sparked off a strong public debate, but the order was filled despite public criticism. France has bluntly declared that it wants to have relations as close and friendly as possible with all countries, regardless of the character of their governments. The French government has sold a number of gunboats to Greece and has made it clear that it is also willing to supply 30 Mirage fighter bombers, and armoured vehicles, although the payment terms offered seem to be unacceptable to the Greek government at present.[19]

The West German government agreed in 1969 to build four submarines for Greece at the state-owned Howalt shipyards in Kiel: they were delivered in 1971. This agreement had been negotiated in the strictest secrecy.[20] In June 1971 the official spokesman for the Bonn government, Conrad Ahlers, indicated that even if Willy Brandt did have strong opinions about present conditions in Greece, the fact that Greece is an important ally of NATO needed to be taken into consideration in the matter of weapon deliveries to the country.[21]

The British government was also reported in March 1969 to have secretly negotiated substantial deliveries of different kinds of weapons. In 1971 the British Minister of Defence, Lord Carrington, arrived in Athens – in secrecy – for talks with Greek government officials.[22] All these examples show that what is going on at an official level is one thing, and what is happening on a practical level quite another, especially when a country's own interests are involved.

We turn now to the relations between communist Europe and the Greek military junta. A great deal has been written on this during the last two years, and much of it has been exaggerated and sensationalized. The trade figures, however, clearly show that there is no reason whatsoever to exaggerate these relations. In comparison with the relations between Greece and the Western European countries, they have been of a limited nature, in both political and economic terms. The available trade figures clearly illustrate this. The misunderstanding as to these relations stems from the essentially different situations with which Eastern and Western Europe were confronted in 1967 when the Greek *coup* took place. The Western European countries, by belonging to the same family of nations, had a moral responsibility for the *coup* that made it necessary for them to react publicly in a strong manner.

Eastern Europe was in a different position. The *coup* was, for them, a more or less natural result of the development of the bourgeois state – a symptom of the crisis within the capitalist world. The *coup* nevertheless offered interesting possibilities for them, especially the Soviet Union, to increase their influence in an important strategic area. The new rulers in Athens were completely unknown to the outside world. Their foreign-policy orientation was an open question. And in spite of their declared anti-communism, earlier experience of Mediterranean countries showed that a strong domestic anti-communism was no obstacle to close and friendly relations with communist countries.

What we therefore see demonstrated in relations between Eastern Europe and Greece is a particular form of non-ideological pragmatism in international foreign relations. The Colonels domestically present themselves as crusaders for the West. They are strongly anti-communist, harassing all progressive elements within their country. This is in accordance with the very essence of their *coup*, which in fact was based on anti-communism. But this is on the domestic level. In foreign relations they have co-operated closely with countries of different political and social systems. They are even very careful not to do anything that could harm or destroy these relations. While the Greek propaganda apparatus has steadily criticized the Western leaders, they have been very careful in their attacks on the East. As early as 1968 Panayotis Pipinelis advocated non-interference and close relations with Eastern Europe. Six months later Stylianos Pattakos proposed a 'peace plan' for south-east Europe, regardless of differing political and social systems.

Far from being idealistic, this Greek policy is an expression of realism. In their morally isolated position in Western Europe it has been necessary for them not to provoke further isolation through difficult relations with their Eastern neighbours. The Cyprus crisis in the autumn of 1967 was a hard lesson for the Colonels, who found themselves in such a weak internal position that an outward policy of confrontation proved in fact impossible. There is reason to believe that the Colonels at this time were frightened by the prospect that their struggle against the left wing at home would develop into a fight with established communism in Eastern Europe. In this way the Greek problem could easily develop from an internal struggle into an international problem, as was more or less the case during the Greek civil war. The regime in its isolated position would naturally try to avoid such a development, and 'appeasement' towards the East was therefore a logical policy.

Another important factor should be mentioned. Ever since taking over power, the Greek Colonels have stressed Greece's importance for its NATO allies and its Western trade partners, both in military and in economic terms. The strong criticism from many of its allies and closest associates has caused the regime to stress the need for Greece to develop its trade relations with other countries as well. This was especially strong after their expulsion from the Council of Europe, and it was then accompanied by a more active Eastern policy. By using a kind of blackmail the Colonels were trying to silence their critics by pointing to the 'dangerous' consequences of their criticism. This 'ultimatum' was also a deliberate attempt to fool public opinion and create doubts as to the real orientation of the regime. It led, furthermore, to an even greater split in the Greek communist camp.

Greek policy has suited the Eastern European countries excellently. They have accepted the present status quo between the two blocs, and therefore peaceful co-existence between different political and social systems gives a natural framework for their relations with the Greek regime. Even if they have urged a 'fight against fascism and for democracy in Greece' they have behaved 'correctly' and continued to build up their relations with Greece. Support for the Greek communists has not been seen as an obstacle to good relations at the official level. It is understandable that this sort of 'realism' should tend to create confusion and some disillusionment within the Greek communist movement.

The Soviet Union has given some support for the construction of industrial projects. There has also been a certain development in trade between the two countries, although this development stagnated during the first two years after the *coup* and is still limited in comparison with the development in trade relations, for instance, between Greece and the

EEC countries, Great Britain or the United States. It is interesting to note that the Greek government in January 1970 unilaterally reduced duties on many Soviet products by 50%. For their part, the Russians promised to give Greece technical aid for projects along the Bulgarian border. In addition, the Soviet Union is increasingly buying more Greek tobacco.

Much more remarkable are the developments between Greece and Bulgaria. There have been reciprocal visits at a high government level. Radio Sofia at the beginning of 1970 described their relations as follows: 'They are correct and pragmatic. A number of agreements of interest to both parties have been signed or prepared during recent years and our economic and trade relations have been developing rapidly. Both countries are interested in new forms of co-operation in the technical field.'

It is worth noticing, too, that the Bulgarian press has avoided attacking the military regime in Athens. This led Pipinelis to say that the Bulgarian press took a far more correct attitude to what is happening in Greece than did, for instance, the Swedish. A Norwegian colleague once discussed the Greek situation with a Bulgarian journalist who was alarmed to hear what the Norwegian press was writing about the situation in Greece. The Bulgarian, somewhat puzzled, asked, 'What is the real motive behind your anti-Greek campaign?'[23]

On the level of rhetoric the German Democratic Republic takes a different stand. The East German press has condemned the Colonels and their regime as consistently as has the Scandinavian. These attacks have been of a very harsh nature but they have proved no obstacle to the signing of a treaty establishing chambers of commerce in both countries in the winter of 1970. This created some confusion among West German diplomats in Athens, who feared that this was a token of official recognition of the Pankow government. The West German ambassador, however, was informed that this move signified nothing in connection with the question of recognition.

Poland enjoys a thriving trade with Greece. The country has been well represented at the Salonica International Fair since the *coup*. In February 1970 there was a major Polish book exhibition in Athens. On the occasion of its opening the Polish Ambassador exchanged courtesies with the Greek Deputy Premier, Pattakos.

One of the agreements which has attracted widespread attention is that between Albania and the Greek regime, which was signed in May 1971. The two countries had up till then in principle been technically at war since the Italian attack on Greece on 28 October 1940, for which Greece held Albania also responsible. Moreover, the border question concerning Northern Epirus and the Greek minority population living in this area has been the source of much friction between the two countries.

Since the communist take-over Albania has never been willing to accept responsibility for Mussolini's attack on Greece. Neither has Enver Hoxha been prepared to accept the Greek view that the two countries were still in a permanent state of war. The Albanians therefore, as early as 1955, proposed the establishment of diplomatic relations to break the deadlock.[24] At that time this was not acceptable to Greece. It may seem somewhat paradoxical that this anomalous situation has been ended by a Greek military regime. With its nationalistic attitudes and its emphasis on Pan-Hellenism, it is strange that this regime should abandon the idea of the union of Northern Epirus with Greece. Particularly as Theophylaktos Papakonstantinou in his officially sponsored book *Politiki Agogi* (Civics) states that 'Northern Epirus, for historical, ethnic and other reasons, must be united with Greece.'

Papakonstantinou's book has also provoked a negative reaction in Yugoslavia, because of its remarks on the 'Macedonian Question'. The official party newspaper *Borba* criticized the book strongly and accused the author of using arguments which ran counter to the interests of other nations. As a result, Pipinelis, at a press conference some days later, stated that the book reflects the author's own private views on foreign policy. He added that 'this incident should not harm the sympathetic feelings which the Greek government and people entertain towards Yugoslavia'. But after Pipinelis' statement, Papakonstantinou himself again criticized the Yugoslav attitude and said that the comments in *Borba* indicated that this had undergone no change. If Yugoslavia, he continued, really did want friendly relations with Greece then once and for all the Yugoslav government should declare that its Macedonian ambitions did not involve Greece.

These examples show what tensions lie below the surface of the seemingly good relations which exist between the two countries. Trade continues as before, while on 9 September 1970, the Greek deputy Foreign Minister Xanthopoulos-Palamas visited Belgrade, the first such visit since the coup. Some months later his Yugoslav opposite number, Tepavac, made a brief visit to Athens.

Rumania has also developed good relations with Greece. A year before the *coup d'état* Premier Maurer, together with the Minister of Foreign Affairs, Manescu, visited Athens at the invitation of the Stefanopoulos government.[25] At this time a treaty concerning co-operation in trade, shipping, industry, communications and cultural relations was concluded.

After a short break these relations were resumed and in October 1969 the Greek Minister of Trade paid an official visit to Bucharest. In December 1970 the Rumanians paid a return visit. In connection with this a five-year trade treaty was signed. In 1971 Manescu again visited Athens[26] and there were discussions about further technical, economic and cultural co-operation. The attitudes of Yugoslavia and Rumania are of some interest in connection with internal problems in the Greek communist party. The dissenting Brillakis–Theodorakis group has worked hard to win full support for the Greek resistance, particularly from Rumania.

In conclusion, I hope that I have been able to point to some of the features that characterize the way the different countries of Europe have reacted towards Greece since the *coup*. My main thesis is that the many powerful verbal reactions have not been followed up on a practical political level with regard to matters such as a boycott of trade, investment and military co-operation, the essential preconditions for the survival of any regime. It seems quite clear that an attitude of strong moral condemnation has not been an obstacle to close co-operation in many fields. If there has been a choice between what has been morally right and what has been expedient the latter has always won. Moral indignation has never been allowed to affect the self-interest of the countries involved. This has sometimes reached the point of pure hypocrisy. Pragmatism has dominated the scene, although there have been idealistic overtones, and some genuine exceptions.

The establishment of a dictatorship in Greece has taught a hard lesson. It unfortunately appears that bloodshed is necessary before the world begins to think and react seriously. In the five years of dictatorship in Greece, Europe has had a chance to grasp the evil by its roots and thus avoid a new Vietnam in Europe. But little has happened, and now it may already be too late.

Oslo, September 1971   *Arne Treholt*

NOTES

1 An eloquent example of this attitude is demonstrated in the statement made by Sir Hugh Greene before the European Sub-Committee of the Committee on Foreign Relations of the House of Representatives on 14 July 1971.

2   A Danish public opinion poll in November 1967 listed 58% as being in favour of the Government line of condemnation, 27% against and 15% as undecided. (Published in the Danish newspaper *Aktuell* on the basis of an analysis by the *Observa* institute.)

3   *Le Monde*, 11 Dec. 1969.

4   *Arbeiderbladet*, Oslo, 16 Apr. 1970.

5   30 Apr. 1967.

6   The Scandinavian parliamentary delegation to Greece was made up of delegates from Sweden, Norway, Finland and Denmark. The Norwegian Labour MP, Aase Lionaes, was elected head of the delegation. They made thoroughgoing investigations in Athens for a week, and met among others, Premier Kollias, Pattakos, the Minister of Justice, the Minister of Foreign Affairs and Totomis along with many Greek politicians. They obtained permission to see Andreas Papandreou in Averoff prison and thirteen prisoners in Amaroussi, among them generals, newspapermen, parliamentarians and university teachers. Their report created a sensation in all the Nordic countries, and was published in all the Scandinavian languages in 1967.

7   17 Sept. 1967. Foreign policy editorial.

8   Among others, Robert Mauthner in the *Financial Times Survey* on 26 Feb. 1969.

9   *Arbeiderbladet*, 15 July 1969.

10 Reports in the Norwegian dailies *Arbeiderbladet* and *Dagbladet* on 8 Dec. 1969 from their correspondents in Bonn describing increased pressure on the Brandt government by the Americans.

11 Quoted from the Danish *Politiken*, 27 Aug. 1967.

12 This has been stressed by many insiders, among them Cyrus L. Sulzberger, in an article in the *New York Times* which was later referred to in hearings of the Committee on Foreign Relations of the US Senate (1970).

13 When the leader of PAK, Andreas Papandreou, mentioned this during a speech in Oslo in April 1970, the Secretary-General of NATO, Manlio Brosio, made a statement a week later denying categorically that any such plans existed for any of the NATO countries, and claiming that the allegation was pure fabrication.

14 In his book *Juntaen ut av NATO* (The Junta out of NATO), 1970, the former Minister of Justice and now President of the Committee on Legal Affairs in the Norwegian Parliament, Labour MP Jens Haugland, who was a member of the Norwegian government from 1955 to 1965, claims 'that such plans do exist for all NATO countries'. The Minister of Defence at that time, Gunnar Hellesen, denied the existence of such a plan. But Mr Haugland refused to withdraw his statement and said that his 'solemn oath' as a minister prevented him from making further comment.

15 The Danish newspapers *Berlingske Tidende* and *Politiken* on 6 May 1967

claimed that Brosio in a private meeting with the Danish ambassador to NATO, Hiorth-Nielsen, had urged Denmark not to raise the question. When it became apparent that the Ambassador had clear instructions in the matter, Brosio adjourned the meeting until the following day.

16 The *Greek Observer*, No. 15–16, June–July 1970.

17 Lady Fleming, the widow of Sir Alexander Fleming, was arrested in Athens on 2 Sept. 1971 for allegedly trying to organize the escape of Alexander Panagoulis.

18 OECD, *Statistics of Foreign Trade:* Overall trade by countries, Apr. 1971.

19 Reuters dispatch from Athens, 29 Aug. 1970.

20 *Dagbladet*, Oslo, 8 July 1969.

21 Reuters dispatch from Bonn, 28 June 1971.

22 According to the Thessaloniki newspaper *Ellinikos Vorras.*

23 Jahn Otto Johansen in *Arbeiderbladet* on 9 June 1970.

24 *Neue Züricher Zeitung*, 11 May 1971.

25 *Neue Züricher Zeitung*, 15 June 1971.

26 *Frankfurter Allgemeine Zeitung*, 16 June 1971.

CHAPTER TWELVE

United States Policy in Post-War Greece

With few exceptions, American policy in regard to Greece has been only incidentally a policy directed *toward* Greece. Rather, it has tended to be a more or less mechanical local application of a world-wide line, adopted for reasons often quite irrelevant to actual Greek circumstances. This was true even of the Truman doctrine, for which Greece was not so much the reason as the occasion.

During the last years of World War II and in the immediate post-war period, American policy was based on the Teheran agreement – or rather on an interpretation of it which differed in some important respects from that given it by the Russians and most British Conservatives, but was rather closer to that of the British Labour Party. According to this interpretation, the lines on which Europe was partitioned at Teheran represented primarily a military division of labour, and only secondarily a recognition of spheres of interest. Within their respective spheres, the powers were under an obligation to act in the interests of democracy – an obligation which was, in fact, subsequently spelled out in the Yalta agreement. Underlying this interpretation was the assumption that the powers would maintain a basically harmonious relationship in the post-war period, and that this harmony would be reflected in the internal politics of the liberated nations.

To both Stalin and Churchill, in contrast, post-war rivalry seemed inevitable. Teheran and Yalta were for them efforts to delimit the area of conflict by conceding each other primacy in certain parts of Europe. (Not *every* place which could become an area of conflict was covered; the case of Trieste is an obvious example.) Nor did either expect the other to risk control of the allotted satellites by giving too literal an interpretation to the guarantees of freedom and independence which formed part of the standard verbiage of inter-allied agreements. (To be sure, there were

228

Americans – both critics of the agreements such as the present writer and some of their architects, such as Dean Acheson – who also regarded the agreements as a simple deal between empires, in which lip-service to democratic goals did not imply any readiness to let the populations concerned determine their own fates. But this was not the predominant view either of the American public or, probably, within the Roosevelt administration.)

The consequence was that, while Churchill and Stalin accepted without a murmur each other's actions in Eastern Europe and Greece, most Americans – official as well as unofficial – were shocked. In the case of Greece, Secretary of State Edward Stettinius declared on 5 December 1944, while British troops were fighting ELAS for control of Athens: 'We have reaffirmed to both the British and Italian governments that we expect the Italians to work out their problems of government along democratic lines without influence from the outside. *This policy would apply to an even more pronounced degree with regard to governments of the United Nations in their liberated territories.*' (My italics.) At the same time the detachment of American troops in Athens was showing, according to C. M. Woodhouse, 'a spirit of neutrality with a benevolent bias in favour of EAM/ELAS'.[1]

From the same starting point, Washington became increasingly disenchanted with the type of 'democracy' developing in the countries of the Soviet sphere. British policy took a similar turn after Labour came to power in 1945; the resulting Anglo-American protests over events in Bulgaria and Rumania were a violation of the Teheran and Yalta agreements as Stalin conceived them – though in the eyes of London and Washington they represented an attempt to implement those agreements. The protests did not, of course, produce any change in Soviet policy in East Europe. But they produced a profound change in Western Europe, where the Communist parties became instruments of Soviet retaliation. In France and Italy, they left the governing coalitions in which they had played an unrevolutionary role and initiated a drive to obtain power if possible, and disrupt in any case, through strikes and demonstrations. In Greece, the civil war of 1946–49 – which, in contrast to the situation in December 1944, had the full moral and material support of Greece's northern neighbours – signalled the final collapse of the Teheran agreement on spheres of interest. (In all these cases, of course, the communists were able to muster mass support because of the existence of major and real grievances.) The idea of 'containment' was, in a sense, an effort to restore the boundaries between those spheres. On the one hand, it involved an acceptance of the West's inability to intervene effectively in opposition to the Soviet Union's policies in the countries garrisoned by Soviet troops. On the other, it meant that the United States was prepared to block the extension of the Soviet sphere in Europe by whatever means might seem necessary.

In general, the means envisaged at this time were political and economic rather than military. Only after the communist *coup* in Czechoslovakia in March 1948 did Washington react with the idea of NATO. Moreover, Washington's political perspective at this time envisaged the removal of those conditions which favoured the growth of communist strength. This, in the eyes of most Americans, required social reforms; centrist and Social Democratic parties were in general regarded as the best hope for such policies.

In Greece, this line was exemplified during the civil war by an inflexible veto on the repeated proposals of rightist elements to establish a military dictatorship. And it was at American insistence that Tsaldaris was replaced as Prime Minister by Sophoulis, despite the majority possessed by the Populists and their allies in the parliament elected in 1946. (Loy Henderson of the State Department flew from Washington to Athens to break the news to Tsaldaris that he was out.) After the end of the civil war, United States officials were delighted by the success of left-of-centre groups in the election of 1950. They blocked the attempt of the palace to persuade Sophocles Venizelos to renege on his pre-election agreement with Plastiras and Papandreou, whereby the one whose party did best in the elections would have the support of the other two as Prime Minister. When Venizelos agreed to serve as Prime Minister with Populist support, the ground was cut from under him by an open letter from Ambassador Henry Grady, which in effect warned that a continuation of American aid might depend on the formation of a government which reflected the desires of the Greek people as expressed in the election results.

The series of centre governments which began in the spring of 1950 thus represented a major success for American policy. But, having achieved that goal, the United States changed its policy. This change was not a reflection of anything that was happening in Greece, where it coincided with but was not caused by the replacement of Grady by John Peurifoy. (If Grady had continued somewhat longer in Greece, his personal belief in the earlier line might have brought him into open conflict with Washington, as it later did in Iran. But it would not have prevented the policy in Greece from changing. And while Peurifoy, in Greece as later in Guatemala, was certainly more flamboyant in his interference on behalf of the right than most American diplomats would have been, the policies he carried out in both places were in all essential respects made in Washington.) The catalyst for this change was the Korean War, which convinced Washington that the danger of Soviet expansion was a strictly military one, and that it could be resisted not by political and economic reforms achieved through the democratic left and centre, but by reliance on military elements – not merely in strictly military matters, but in politics as well.

Thus at this time the United States began applying intense pressure on Germany to re-arm, and abandoned any pretence of impartiality between the Social Democrats, who opposed re-armament, and the Christian Democrats, who supported it. In France, American support swung to the so-called 'Fourth Force' – the non-Gaullist right typified by Antoine Pinay and closely allied to the French armament industry. And in Greece the military right, which had always been nurtured and cultivated by some American military men but whose path to power had been blocked by the previous American policy, now became the chosen instrument of the Embassy.

There is good reason to believe that the abortive military *coup* staged in May 1951 by IDEA, an organization of right-wing officers close to the American military mission, was encouraged by the Embassy. It failed, however, partly because key positions in the armed forces were still held by the rival British-sponsored and palace-oriented faction led by General Ventiris, and partly because Marshal Papagos did not want to take power through a *coup*.

The Embassy then turned to other means in order to accomplish the same end. Papagos was prevailed on to enter politics as the leader of a new organization, the Greek Rally (Ellinikos Synagermos). Embassy influence was brought to bear on various right-wing groups to submerge their identity in the Rally; Constantine Tsaldaris, with the support of a few other individuals, refused to join and maintained the shell of the Populist Party. But most former Populist politicians, and almost the entire right-wing press, flocked to the banner of Papagos. Nevertheless, much to the surprise of the Embassy, the Rally came out of the 1951 elections with considerably less than a parliamentary majority. More than half the seats in parliament were held by the two parties which divided between them the mantle of traditional liberalism, Plastiras' EPEK (National Progressive Union of the Centre) and Sophocles Venizelos' Liberals. The Embassy tried to persuade the latter to form a coalition with the Rally, with Papagos as Premier. For once, Sophocles Venizelos was not amenable to an Embassy suggestion; after long bargaining, a Plastiras–Venizelos coalition took office, much to Ambassador Peurifoy's annoyance. In the ensuing months, the Embassy called in individual deputies belonging to the coalition parties and endeavoured to persuade them to defect to the Rally. In some cases the Embassy's arguments were doubtless persuasive by themselves; deputies closely associated with major Greek business interests might even have switched sides without any American intervention, because of their opposition to the economic reforms instituted by George Kartalis as Minister of Co-ordination. But there were also cases in which other American agencies furnished more substantial inducements to defectors. At the same time, the Embassy openly propagandized against the Plastiras–Venizelos government, charging it with endangering security by freeing too many political prisoners, and denouncing it for countering the defections by accepting the support of deputies who had been elected as EDA candidates. Peurifoy also publicly demanded the adoption of the so-called 'majority' (properly plurality) system of election in place of the existing form of 'reinforced' proportional representation. He rightly believed that this change would give the right, united in the Greek Rally, a disproportionate share of the seats in Parliament because the division between left and centre would make it, though a minority, the largest party in most constituencies. When the centre government succumbed to his pressure on this point, it practically assured its own defeat.

The result of the 1952 election was even more of a success for the Rally than Peurifoy had expected. With 49% of the vote, it won 80% of the seats in Parliament. This was, indeed, more of a victory for his efforts than Peurifoy really wanted. For it restricted the Embassy's possibilities of manipulation; a government with a majority of this magnitude could pursue an independent policy *vis-à-vis* the Embassy, if it so desired, without fearing the sort of campaign of attrition which Peurifoy had waged against the Plastiras–Venizelos government. (The Papagos government did in fact stir up the Cyprus issue in a way that certainly ran counter to American desires – even though there is reason to believe that secret American aid went to EOKA because of its 'anti-communism'. On the other hand, its continuation of the policy of amnesty, which had brought American strictures when it was pursued by the Plastiras–Venizelos government, does not seem to have met with any opposition from the Embassy. For the latter did not really object to the release of most political prisoners, as long as it was done in the name of expediency rather than justice.)

Meanwhile, the militarization of American policy had been reflected in the induction of Greece and Turkey into NATO. It took considerable arm-twisting to overcome the objections of some of the original members of the alliance to including the Eastern Mediterranean in the North Atlantic. Like such American experts as George Kennan, they felt that the extension of NATO's protective umbrella to Greece and Turkey made the alliance a riskier thing, and that the abandonment of its original geographic basis gave the Soviet Union legitimate reason to fear that the US was pursuing a policy of encirclement. The original decision to bring Greece and Turkey into NATO was probably at least in part motivated by a desire to create an indirect tie between NATO and Yugoslavia, which had recently entered into a defensive alliance with Greece and Turkey. The Balkan Pact, however, soon went into cold storage, primarily as a result of Greek–Turkish tensions over Cyprus; American relations with Yugoslavia continued to function on a bilateral basis, outside the NATO framework. But Greece and Turkey remained in NATO, a fact which immensely complicated life for both states and for NATO itself. And, because their adherence to NATO had been accompanied by the establishment of NATO (read American) bases in both countries, it created a Pentagonal vested interest which played a major role in American policy decisions.

American intervention was again fairly open in the manoeuvring which followed the death of Marshal Papagos. If the Embassy was no longer in a position to shift power from one party to another, it could nevertheless play a decisive role in the contest of factions within the Greek Rally. The senior leaders of the Rally, Kanellopoulos and Stephanopoulos, were passed over for the succession primarily because of strong American support for Constantine Karamanlis, who held the relatively minor Ministry of Public Works. This support continued throughout the eight years in which Karamanlis served as Premier; for much of this time, the Embassy practically ignored the existence of the opposition parties. (Unlike the British, US diplomats were not normally allowed even informal contacts with members of EDA. But in the late fifties and early sixties, they were also completely out of touch with the Centre. Ambassador Ellis Briggs almost completely broke off private contacts with the opposition, after the elections of 1961, and brought strong pressure to bear on George Papandreou to give up his campaign against the validity of those elections.)

But while successive ambassadors gave their personal flavour to American policy, its underlying basis did not significantly change. This was determined by the obsessively anti-communist and essentially military emphasis which had characterized it since the Korean war. Greece was thought of primarily as a military base, equipped with an army, and only secondarily as a country inhabited by a people. Its military reliability was the first consideration; this, in the eyes of American policy-makers, was to be preserved by insulating the armed forces from 'political control' – in other words, by preserving them as an autonomous authoritarian enclave. When Papagos was Premier, of course, there was no problem; he controlled the armed forces, but since he also represented them, his control was 'non-political'. After his death, the Americans relied on the special relationship which existed between the palace and the military.

This basic attitude did not change even when the Kennedy administration revived, to some extent, the concern with reform as a weapon against communism. President Kennedy's Ambassador to Greece, Henry Labouisse, was himself a man of progressive background and sympathies. He sought to rebuild relations with the Centre Union, not without some success, and when the Papandreou government came to power relations were initially good.

Yet a certain heritage of distrust and estrangement remained. And Labouisse, whatever his personal inclinations, could not alter the basically military orientation of American policy – and hence its built-in bias – in the Greek situation, in favour of the palace and the right. Nor did he have the power to control the activities of the military mission and the CIA, both of which had more resources at their disposal than the Embassy, despite his nominal authority over them.

Moreover, it did not take long for the Papandreou government to come into conflict with the CIA and the United States Information Agency on specific matters. The clash with the CIA resulted from the efforts of Andreas Papandreou, who as Minister to the Prime Minister had nominal supervision over the Greek Central Intelligence Service (KYP), to bring that agency under the effective control of the Greek government. Discovering that it had been funded directly by the CIA, which thus was in a position to exert a decisive influence on its activities, he demanded that all funds supplied to KYP pass through the Prime Minister's office. The CIA blocked this attempt to subject its activities in Greece to a democratic control from which they were exempt in most of the world, but it did not forgive it. The CIA's hostility to Andreas Papandreou in particular and the Centre Union in general was not the sole cause and probably not the principal cause of the American role in 1965 and thereafter. Yet it must certainly have coloured the reports Washington received and on which American decisions were based. And it seems likely to have affected the implementation of American policy in ways that may have been almost as important as the policy itself.

The clash with the CIA related to essentials; that with the USIA was almost accidental in character. The Voice of America, the BBC, and the French radio all relayed programmes through the Greek radio network. Objecting to the BBC's use of this time to broadcast extracts from the British press which presented views on the Cyprus question which differed from those of the Greek government, Andreas Papandreou proposed to end all three agreements; he won Cabinet backing for this. The British and French accepted this decision, though they hardly welcomed it; the director of the USIA in Greece reportedly threatened reprisals. A bitter quarrel ensued, and after the USIA official had gone on home leave, the Greek government requested that he not be sent back to Greece. Although the dispute seems to have been blown up well beyond the proportions that its significance deserved, there can be little question that it contributed to the development of a widespread feeling of resentment against Andreas Papandreou in American official circles. This was all the more intense, one suspects, because of a feeling in those circles that Papandreou's recently surrendered American citizenship imposed some sort of an obligation on him to see things through American eyes. It need hardly be added that there were plenty of Greeks, especially in those circles on which the Americans were accustomed to rely, who had their own reasons for disliking and distrusting Papandreou and were ready to encourage similar sentiments among the Americans. None of this, of course, affected the basic motivations of American policy in Greece. But it certainly had an effect on the form which that policy's implementation took.

A third source of conflict came to a head after President Kennedy's assassination had brought Lyndon Johnson to power. This, which probably loomed a good deal larger in Athens than it did in Washington, was the Cyprus issue. The Papandreou government backed President Makarios in his abrogation of the Cyprus constitution and his conflict with the Turkish community on the island, while Turkey, of course, backed the Cypriot Turks. Greek policy, at least formally, was to insist that the dispute was an internal Cypriot question that had to be settled between the two communities on the island, without the intervention of any outside power. This furnished a theoretical rationale for the refusal of the Papandreou government to enter into negotiations with Turkey for a settlement of the question, although George Papandreou also tended to stress the danger that such negotiations, if unsuccessful, would make the situation worse. Turkey, on the other hand, emphasized her role as protector of the Turkish community on Cyprus, and sought to keep the issue on the international plane. Whatever the theoretical arguments advanced by the two sides, it was clear that each was seeking the forum most favourable to it. The Greeks on Cyprus far outnumbered the Turks, and if there were no foreign interference would presumably be able to win the argument by sheer force. But internationally, the boot was on the other foot; Turkey's military strength far exceeded that of Greece. Realistically, of course, the Cyprus question *was* in the international arena, and both the Greek and Turkish governments were in it up to their necks and had been for years.

From the American point of view, the crucial thing about the quarrel was not the rights and wrongs of the two communities on the island, but the damage it did to relations between Greece and Turkey, both allies of the United States. If the two countries went to war over Cyprus, the security of American bases in both countries would be undermined. Moreover, both countries would be using weapons provided by the United States, as indeed they already were through their proxies on Cyprus. (This, of course, represented the *reductio ad absurdum* of the military-centred foreign policy which the United States had been following and of the assumption that 'anti-communism' was an adequate foundation for a military alliance.) What mattered, therefore, was not the basis on which a solution was reached; it was simply the surmounting of the immediate crisis. The 'Acheson Plan' for a partition of Cyprus was regarded by many Greeks as part of a sinister plot for the extension of American power at the expense of the rights of the Greek Cypriots. But in all probability it was simply the same sort of knee-jerk reaction that has caused advocates of *Realpolitik* to resort to partition – usually with disastrous results – as a 'solution' to communal tensions elsewhere. It was, in any case, less important in American eyes than steps to defuse the immediate situation. These included the imposition of a truce, the establishment of a UN force to supervise it, and the prevention of a Turkish invasion of the island. Such measures certainly helped to preserve the NATO alliance and the American military position in the Eastern Mediterranean by temporarily papering over the Greek–Turkish conflict. But they also averted a war which would have been disastrous for the peoples of the area. Their accomplishment did nothing to secure a permanent solution of the Cyprus problem, and it left both Greeks and Turks resentful; each side felt that the United States had betrayed it by not giving it unlimited backing against the other. On the whole, the Turkish resentment was probably greater because most Turks felt that without international intervention they would have been able to 'solve' the Cyprus problem by force of arms. One result was a significant rapprochement between Ankara and Moscow. But there was enough resentment in Greece to exacerbate still further the tensions which existed in Greek–American relations.

The Cyprus crisis also had another result, primarily affecting the internal politics of Greece and the Greek military, but soon deeply involving the Americans. This was the 'Aspida' case, which had its origins in the Greek forces illegally on Cyprus as a result of the crisis. It was precipitated by the intrigues of George Grivas, who commanded those forces, and quickly taken up by circles close to the palace. Many right-wing Greeks certainly believed that there really was a secret Aspida organization sponsored by Andreas Papandreou to prepare the way for a left-wing military *coup*; this belief found a ready echo among at least some of the Americans who had developed an antagonism to him. Any such undermining of the anti-communist reliability of the armed forces would have struck at the basic assumptions of American policy; even the suspicions of it assured substantial American support for any attack on Papandreou, and by extension on the Papandreou government itself.

The same obsessive anti-communism caused many Americans to disapprove of the release of almost all the prisoners still held for offences arising from the civil war. Indeed, the fact that under the Papandreou government the people of Greece had more freedom than at any period since the war, was itself a reason for distrust, in the eyes of some Americans. For they saw this freedom as a relaxation of the barriers against communism. This attitude was, of course, shared by many right-wing Greeks, including a good many military men.

Certainly the existence of these attitudes among Americans must have been one of the factors that encouraged the King to dismiss the Papandreou government in 1965. The issue of royal as against 'political' control of the armed forces was one on which, even without any specific commitments from the Embassy or other American agencies, he knew he could be certain of considerable American sympathy. When to this was added the ingredient of a 'leftist plot' involving the son of the Prime Minister, he could be reasonably sure that the sympathy would take practical forms. And it did.

The formation of the Stephanopoulos government would not have been possible without American support; indeed, it is unlikely that

Stephanopoulos himself would have undertaken it if he had not believed the United States would welcome it. Several of the others who broke away from the Centre Union to support the King were well known for their close ties with the US Embassy. Some were widely believed to have CIA connections. The Embassy's support for the King and its opposition to the Papandreous were evident enough in the background briefings given to American journalists, and often reflected in their articles. Indeed, the Embassy assured the King of American support in any steps he might take, short of a military *coup*. Some of the other American agencies involved made no such exception.

As the conflict continued, and the Stephanopoulos government maintained a tenuous parliamentary majority in the face of the Centre Union's solid support in the country, the possibility of a military coup by IDEA (whose leadership dominated the Army high command) became a recurrent theme. The attitude of the United States seemed likely to be crucial in determining whether one took place. And that attitude was by no means clear. Certainly the idea of elections, leading to a Centre Union victory which not only would deprive the King of control over the armed forces but seemed increasingly likely to threaten the monarchy itself, was not a welcome one to Washington. Certainly, too, the Johnson administration had no insuperable objections of principle to a military *coup* at the expense of a 'leftist' though non-communist government; it had shown this in Brazil and the Dominican Republic. But it was hardly desirous of a second Dominican adventure, particularly in Europe; the international and domestic repercussions of the first one were still reverberating.

So the official American position continued to be one of opposition to military intervention in the situation. Few Greeks, however, believed that the position was an immutable one, or that it was shared by the US military mission or the Athens representatives of the CIA. Certainly the military mission and CIA were privy to the plans for a military takeover which were under consideration in the upper reaches of the Army. At one point, the Johnson administration seems to have been resigned to such a *coup*; while its precise implications were never quite clear, it would apparently have involved the imposition of a state of siege, a sharp curtailment of civil liberties, a postponement of elections beyond the constitutionally prescribed time, and their 'management' by a new electoral law and perhaps by other means as well. But the administration appears finally to have decided that for the time being there were other and preferable options available, and to have so informed the King and the leaders of the armed forces. And for the King, at least, American support was a pre-requisite for a *coup*.

The decision to permit the scheduled elections to take place appears to have become definite at about the beginning of April. The designation of Kanellopoulos as Prime Minister on 3 April would have been extremely unlikely if the King and the officers who followed his lead were contemplating a *coup*. Kanellopoulos was strongly opposed to any such step and his presence as Prime Minister would have been a major obstacle to its legitimation.

The Embassy's expectation was that the elections scheduled for 28 May would not give a clear majority to any party, and that they would then be followed by a Papandreou–Kanellopoulos coalition, supported by the 'moderate' elements of both parties – that is, the right wing of the Centre Union and the democratic right which followed Kanellopoulos. If the Centre Union remained united, and Andreas Papandreou participated in such a coalition, he would be 'contained'. If he refused, he would be out of the government, and would cease to represent a threat.

Some aspects of this assessment were probably unrealistic; the probability was that the Centre Union would sweep the elections by a substantially greater margin than in 1964, primarily because it had succeeded in winning over a good many of the non-communists who had in the past supported EDA because they had lost faith in the Centre. Moreover, because of the role Andreas Papandreou had won in the selection of candidates, most of the new Centre Union deputies were likely to belong to the left wing of the party. The Embassy had long had a tendency to overestimate the strength of the right-centre, perhaps because members of this group were usually ready to tell the Embassy what it wanted to hear.

Nevertheless, the Embassy may well have been right in expecting a Papandreou–Kanellopoulos coalition to emerge from the elections, since both George Papandreou and Panayotis Kanellopoulos seem to have been favourably disposed to the idea. One indication that there was a substantial factual basis for the reports of a pre-election agreement between the two leaders was Kanellopoulos' decision not to prosecute Andreas Papandreou during the election period on charges arising from the Aspida case. (This is scarcely conclusive evidence, however. Papandreou and Kanellopoulos were after all old friends, and had been political allies as well as rivals in the past; the idea of prosecuting George Papandreou's son may well have been distasteful to Kanellopoulos – particularly since he probably at least suspected that the charges were false. It should be added that Washington

was probably relieved by the decision, since Andreas had many influential
friends in the United States.) And avoiding a pre-election *coup* did not
foreclose the possibility of one at a subsequent date if things did not turn
out according to the Embassy's scenario. There is, however, no reason
to believe that any decision on the American attitude toward such a
post-election *coup* had been reached; it was a contingency which could be
dealt with if the occasion arose.

But the decision not to carry out the so-called 'big *coup*' opened the
way for action by the small group of officers in EENA; the decision not to
prosecute Andreas Papandreou probably precipitated it, since Andreas
had come to be the personification of evil in the eyes of right-wing
know-nothings such as those in EENA. Because the American opposition
to the Centre Union had been so open in the preceding two years, because
the Greeks had come to attribute anything that happened in their country
to American influence whatever the facts might be in any particular case,
and because the CIA had a well-earned reputation for arranging or seeking
to arrange the overthrow of inconvenient governments, most Greeks
initially believed that the United States was behind the *coup*. Many
certainly still do. It is a belief which the junta at first went out of its way
to encourage, since by identifying itself with the Americans it hoped to
bolster its originally meagre support in the armed forces and on the
political right. (More recently, adopting a nationalist posture, it has
stressed its independence *vis-à-vis* the Americans.) But the available
evidence suggests very strongly, though in the nature of the situation it
cannot prove absolutely, that it is a mistaken belief.

It was not merely that American officials in Athens in the period
immediately after the *coup* of 21 April disclaimed any part in its preparation, but that their obvious discomfiture could simply not have been
feigned. The *coup* that the United States had considered and ultimately
rejected as a solution was a *coup* involving the King and the top leadership
of the armed forces. But the first thing the conspirators did on 21 April
was to lock up the generals who would have headed that *coup* if it had
taken place. True, their success depended in large part on the fact that
Papadopoulos had been slated for a key role in the other *coup*, and most
of those who received his orders on 21 April thought that they came from
the generals and had the blessing of the King.

It has been argued that because Papadopoulos had served in the Greek
Central Intelligence Service, KYP, and had thus worked under CIA direction, the CIA must have known and by implication participated in his
preparations for the *coup*. But there is no reason to believe that Papado-

poulos would have had any more hesitation about deceiving his American contacts than about deceiving his Greek military superiors and – in the 'big *coup*' – co-conspirators. Nor is there anything in the CIA's record to suggest that it could not be deceived rather easily.

A second fact that was quite obvious was the general American contempt for the new rulers of Greece. The Embassy was clearly counting on out-manoeuvring them and inducing them to surrender power in short order; the chosen instruments for this purpose were the King and the generals – those who were not under lock and key. (Within the junta, the Embassy expected Vice-Premier Pattakos to carry the ball for a restoration of parliamentary government, although there was no reason whatever to believe that he had either the intention or the power to do so.) At the same time, however, the Embassy and its superiors in Washington preferred the junta's rule to a possible civil war; advice from the Embassy was at least one factor in the decision of the King not to attempt to resist the *coup*, as some of his close associates had urged. The King's acceptance of the new regime then permitted the State Department (and its opposite numbers in other countries) to assert that, since their ambassadors were accredited to the King, no question of recognition arose. Later, after the King's flight, the argument changed; the ambassadors were accredited to the King *in Athens* and not in Rome, so that it was only normal for them to continue relations with the government and regent who acted in his name.

Meanwhile, Embassy and State Department began a pattern of looking on the bright side which was to persist, year after year, in the face of the facts. Thus they hailed the junta's appointment of a committee to draft a new constitution as a major step toward the return of democracy, stressing that the committee was under instructions to report within six months. The new constitution which it was to draw up would then, in their view, furnish the basis for a prompt return to democracy. They skipped lightly over such minor questions as why Greece needed a new constitution, what validity one drawn up under military rule could have, how much democracy it was likely to contain, and what guarantees there were that the men who had seized and were exercising power in violation of the existing constitution would respect the new one if it got in their way.

At the same time, the United States continued to supply military aid to the junta, and thereby accepted the role of accomplice in its crimes. To be sure, Defense Secretary Robert McNamara did warn his counterpart, General Spandidakis, that it would be very difficult to continue aid if democracy were not restored. When Ambassador Xanthopoulos-Palamas presented his credentials in September, President Johnson spoke to him in similar terms. The President was speaking with the voice of experience; he had reportedly been prepared to lift the partial embargo in July, but found that the public reaction to the revocation of Melina Mercouri's Greek citizenship made restoration of full arms aid politically unhealthy. McNamara himself is reported to have favoured a suspension of aid, but its continuation had the support of both the State Department and the military establishment. The position of the advocates of continued aid and the reluctance of Washington to do anything to upset the Greek apple-cart were reinforced by the outbreak of war between Israel and her Arab neighbours. The proximity of Greek bases to the fighting increased their apparent importance, even though they did not in fact serve any purpose during the conflict and were unlikely to be of much use in any future crisis in the Middle East because of the close ties which any Greek government had to maintain with the Arab states. And the advocates of continued military aid added – it was an argument that was to be used again and again over the years – that giving aid enabled the United States to influence the junta in the direction of a return to democracy. The result of the conflicting pressures within the United States government was a suspension of shipments of heavy weapons but a continuation (and in many categories an actual increase) in all other forms of aid. The weapons cut off were those which would have been useful primarily against a foreign foe; those which continued to flow were the ones most important for domestic repression.

This policy must be judged in the light of the fact that a decision had been reached *before* the *coup* to phase out military aid to Greece, or at least to reduce it sharply, over the four-year period 1967–70. This decision was non-political in origin; it was based on the belief that some of the aid Greece was receiving was unnecessary for the fulfilment of her NATO role, and that her improved economic situation would enable her to pay for the rest from her own resources. Thus even when arms shipments fell below the pre-*coup* figure, the reduction did not bring the level below what had been planned before 21 April 1967. Indeed, for most of the period when the 'reduction' was in effect, aid was actually greater than had been planned before the *coup*. Of course, it must be recognised that one of the assumptions on which the cuts had been planned turned out to be false; the economic improvement that had been taking place did not continue, and Greece faced serious balance-of-payments difficulties even without the added burden of paying for arms. The increase in military aid over what had previously been planned may thus have been a reward to the Colonels not for destroying Greek democracy, but merely for damaging the Greek economy. This would at least have been in line with the Pentagon's domestic policy of giving special subsidies to inefficient suppliers.

The CIA seems, like the State Department, to have relied on the King and the generals to bring back a parliamentary regime of some sort. It did not, however, expect them to persuade the junta to surrender power voluntarily. It appears to have had a plan which bore a striking resemblance – except in respect to the regime it was designed to displace – to the plan for the generals' *coup* which had been considered early in 1967.[2] The trouble with this was that the junta assumed from the beginning that it could not rely on the King and his friends in the armed forces, and acted accordingly. By increasing the officer corps by 10%, giving large-scale promotions to its own adherents – or those who became its adherents when they got the promotions, removing large numbers of high-ranking officers loyal to the King, and assigning its own people to key positions, it strengthened its own position in the armed forces and eroded that of the King.

Whatever the role of the CIA in the original plans for the King's *coup* of December, there is nothing to indicate that it had a hand in the fiasco of its execution. Some Greeks have suggested that it even tipped the junta off to the King's plans. This seems improbable; everybody in Athens had been talking about the prospective royal *coup* for months, the foreign press had carried numerous articles on it, and there had been little doubt about anything except the precise date. The CIA's non-involvement may have been due to an unwillingness in Washington to take part in an attempt to overthrow the junta, or simply to a belief that the junta's preparations had doomed the *coup* before it was launched. Whatever the reason, when the King finally did move he had no support from any part of the American government, however much the United States might have welcomed a royal victory if by some miracle it had occurred.

To be sure, the United States did wait until 23 January to resume full diplomatic relations with the junta, an act reportedly greeted by the latter with 'enormous relief'. (Up to that time only two other countries had taken similar action: Turkey, which felt it necessary to continue negotiations over Cyprus, and the Congo.) Presumably it took the State Department that long to think up a rationale for the action, since it had originally predicated its immediate recognition of the junta after 21 April on the continued presence of the King. To be sure, the absence of 'full diplomatic contacts' in the previous month had not prevented Ambassador Talbot from meeting the Greek Foreign Minister Pipinelis, or Admiral Griffin from officially calling on the government and exchanging compliments with it when he left his post as NATO Mediterranean commander. But the resumption was symbolically significant; it represented the abandonment of any reservations in American acceptance of the junta's legitimacy.

A further step in this direction came when, on 15 March 1968, the junta published the draft constitution submitted to it three months earlier by the committee appointed in May 1967, announcing at the same time that it would present its own draft in June and submit it to a plebiscite in September. The State Department 'welcomed' the news; its spokesman added: 'We are further pleased to note that comments from the Greek people and the press on the draft of the Constitution are being encouraged.' The *New York Times* commented editorially: 'This blessing, bestowed with such unseemly haste, is simply the latest in a series of moves that point to one conclusion: Washington has decided to do everything it can to provide the Athens junta with the prestige and respectability it has hungered after since its putsch of last April.'

This acceptance took place despite the fact that the defeat of the King's *coup* was followed by a stepped-up purge of the armed services, which retired almost all those senior officers who had NATO experience or American training. 'Political interference' with the armed forces was apparently objectionable only when it came from a *democratic* government; from a dictatorship it was regarded as normal and proper. There is no recorded instance of any action by the United States to discourage the junta's military purges, though one can imagine the uproar which would have emanated from Washington if the Papandreou government had attempted anything comparable. It is perhaps more than a coincidence that this complete acceptance of the junta followed closely on the departure from President Johnson's cabinet of Defense Secretary Robert McNamara, who had been responsible for the original cut in military aid.

Deliveries of heavy weapons were resumed on 21 October 1968, thus abandoning the one remaining anti-junta aspect of US policy. The ostensible reason for this was the Soviet invasion of Czechoslovakia. It was true that Greece's neighbours, Yugoslavia and Albania, feared that the Soviet Union might exert military pressure to bring them back to Communist orthodoxy. But nobody suggested that Greece was in danger of a Soviet invasion; Russian troops might be sent to the lost sheep of the house of Lenin, but they would not cross the lines set at Yalta – any more than American troops would cross them in the other direction to defend the independence of a Hungary or a Czechoslovakia. Czechoslovakia would thus seem to be the excuse, rather than the reason, for the renewed shipment of heavy arms to Greece.

Greece played only a very minor role in the 1968 presidential election. Neither party mentioned the subject in its platform, and there was no discussion of it on the floor of either party's convention, although three anti-junta organizations presented proposals before the Democratic platform committee. In the pre-convention period Senator Eugene McCarthy cited President Eisenhower's warning against the military-industrial complex and said: 'This is not a danger at home yet, but its force and power – conscious or unconscious, sought or unsought – is already manifest in our foreign policy and reflected in what has happened in Greece.' And Robert Kennedy, after a long conversation with Andreas Papandreou, took the latter out with him to the press conference at which he announced his candidacy. But neither Hubert Humphrey nor Richard Nixon mentioned the subject.

One candidate did, however, discuss it at some length, with the gracious liberalism for which he was to become famous. In answer to a question the Republican Vice-Presidential candidate, Spiro Agnew, declared on 27 September: 'I think the Greek military government that took over in 1967 has not proven itself to be as horrendous a spectre to contemplate as most people thought it would. I think as long as they are seriously living up to their obligations – there is supposed to be a referendum this Sunday on the constitution and I think they have promised free elections thereafter – that particularly with that information and that performance along with the recent disclosures of the PAK (Panhellenic Liberation Front) involving Mr Andreas Papandreou and Mr Brillakis based in Italy and Mr Papandreou in Sweden, I think we have got to believe that although we don't want a military government, we look for the return of a free elective system in the tradition of Greece, that this particular military government has done a bit to stabilize the communist threat in Greece. That they have, for example, encouraged the return of Greek shipbuilding interests, which is one of the most important economic factors in the country; that the Greek government, when the Arab–Israeli crisis broke and the Soviet build-up began and as it continues in the Mediterranean, have immediately made their bases available to us for refuelling and that the communist forces under

Andreas Papandreou, which incidentally Andreas is now not operating with the consent of George. The former Premier indicates that they are totally identified with the communist movement, which gives their cause a lot less sanctity in our eyes. Also I think that there have been recent amnesties granted to former Prime Ministers which indicates that the government does not wish to control the country absolutely but only to provide a salutary climate in which a free elective system can take place.'

Nevertheless the Nixon administration appeared initially to be following a line a good deal less favourable to the junta than that which President Johnson was pursuing at the end of his term. The embargo on heavy weapons was re-imposed, the post of Ambassador was left open for almost a year, and a number of highly critical statements were made by key officials. (Vice-President Agnew, on the other hand, said nothing publicly. Privately, he reportedly told pro-junta visitors that the Nixon administration did not support the junta, and that he himself would not visit Greece as long as the junta was in power.)

Testifying before the Senate Foreign Relations Committee on 27 March 1969, Secretary of State William Rogers answered a question from Senator Claiborne Pell by declaring: 'Yes, Senator! We share your concern not only for the torture but for other civil liberties. We are doing what we can to that effect. And we will be conscious of the factors that you mention in our subsequent negotiations.'

On 14 July, Rogers told the Foreign Relations Committee: 'As you know we did not last year obligate all the money that was appropriated, and if the suspension continues then we would not obligate as much money as has been requested this year. On the other hand we would hope that the Greek Government will make progress toward parliamentary government, that it will implement the constitutional provisions, and that we would be able to somewhere along the line, to remove the suspension. If so we would like to have the money available. . . . I would not want them to think that no matter what they did, that their money was unavailable. But . . . the money will not be obligated unless the suspension is removed, and the suspension will not be removed unless they make some progress toward more parliamentary government.'

On the following day, Secretary of Defense Melvin Laird told the Committee: 'I want it understood at the present time we have a freeze on the aid as far as Greece is concerned, and that freeze is being continued and will be continued until progress is made toward more democratic procedures in that country. We have not released any military equipment to Greece since I have been Secretary of Defense, and the freeze is currently on the program as far as Greece is concerned . . . and since this administration has been in office, there has been no relaxing, no relaxation of that freeze. We are hopeful that the Greek government will move in the direction of democratic procedures, and this would be reviewed at that time.' The Defense Department later explained that Laird meant that no *heavy* arms had been sent to Greece during his term of office. Again, in response to a letter from fifty members of Congress expressing concern about American policy toward Greece, Assistant Secretary of State William B. Macomber, Jr, wrote on 5 August: 'Your letter points up the dilemma we face in determining our policy toward Greece. On the one hand we see an autocratic government denying basic civil liberties to the citizens of Greece. We think such an internal order does not coincide with the best interests of Greece, whose stability in the long run, we believe, depends upon the free play of democratic forces. We have been pressing this viewpoint upon the Greek Government, and our policy on military assistance has been motivated by our desire to see Greece evolve toward representative government.

'On the other hand, Greece is a NATO ally which has scrupulously fulfilled its treaty obligations. It is important to our strategic interests in the Mediterranean area and has extended full co-operation in this field.

'This, then, is the dilemma – how to deal with an ally with whose internal order we disagree yet who is a loyal NATO partner working closely with the United States in furtherance of the purposes and obligations of the NATO Treaty.

'Our policy toward Greece is now under intensive review. As we consider this difficult problem we will keep the suggestions of yourself and your colleagues very much in mind.'

In retrospect, it seems likely that the Nixon administration began to shift toward a more favourable attitude toward the junta in September 1969. On 30 September, former Premier Constantine Karamanlis issued a sharp denunciation of the junta and indicated his readiness to take up the fight against it. It was widely felt that Karamanlis, who had made no public statement for two years and had not previously indicated a readiness to return to an active role on the Greek political scene, would not have done so at this point without some indication of support from Washington. But his statement elicited no public response from anyone in the Nixon administration. It seems likely that he may have been encouraged to act by some officials in the State Department or CIA, but that their initiative was subsequently overruled in the National Security Council or by the President himself.

September was also the month in which the President finally nominated Henry Tasca to fill the long-vacant post of Ambassador to Greece. It is at least probable that Tasca was chosen to implement a policy already decided on. Tasca's own answers, during his interrogation by the Senate Foreign Relations Committee on 4 November prior to confirmation, were inevitably extremely guarded. Yet they left an impression of much greater readiness to defend the junta than Rogers and Laird had shown in July. In November, too, American diplomats in Europe were actively – and unsuccessfully – lobbying against a condemnation of Greece by the Council of Europe.

Perhaps partly because its members sensed the direction in which administration policy was moving, the Senate Foreign Relations Committee coupled its approval of the Tasca appointment on 8 December with the insertion in the Foreign Assistance Authorization Bill of the Pell Amendment banning aid to Greece. But on a motion of Senator Dodd of Connecticut, this ban was removed from the bill by a vote of 45 to 38. The Senate then unanimously passed a motion, also by Dodd, 'That it is the sense of the Senate that the United States Government exert all possible effort to influence a speedy return to a constitutional government in Greece.' Since the Senate had just rejected the most important type of pressure available to it, this resolution made little impression on either the administration or the junta.

It gradually became clear during 1970 that the policy Tasca was implementing was one of rapprochement with the junta. Almost as soon as he arrived in Greece, he began to transfer out those members of the Embassy staff whose understanding of the Greek situation had made them *persona non grata* to the junta. By August there was apparently nobody left on his staff who knew enough to correct him when he wrote to Dean Le Roy C. Breunig of Barnard College that Phoivos Ioannidis, the former Herakleion youth leader of the Centre Union whom the junta had tortured and imprisoned, had 'been a member of a United Democratic Left (EDA) Youth Group (EDIN)'.[3]

Meanwhile, in Washington, the atmosphere was also clearly changing for the worse. After visiting a number of high administration officials in May 1970, Helen Vlachos reported: 'In Athens, the walls have ears; in Washington, the ears have walls.' And in June, when Senator Vance Hartke of Indiana introduced an amendment to the Military Sales Act to cut off aid to Greece, the administration came out squarely in defence of the junta. A memorandum from the Defense Department, introduced by Senator Strom Thurmond, asserted: 'Most importantly, the Greek Government announced that in accordance with a specific timetable, to which it has thus far carefully adhered, the institutional structure of a democracy prerequisite to elections will be in place by the end of this year. This timetable is a public commitment on the part of the Greek Government. It seems to be a reasonable time element, i.e., the end of this year. A yardstick has now been established to measure the Greek regime's performance. Some patience and restraint should be exercised by all, as the Greek regime seems to be moving ahead in the direction to establish democratic norms. . . . Greece can be helped by sympathetic understanding rather than by censure.' On 29 June, the Hartke Amendment was defeated by a vote of 50 to 42.

Throughout the summer, reports circulated – and were repeatedly denied – that the administration was about to lift the embargo on heavy arms again. On 22 September the announcement finally came. It was, of course, a direct violation of the pledge Secretaries Rogers and Laird had given the Senate Foreign Relations Committee in July 1969. Even the official announcement did not claim that Greece had made 'progress toward more parliamentary government' or 'more democratic procedures', but only that 'the trend toward a constitutional order is established' and 'the Government of Greece has stated that it intends to establish parliamentary democracy'. Both these statements were just as true in September 1970 as they had been in July 1969 or May 1967 – and no truer. Indeed, the official announcement itself confessed that 'the United States had hoped for a more rapid return to representative government in Greece'. Senator J. W. Fulbright commented: 'We espouse high-sounding principles on the one hand, while dealing with dictators for military bases on the other. The administration might at least spare us the pain of its rhetoric and get on with the deal – provided, of course, the price is right.' State Department spokesman Robert McCloskey specifically denied that the aid decision was related to the internal crisis then erupting in Jordan. Fulbright, however, suggested that it was – the administration thought that the public would not notice what was done about Greece because its attention was focused on Jordan.

The arms decision was quickly followed by Secretary Laird's visit to Athens, the first of a series of high-level pilgrimages to the shrine of the junta. (The Colonels had already received one interesting unofficial guest; in March the President's brother Donald Nixon had come to see them in search of contracts for the Marriott Company, of which he had recently become Vice-President. Shepherded around by Tom Papas, he did not leave Athens empty-handed.) There was, indeed, one legitimate reason that might have inspired cabinet-level visits to Athens; Washington could not hope to get the truth of what was happening there from the Embassy under Henry Tasca, in the unlikely event that it wanted to. Thus in February 1971 the Senate Foreign Relations Committee's investigators, James G. Lowenstein and Richard Moose, reported: 'Many in the Embassy tend to rationalize the actions of the regime in terms similar to those the regime itself uses. For example, the Embassy apparently believes that the proposed law on political parties is basically democratic and compatible with local conditions despite the fact that under Article 58 of the new constitution, which the law would implement when put into force, the charter of every political party must be approved by the Constitutional Court which also can supervise the functioning of the parties and has the power to dissolve any party whose "aims or activities are manifestly or covertly opposed to the form of government. . . ."

'In this same connection, we noted that in Embassy meetings the *coup* and its aftermath was often referred to as the "revolution". Those Greeks opposed to the regime in Athens refer not to the "revolution" but to the "junta" or the "Colonels". Others, less partisan, refer to the "government" or the "leadership" or the "regime". It is only those who support the government who refer to the "revolution". The term is certainly not neutral.' They also noted that the Embassy had stated that it assumed that the continuing arrests under martial law were being carried out under the letter if not the spirit of the law, and commented: 'Yet no one in Athens was able to cite to us any provisions of the military or civil penal code which permits holding persons in detention incommunicado for more than 20 days.'

Lowenstein and Moose also analysed the contents of a document put out by the State Department in January 1971 for the use of the public, entitled *Greece: US Policy*. This document asserted: 'From a high of over 6,000 in 1967, there are now approximately 300 political prisoners. The Prime Minister has pledged to free all remaining political detainees by the end of April 1971 if security conditions permit.' The Senate's investigators pointed out: 'There are, of course, far more than 300 political prisoners if the numbers of those in exile (of which there are 60), detainees (of which there are about 345) and sentenced prisoners (of which there are about 350) are combined. The 6,000 figure refers, moreover, to those suspected of communist sympathies who were detained immediately after the *coup*. The Prime Minister's statement applied to the remaining detainees from among that group, but not to those sentenced for political crimes, to say nothing of those arrested since November.' The numbers cited by Lowenstein and Moose were themselves minimum figures for all categories; other estimates ran much higher.

'The State Department paper,' they also noted, 'includes the remarkable sentence that "With minor exceptions, all institutional laws necessary to put into force the constitution were promulgated by the end of 1970 as pledged by the Greek Government." As we have noted in this report, the institutional laws not yet put in force are hardly minor since they relate to the state of siege, political parties, parliament and the constitutional court. Furthermore, the constitution is by no means yet in effect; elections have not been scheduled or even promised and martial law is still in effect superseding the guarantees of due process for which the constitution provides.

'Finally, on the question of torture, the paper states that during the operative period of the agreement between the Greek Government and the International Committee of the Red Cross, "no instances of torture of prisoners were confirmed by the Red Cross." The fact of the matter is that, as a matter of policy, the Red Cross never confirms or denies instances of torture or indeed ever issues public reports. Its reports were made to the Greek Government and were confidential. The implication of the statement quoted is that no torture has taken place when in fact it seems far more probable that some tortures have occurred.' It should be noted that the document in question is not an isolated case, but rather is fairly typical of official American statements on Greece.

For a while in March it seemed that the administration was again veering away from the junta. Secretary of State Rogers once more expressed 'disappointment' with the lack of progress toward constitutional government. (It seems quite likely, in fact, that the Secretary of State really *is* disappointed and would like to do something about it. But in the Nixon administration the State Department's function is not to make foreign policy, but merely to apologize for it.) Two representatives of the Washington Institute of Strategic Studies – a government 'think-tank' – visited Athens and conferred with leaders of the Centre Union and ERE. For the first time, President Nixon sent greetings to the exiled King Constantine on Greek Independence Day. But it turned out to be a false dawn.

A more significant indicator of American policy came with the visit to Athens of Secretary of Commerce, Maurice Stans. Secretary Laird had limited his Athens utterances to platitudes. Not so Stans. He told a luncheon audience: 'We in the United States Government, particularly in American business, greatly appreciate Greece's attitude toward American investment, and we appreciate the welcome that is given here to American companies and the sense of security that the Government of Greece is imparting to them.' He went on to praise the 'economic stability' and 'political stability' and credit the junta with an 'economic miracle'. And he declared: 'I am particularly complimented by the fact that there are nine ministers and deputy ministers of the Government of Greece who hear me address you today. It is a compliment to me and it is a compliment to the Government of the United States and to the wonderfully close relations that exist today between our two countries.' After Stans visited the Ministry of Co-ordination, a ministry communiqué asserted that Stans had conveyed President Nixon's 'warm love to the Greek Government and the Greek people'. Pressed by reporters, the Embassy unofficially denied that Stans had spoken of 'warm love' and suggested that he had used the phrase 'warmth and confidence'. But there was never any official denial or clarification. On 12 July, Representative Benjamin Rosenthal queried Deputy Assistant Secretary of State Rodger Davies on the Stans statement, as follows:

> DAVIES: I don't have the text of that letter. It was not warm love, as the Embassy correctly stated.
> ROSENTHAL: Did we send a letter to the Greek Government clarifying Mr Stans' remarks?
> DAVIES: I believe we stand on the Embassy statement, sir.

*   *   *

> ROSENTHAL: Has the Secretary or the President issued any statement at least since Stans' remarks in Athens in April 1971?
> DAVIES: Not since April, sir.

Davies nevertheless asserted: 'We have made clear, I think, publicly and certainly in statements that have been reproduced in the Greek press, that the United States Government does not support the authoritarian nature of the regime in Greece.' But he admitted: 'It is probably true, sir, that a great many of the Greek people have interpreted our continued working relationship with their government as evidence of across-the-board support for the government. In the cases of those persons who are strongly opposed to their government, this has probably been reflected in some anti-Americanism.'

The testimony of Davies, as well as that of James H. Noyes, the Deputy Assistant Secretary of Defense with responsibility for Pentagon policy toward Greece, helped to convince members of the House of Representatives Foreign Affairs Committee that the administration simply could not offer a valid defence of its continuance of US military aid for the junta. This view was strongly reinforced by the testimony of Colonel Oliver Marshall, who had been Army and Defense Attaché of the US Embassy in Athens at the time of the *coup*; he urged that the United States do everything it could to dissociate itself from the junta and exert pressure for the restoration of Greek democracy, even at the cost of sacrificing immediate military advantages. (Colonel Marshall's testimony also described in some detail the events surrounding the *coup*, and how completely taken by surprise he and other Americans in Athens had been. He described the *coup* as 'open mutiny' and, on the question of American relations with the junta, said: 'I don't know how you deal honourably with dishonourable men.') Largely as a result of the testimony of these and other witnesses, the House Foreign Affairs Committee, by a vote of 17 to 12, approved the Hays Amendment to the Foreign Assistance Act. This banned aid to Greece unless the President certified in writing that it was required by overriding considerations of national security. On 3 August this action was ratified by the House by a vote of 122 to 57; it was the first time since the end of World War II that either house of Congress had taken action against a right-wing dictatorship. Despite the clear intention of the President to use his authority to override the ban, it was a significant blow to the junta.

While the State Department seemed ready to accept the inclusion of the Hays Amendment in the Foreign Assistance Act, the Pentagon and White House apparently felt it necessary to reassure the junta. To this end they lobbied intensively in the Senate; although the Foreign Relations Committee approved the Hays Amendment, the full Senate voted it down by 49 to 31. Two things are noteworthy in regard to the vote. The intensity of administration pressure is indicated by the defection of certain Republican Senators who had hitherto not merely opposed aid for the junta but actively fought against it. And *all* the prospective candidates for the Democratic presidential nomination, either in connection with the Senate vote or otherwise, have now recorded themselves against aid to the junta. This includes not only Senators Muskie, McGovern, and Humphrey, but the two most conservative: Senator Henry Jackson and Representative Wilbur Mills. This reflects the general reaction against a military-oriented interventionist foreign policy in any part of the world. A Democratic victory in the 1972 elections therefore seems likely to herald a major change in US policy toward Greece.

The implications of the visit to Greece of Vice-President Agnew, and his public praise of the junta, are less clear. The State Department is known to have opposed the trip; what is not certain is whether the Vice-President simply disregarded the Department's advice, or whether the President wanted him to shore up the junta as a matter of policy. (It has been suggested that Mr Agnew was simply looking for a congenial place to live after 1972.) There are, indeed, reports that he was the bearer of a message from the President asking assurances on a date for elections, and that he obtained them. But as of this writing, there is no evidence that he actually either obtained or sought any assurance other than the meaninglessly general ones which the junta has been providing ever since 1967.

New York, November 1971   *Maurice Goldbloom*

NOTES

1 WOODHOUSE, C. M., *Apple of Discord. A survey of recent Greek politics in their international setting*, London 1948, p. 218.
2 *Le Monde*, 13–14 August 1967, described this prospective *coup* and the junta's counter-measures. The events of December followed *Le Monde's* script.
3 EDIN was of course the youth group of the Centre Union.

Bibliography

This bibliography cannot for obvious reasons be considered as complete, although it does include most of the more significant books published on Greece since 1967. To keep it at a manageable length periodical articles have been excluded. General works on Greek history and politics have been included if they also cover the post-1967 period. Only periodicals dealing with Greece which have commenced publication since 1967 are listed.

THE REGIME'S 'CREDO': BOOKS

GEORGALAS, G., *I Ideologia tis Epanastaseos* (The Ideology of the Revolution), Athens, 1971, 76 pp.

GEORGALAS, G., *I krisis tis Katanalotikis Kinonoias* (The Crisis of the Consumer Society), Athens, 1971 (Viper), 202 pp.

PAPAKONSTANTINOU, T., *Politiki Agogi* (Civics), Athens, 1970 (Kavanas-Ellas), 698 pp.

PAPADOPOULOS, G., *To Pistevo Mas* (Our Credo), Athens, 1968–, 6 vols. continuing.

TSAKONAS, D. G., *Eisagogi eis ton neon Ellinismon* (Introduction to Modern Hellenism), Athens, 1971, 126 pp.

PERIODICALS

Theseis kai ideai (Theses and ideas), Athens, 1968– , monthly.

DISSENTING VOICES

AVGERIS, Markos, *Antitheseis kai parallilismi* (Contrasts and parallels), Athens, 1970 (circulated privately).

Dekaochto Keimena (Eighteen Texts), Athens, 1970 (Kedros), 210 pp. English edition by Harvard University Press (to be published).

ABATZOGLU, Petros, *Thanatos misthotou* (Death of a salary earner), Athens, 1970, 144 pp.

Nea Keimena (New Texts), Athens, 1970 (Kedros), 264 pp.

MARONITIS, D. N. (ed.) *O Fovos tis Eleftherias. Dokimes Anthropismou* (The Fear of Liberty. Essays on Humanism), Athens, 1971 (Papazisis), 334 pp.

RALLIS, G., *I Alithia ya tous Ellines Politikous* (The truth about the Greek politicians), Athens, 1971.

PAZ, *Anazitontas . . .* (Searching . . .), Athens, 1971 (Iridanos), 40 pp. (Written in Aegina prison in 1970.)

CLANDESTINE PRESS

Antistasi (Resistance) – Peasants' Front Against Dictatorship (AAMY), appears irregularly, 1969–.

Avgi (Dawn) – United Democratic Left (EDA), monthly, sometimes appears irregularly, 1968–.

Dimokratiki Amyna (Democratic Defence), Bulletin, appears irregularly, 1968–.

Eleftheri Ellines (Free Greeks) Bulletin, appears irregularly, 1969–.

I Genia mas (Our generation) – Lambrakis Youth Movement, appears irregularly, 1968–.

Nea Ellada (New Greece) – Patriotic Front (PAM), monthly, 1967–. (Also *Agonistis* (Fighter) – PAM of Western Greece, *Achaya* (Achaia) – PAM of Northern Peloponnese, etc. These publications appear irregularly.)

Rizospastis (Radical) – Greek Communist Party (KKE), monthly, 1967–.

Rizospastis/Mahitis (Radical/Fighter) – Greek Communist Party inside the Country (KKE/Interior), monthly, 1968–.

Thourios – Student Resistance Organization 'RIGAS FERAIOS', appears irregularly, 1968–.

Nitis, *Kraniotrypano-Katopsi* (Head-drill – Katopsis) (Poems), Athens, 1971; (*Poligrafos* – [Duplicating Machine]), first in the series 'Present Day Library'.

BOOKS ON POST-1967 GREECE, PUBLISHED ABROAD

ARGIRAKIS, Minos, *Gribbe Over Byen* (The City swam in Black Flags) Copenhagen, 1969 (Sirius). Also published in Sweden.

ARSENI, Kitty, *Nelle Carceri dei Colonnelli*, Roma, 1970 (Editori Riuniti),

118 pp. (with an introduction by Mikis Theodorakis). Also published in Denmark.

Athènes – presse libre, (ed.) *Livre noir de la dictature en Grèce*, Paris, 1969 (du Seuil), 206 pp.

BAKOYANNIS, P., *Milisate ya Dimokratia kirioi Sintagmatarches?* (Colonels, did you speak of Democracy?), Frankfurt am Main, 1968 (Hellas), 164 pp.

BECKET, James, *Barbarism in Greece*, New York, 1970 (Walker and Co.), 148 pp. (Foreword by Senator Clairborne Pell). Also in paperback.

CAMPBELL, J. and SHERRARD, P., *Modern Greece*, London, 1968 (Ernest Benn), 426 pp. Illustrated.

CAREY, J. P. C., and CAREY, A. G., *The Web of Modern Greek Politics*, New York, 1968 (Columbia University Press), 240 pp.

CASSANDRAS, Nicolas, *Zwischen Skylla und Charybdis, Griechenland unter der Diktatur*, Wien, 1968 (Österreichischen Gewerkschaftsbundes), 122 pp.

CERVI, Mario, *Dove va la Grecia? (Dal colpo di stato al referendum)*, Milano, 1968 (U. Mursia), 324 pp. Illustrated.

CHAUVEL, J. F., *La Grèce à l'ombre des épées*, Paris, 1968 (Robert Laffont), 274 pp. Illustrated.

COUBARD, Jacques, *Mikis Theodorakis, ou la Grèce entre le rêve et le cauchemar*, Paris, 1969 (Juillard), 344 pp. Illustrated.

Council of Europe, European Commission on Human Rights, *The Greek Case, Report of the Commission*, 4 vols., Strasbourg, 1969 (Council of Europe).

DE JACO, Aldo, *Colonnelli e resistenza in Grecia*, Roma, 1970 (Editori Riuniti), 250 pp.

DIAKOYANNIS, Kiriakos, *Yati pira meros sti sinomosia tis huntas kai tis C.I.A. kata tau Andrea Papandreou kai tis Ellinikis Dimokratias* (Why I participated in the conspiracy of the Junta and the CIA against Andreas Papandreou and Greek Democracy), Montreal, 1967 (Patris), 608 pp.

DOGAS, Elias, *De Toestand in Griekenland* (The Situation in Greece), Amsterdam, 1969 (Stichting Uiterverij Bevrijding).

DREYFUS, N., *Les étudiants grecs accusent*, Paris, 1961 (Editeurs Français Réunis), 128 pp.

FILINIS, Kostas, *Theoria dei giochi e strategia politica*, Roma, 1971 (Editori Riuniti), 192 pp. (Written in 1969 in Aegina prison.)

FRANGOS, George and SCHWAB, Peter, *Greece under the Junta*, New York, 1969 (Facts on File).

FREDERIKA, Queen, *A Measure of Understanding*, London, 1971 (Macmillan), 270 pp. Illustrated.

Greece: Royal Ministry of Foreign Affairs, *The Greek Case before the Commission of Human Rights of the Council of Europe*, vol. I, Athens, 1970.

GRITSI-MILLIEX, Tatiana, *Chroniko* (Chronicle) 1966–1971, Nicosia, 1971, duplicated.

GSTREIM, Heinz (ed.), *Zum Beispiel Griechenland*, München, 1969 (Delp), 172 pp.

KATRIS, Yannis, *I genisi tou neofasismou. Ellada, 1960–70* (The genesis of neofascism, Greece, 1960–1970), Geneva 1971 (Editex), 390 pp. Also to be published in the USA: Katris, John, *Eyewitness in Greece: the colonels come to power*, St Louis, Missouri, 1971 (New Critics Press).

KOCH, Erwin E., *Griechenland im Umbruch*, Frankfurt am Main, 1970 (Maindruck), 264 pp.

KOROVESSIS, Pericles, *The Method*, London, 1970 (Allison and Busby), 88 pp. Also in paperback, London, 1970 (Panther).

KOROVESSIS, Pericles, *La Filière. Témoignage sur les tortures en Grèce*, Paris, 1969 (du Seuil), 122 pp.

KOROVESSIS, Pericles, *Anthropofilakes* (Guards of Human Beings), Lund, 1970 (Rabén and Sjögren), 110 pp. (Cover design by Voula Costopoulos.) Also published in Swedish, Danish, Portuguese and Finnish.

LANGLOIS, D., *Panagoulis: le sang de la Grèce*, Paris, 1969 (Maspero), 128 pp.

LEGG, Keith, R., *Politics in Modern Greece*, Stanford, California, 1969 (Stanford University Press), 368 pp.

MANGAKIS George, *Eleftheria agapi mou* (Liberty, my love), Frankfurt am Main, 1971.

MARCEAU, Marc, *La Grèce des colonels*, Paris, 1967 (Robert Laffont), 274 pp. Illustrated.

MATHIOPOULOS, B. P., *Athen brennt*, Darmstadt, 1967 (Schneekluth), 224 pp. Illustrated. Also published in Italy, Milano, 1968 (Mondadori).

MEESTER, J., *Verslag van een diktatur* (Report on a dictatorship), Amsterdam, 1969 (De Bezige Bij), 128 pp.

MERCOURI, Melina, *I was born Greek*, London, 1971 (Hodder & Stoughton), 224 pp. Illustrated. Also published in USA, New York, 1971 (Doubleday & Co); in France, Paris, 1971 (Stock); in the Federal Republic of Germany, 1971 (Blanvalet); in Holland, 1971 (Bruna); in Norway, 1971 (Gyldendal Norsk), and Finland, 1971 (Kirjayhtymä).

MEYNAUD, Jean, *Rapport sur l'abolition de la démocratie en Grèce. 15 juillet 1965–21 avril 1967*, Montreal, 1967 (Etudes de Science Politique), 128 pp. First part of this book (pp. 1–52) translated into Greek: *I vasiliki ektropi apo ton koinovouleftismo tou Iouliou tou 1965* (The royal deviation from constitutionalism of July 1965), London, 1970, 200 pp. Greek translation of second part now in preparation. Also in German: *Bericht über die Abschaffung der Democratie in Griechenland*, Berlin, 1969 (Klaus Wagenbach), 112 pp.

MINUZZO, Nerio, *Quando arrivano i colonnelli, Rapporto dalla Grecia*, Milan, 1970 (Bompiani), 262 pp.

Nederlandse Studenten Raad/NSR (National Union of Dutch Students), (ed.), *Griekenland 21 April 1967, dossiers van een dictatuur* (Greece, 21 April 1967, the dossier of a dictatorship), Leiden, 1969.

NIKOLINAKOS, M. and NIKOLAOU, K. (ed.) *Die verhinderte Demokratie: Modell Griechenland*, Frankfurt am Main, 1969 (Suhrkamp), 184 pp.

NIZZA, Enzo (ed.) *La Grecia dei colonnelli e documenti de la resistenza greca*, Milano, 1969 (Le Pietra), 68 pp. (Posters, photographs, clandestine Greek press, etc.)

PAPANDREOU, Andreas, *Democracy at gunpoint. The Greek Front*, New York, 1970 (Doubleday & Co), 364 pp. English revised edition, same title, London, 1971 (André Deutsch), 338 pp.

PAPANDREOU, Andreas, *Man's Freedom*, New York, 1970 (Columbia University Press), 72 pp.

PAPANDREOU, Margaret, *Nightmare in Athens*, Englewood Cliffs, New Jersey, 1970 (Prentice-Hall), 390 pp.

PONTANI, Filipo M. (ed.), *L'altra Grecia*, Padova, 1969 (La nuova Italia).

ROUSSEAS, Stephen, *The Death of a Democracy, Greece and the American Conscience*, New York, 1967 (Grove Press), 268pp. Revised edition, same title, New York, 1968 (Grove Press), 242 pp. (both with the collaboration of Herman Starobin and Gertrud Lenzer). Also published in the Federal Republic of Germany, Reinbeck bei Hamburg, 1968.

SEYPPEL, Joachim, *Hellas Geburt einer Tyrannis. Impressionen, Analysen, Documente*, Berlin, 1968 (Lothar Blanvalet), 240 pp.

SKRIVER, Ansgar, *Soldaten gegen Demokraten, Militärdiktatur in Griechenland*, Köln/Berlin, 1968 (Kippenheuer und Witsch), 198 pp. Also published in Denmark.

STARAKIS, Jean, *Dans les prisons des colonels*, Paris, 1971 (Bernard Grasset).

STOCKTON, Bayard, *Phoenix with a Bayonet*, Ann Arbor, Michigan, 1971 (Georgetown Publications), 306 pp. Illustrated.

THEODORAKIS, Mikis, *Conquistare la Liberta*, Roma, 1968 (Editori Riuniti).

THEODORAKIS, Mikis, *Journal de Résistance. La dette*, Paris, 1971 (Flammarion). (Also in Greek, *To chreos*.)

TREHOLT, Arne, *Marketakis og Juntaen* (Marketakis and the Junta), Oslo, 1969 (J. W. Cappelens), 216 pp.

TSOUCALAS, Constantine, *The Greek Tragedy*, London, 1969 (Penguin), 208 pp. Also published in France: *La Grèce de l'Indépendence aux colonels*, Paris, 1970 (Maspero), 192 pp. With a short bibliography.

US Senate, Greece, February, 1971. *A Staff Report for the use of the Committee on Foreign Relations*, Washington, 1971 (US Government Printing Office), 16 pp. Compiled by R. Moose and J. Lowenstein.

US Senate, *Hearings before the Sub-committee on United States Security Agreements and Commitments Abroad of the Committee on Foreign Relations, US Senate 91st Congress, 2nd Session, Part Seven, June 9 and 11, 1970*, Washington, 1970 (US Government Printing Office), pp. 1769–1880.

VAN HASSELT (ed.), *Griekenland Vrij* (*Greece Free*), Amsterdam, 1967, (Polak & van Gennep), 140 pp.

Vérité sur la Grèce, Anon. Lausanne, 1970, (La Cité Editeur), 252 pp. Also to be published in London, 1972, as 'Athenian', *Inside The Colonels' Greece* (Chatto and Windus) and New York, 1972 (Norton).

VLACHOS, Helen, *House Arrest*, London, 1970 (André Deutsch), 158 pp. Illustrated.

VLACHOS, Helen (ed.), *Free Greek Voices*, London, 1971 (Doric Publications), 168 pp. (Cover design by Marylena Siotis.)

YANNATOS, Spiros, *O Georgios Papandreou stis krisimes ores tis Elladas ke tis Ellinikis Dimokratias* (George Papandreou during the critical hours for Greece and Greek Democracy), Toronto, 1971 (Greek Cultural Press), 238 pp.

Ya tin anaptixi tis antistasis, ya tin ananeosi tou KKE. Gnomes kratoumenon Kommouniston (For the strengthening of the Resistance, for the renewal of the Greek Communist Party. Opinions of imprisoned communists), 1971 (KOM–EP, Communist Review), 288 pp.

YOUNG, Kenneth, *The Greek Passion*, London, 1968, (Dent), 542 pp.

WOODHOUSE, C. M., *The Story of Modern Greece*, London, 1968 (Faber and Faber), 318 pp. Illustrated.

PAMPHLETS

Athènes – presse libre, *Affaire Christos Sartzetakis*, Paris, 1971, 11 pp.

The Cambridge Greek Affair, London, 1969 ('Group of Cambridge students on the Left'), 36 pp. (with drawings).

Grèce, Grecia, Griechenland, Hellas by KIRO (cartoons), Paris, 1969 (Association of Greek Students in Paris–EPES), 58 pp.

Greece, 1963–1970, (photographs with text), London, 1970 (National Union of Greek Students–EFEE/Abroad), 64 pp.

KATEPHORES, G. and ZIS, G., *Fascism in Greece and why it happened*, London, 1967 (League for Democracy in Greece), 26 pp. (Foreword by R. Miliband.)

MASPERO, F., *Youra, liberté pour la Grèce*, Paris, 1967 (Maspero).

MESEMVRINOS, *I Vasilia stin Ellada* (Monarchy in Greece), Lund, 1968 (The 'Cahiers' of RIGAS), 62 pp.

Moment of Truth, Athens 3 November 1968, (G. Papandreou's funeral), London, 1969 (Patriotic Front Publications), 30 pp. Also in Greek as *To mega pathos* (The great passion). Illustrated.

POTTER, Bob, *Greek Tragedy (The failure of the Left)*, Bromley, Kent, 1968 (Solidarity pamphlet, No. 29), 38 pp.

Swedish National Union of Students – SFS, *Report on Greece*, Stockholm, 1968, 51 pp.

VASILIOU, K. S., *'To Sintagma' ton nomikon tis huntas* (The 'Constitution' of the Junta's lawyers), London, 1968 (United Democratic Left – EDA London Section), 68 pp.

WILLIAMS, Philip, *Athens under the Spartans*, London, 1967 (Fabian Society Research Pamphlet, No. 264), 24 pp.

PERIODICAL PUBLICATIONS

Athènes – presse libre, Bulletin, ed. R. Someritis, weekly, Paris, 1967–.

L'Autre Grèce, Paris, monthly, 1971–.

Cahiers du 20ème Octobre, Paris, monthly, 1971–.

Comité Central des réfugiés politiques Grecs, Bulletin d'Information, München, monthly, 1970–.

Comité soviétique de solidarité avec les démocrats grecs, Bulletin, Moscow, appears irregularly, 1968–.

Comité Suisse pour le rétablissement de la démocratie en Grèce, Bulletin, Geneva, eight times a year, 1968–.

Communist Party of Greece (KKE/Interior), Bulletin, monthly, 1968–. Also in French.

Eleftheria, Waltham, Mass., ed. Stratis Haviaras, monthly, 1970–.

European–Atlantic Action Committee on Greece, Bulletin, to appear irregularly, 1971–.

Free Voice of Greece, broadcast transcripts, WBAI New York, weekly, 1969–.

Grecia, Rome/Bologna, monthly, 1969–.

The Greek Observer, London, ed. George Yannopoulos, monthly, 1969–1970.

Greek–American Solidarity, Minneapolis, Minnesota, monthly, 1971–.

Greek Report, London, ed. Panayotis Lambrias, monthly, 1969–.

Griechische Dokumente und Informationen, Köln, ed. Vassili Mavridis, monthly, 1968–.

Griekenland Bulletin, Amsterdam, ed. Dutch–Belgian Committee for Democracy in Greece, monthly, 1969–.

Hellenic Review, London, ed. Helen Vlachos, monthly, 1968.

National Union of Greek Students – EFEE/Abroad, Information bulletin, London, monthly, 1969–.

Information Bulletin of the Academic Community for a Free Greece, Philadelphia, Pa. USA, 1970–.

News of Greece, New York, ed. Maurice Goldbloom (US Committee for Democracy in Greece), bi-monthly, 1968–.

(North) London Group for the Restoration of Democracy in Greece, Bulletin, London, monthly, 1967–68.

Pressedienst der Zentrumsunion und EDIN in Süddeutschland, edited by Dr N. Grammenos, Esslingen, W. Germany, 1969–.

Quaderni della Resistenza Greca, Bologna, bi-monthly, 1970–.

Report on Greece, Berkeley, California, ed. West Coast Committee for Democracy in Greece, monthly, 1967– .

IN GREEK

Agonas (Struggle), Paris, quarterly, 1970–.

Deltio eleftheron eidiseon, Toronto, appears irregularly, 1971–.

Deltion Enemeroseos (Information Bulletin), edited by Spyros Gisdakis on behalf of the Munich branch of the Centre Union party, 1971–.

Desmotis (Bound), published by the Stockholm office of PAK, 1968–1970, editor: C. Goulos.

Dimokratia (Democracy), Bonn, monthly, 1967–.

Epanastasi (Revolution), bi-monthly, 1969–.

Ethniki Enotis (National Unity), London, ed. George Plytas, monthly, 1971–.

Exodus (Exodus), Paris, monthly, 1970–.

IG-Metal, *Presse Spiegel für Griechische Kollegen*, Bulletin, weekly (in Greek).
Kommunistiki Epitheorisi (KOM–EP, Communist Review), ed. KKE/Interior, monthly, 1969–.
Nea Poreia (New Course), Trieste, bi-monthly, 1969–.
Neos Kosmos (New World), monthly, ed. KKE, 1967–.
Politiki (Politics), Rome, appears irregularly, 1969–.
Poreia (March), Paris, ed. Association des Etudiants Hellènes de Paris, bi-monthly, 1967–.
Propylaia, Zurich, ed. Greek Student Union of Zurich, 1968–1969.

NEWSPAPERS

Agonas (Struggle), München, fortnightly, 1969–.
Antistasi (Resistance), Paris, monthly, 1967–68.
Eleftheri Patrida (Free Motherland), Rome, weekly (1967–1970), continues as *Eleftheri Ellada* (Free Greece), Rome, weekly, 1970–.
Eleftheri Patrida (Free Motherland), London, weekly, 1968–.
Eleftheros Naftergatis (Free Seaman), Hamburg, monthly, 1968–.
Hellas, London, fortnightly, 1967–1969.
Laiki Foni (People's Voice), London, monthly, 1971–.
Makriyannis, Montreal, monthly, 1968–.
Mami (Midwife [of the Revolution]), London, monthly, 1970–.
Neos Kosmos (New World), Toronto, weekly, 1968–69.
Ora tis Allagis (Hour of Change), London, fortnightly, 1967–.
Spitha (Spark), Frankfurt am Main, monthly, 1969–70.
Ta alla nea (The other news), Rome, monthly, 1971–.

SPECIAL ISSUES

Akzente, special issue on Greece, April, 1971.
The Economist, London, 31 July/6 August 1971, 40-page pull-out section on Greece.
Nouvelles Littéraires, Paris, Special issue on Greece, May, 1971.
Les Temps Modernes, (ed. J. P. Sartre), 'Aujourd'hui la Grèce, Dossier'. Paris, September, 1969, 364 pp. In German as *Griechenland. Der Weg in der Faschismus. Dokumentation zur politischen Situation*, Frankfurt am Main, 1970 (Joseph Melzer Verlag).

LITERATURE

KALLIFATIDIS, T., *Xenos* (Foreigner), Stockholm, 1970,

MESEMVRINOS, (ed.) *Poiimata tis neas antistasis* (Poems of the new Resistance), Lund, 1968 (The 'Cahiers' of Rigas), 32 pp.

PANAGOULIS, Alexandros, *Sinechiste* (Carry On), 29 poems, London, n.d. (8½), 32 pp.

PAPANDREOU, Chrysa, *Yannis Ritsos*, Paris, 1968 (Seghers), 190 pp. There are several post-1967 translations of the works of Ritsos in French, Italian, German, Dutch, Spanish, etc. Latest unpublished works of Ritsos: Pierres-Repetitions-Barreaux (bi-lingual edition), Paris, 1971 (Gallimard). Preface by Louis Aragon, and London, 1971 (Jonathan Cape).

SEFERIS, George, *The Land within a Wall*, Montreal, 1969 (Anthelion Press). Translation and notes by Dr John Richmond.

THEODORAKIS, Mikis, *Fern meter fra min cele* (Five yards from my cell), Copenhagen, 1970 (Sigvaldis), 92 pp. (Drawings by Minos Argirakis.)

VASSILIKOS, Vasilis, *Mesa sti nychta tis asfaleias* (In the darkness of the Security Police Headquarters), *Lakka-Souli*, *Bella-Ciao*, Collections of poems, London, 1969, 1970 (8½).

VASSILIKOS, Vasilis, *To psarotonfeko* (The Harpoon), London, 1971 (8½).

VRETTAKOS, Nikiforos, *Odyni* (Sorrow), New York, 1969 (Association of Greek University Graduates).

Index